Your Job Rights

The Federal Employees Guide to Appeals and Grievances

Don Mace and Eric Yoder

Published by
Federal Employees News Digest, Inc.
1850 Centennial Park Dr., Suite 520
Reston, VA 22091-1517
Telephone (703) 648-9551
FAX: (703) 648-0265

Publisher of
Federal Employees Almanac
Federal Employees News Digest
Your Retirement: How to Prepare for It—How to Enjoy It
Your Financial Guide: The Estate and Financial Planner for Federal
and Postal Employees

Copyright ©1993 by Federal Employees News Digest, Inc.

ISBN 0-910582-17-3
Printed in U.S.A.

P robably no area of federal employment is more important and less understood than appeal rights.

Many employees have a kind of vague understanding that certain personnel actions are or aren't allowed, or that certain agency decisions can or can't be contested. But they are confused by the alphabet-soup of agencies involved, unfamiliar with the overlapping laws, rules and decisions from courts and administrative bodies, unable to find the information they need, frightened by the prospects of pursuing an appeal—in short, intimidated by the whole process.

Some of them try fruitlessly to bring appeals that the law doesn't allow, while others pass up their rights because fighting the system simply seems like too much trouble.

That's the message that the editors of *Federal Employees News Digest* have received during the four decades our publications have been around. Time and again, employees call or write to ask for an explanation of what their appeal rights might be in a given situation, how the process works, how they can research their rights and how they can exercise them.

Most of all they wanted that information in plain English, a language all too rare in the field of government personnel.

We designed *Your Job Rights* for you, whether you are an individual employee, a management official, a shop steward, an attorney involved in such disputes, or simply an interested observer of the government. We have pulled together information from the widely scattered sources into the only comprehensive volume of its kind.

You'll find descriptions of the roles of the various agencies, what may be contested before them, and who may bring such appeals. We discuss alternatives to bringing formal complaints but also describe what happens if a person decides to pursue one. We provide points of contact for more information, advice on research and an extensive index of important legal precedents of recent years.

Your Job Rights was designed to aid both the individual employee and agency officials. It is thorough enough to help an attorney or union representative who may become involved in such a case, yet clear enough to be understood by those who have no legal training.

The book is neutral on who may be right or wrong in a given situation, instead describing the process by which a decision on that question is reached.

While *Your Job Rights* concentrates on rights of executive branch employees, U.S. Postal Service employees also will find it useful. Most problems involving postal employees are handled through the grievance procedure that has been negotiated in contracts or consultations between their unions and other organizations and management. However, postal employees do have certain rights of access to other appeals routes, and these are described when pertinent.

Also, the right to appeal certain actions or to bring appeals to certain agencies depends on the employee's job status. You'll find that in most cases, a notable exception being discrimination appeals rights are reserved for tenured employees in the competitive service.

This book does not attempt to anticipate every type of situation that may arise. Personnel disputes usually are very complicated matters involving many laws and rules and numerous events covering a long period. Attempting to create a step-by-step diagram for all the possibilities would be an impossible task and ultimately would be more confusing than enlightening.

It also would be virtually impossible to describe every form of appeal right that a federal employee might encounter. For example, some employees have concerns with veteran's benefits, educational loans or some other form of benefit administered by the government. In such cases the individual agencies involved have their own internal appeals processes, which would have to be explored by contacting those agencies.

Instead, we have provided a road map through the various appeals options available in the large majority of common situations, and guidance on how those options might apply to an individual case. Our thanks to officials of the unions and agencies whose help was so valuable, including the American Federation of Government Employees, National Treasury Employees Union, National Federation of Federal Employees, Office of Special Counsel, Merit Systems Protection Board, Equal Employment Opportunity Commission, Federal Labor Relations Authority, Office of the Comptroller General and Office of Personnel Management. We wish to thank our able staff, as well, including Lisa Pepple and Laurie Baker.

With pride and a hope that it will benefit our readers, we present *Your Job Rights*.

Don Mace
Eric Yoder

Table of Contents

Chapter 1

Overview

As editors of federal employee publications we hear all sorts of horror stories from readers who unexpectedly have found themselves on the short side of disputes with their agencies. Maybe we've heard from you in the past. Aside from letting off a little steam, most simply want to know what to do about their problems—how to get out of a jam.

We, of course, want to help. But since we can't know all the facts (sometimes the individuals themselves don't have their facts straight, either) and aren't in the business of providing direct, individual consultation, we try to help them define the problem and then find the right route of inquiry.

In this book we take the same approach. We offer some general views that can help you to help yourself. If you don't have a formal complaint against your agency yet, maybe this will help you find a solution before it becomes—literally—a "federal case." If you find yourself considering an action against your employer, then the book will help explain pros and cons and how to go about researching the problem, getting help and finding a possible solution.

When we finished the book project we realized that what we had put together after more than a year's work is, to our knowledge, the first and only book to address in depth virtually all ways to defend your rights as a federal worker, including violations of laws, rules, regulations and policies protecting you against unwarranted job actions, discipline, discrimination, disputed financial claims, denied promotions, RIF abuses, sexual discrimination and many other job-related hassles.

The federal appeals landscape is a labyrinth, yet it's not so intricate that a layman can't successfully navigate it—with or without hiring legal help.

Navigating the Maze

At the beginning of this administrative maze is a single door. You should not attempt to open it without first asking yourself the most important question of all: Is what I'm after worth pursuing?

Deceptively simple, this question most certainly is.

This is not a consideration that bothers gamblers much. They wouldn't be gamblers if it did. But it's probably safe to assume that you're not a gambler, at least not where your job is concerned. And, we assume that you don't want to get yourself into deeper trouble than you already may be in or might be in if matters take on a life of their own, as they often do in these cases. You may even be reading this book just to see what kinds of traps might snare you if you're not careful.

If you're not sure you want to pursue a dispute, or clearly decide not to, then you'd better find a way to settle the matter peacefully, because once you've opened the door and taken that first, formal step, it's nearly impossible to go back. (Of course, if the matter involves a dispute over a relatively simple matter, such as the denial of a travel reimbursement, you may find the appeal more cut-and-dried and just press on. You'll find procedures in these pages.)

This advice isn't just for those mad at management. It's also intended for supervisors and managers. We suspect that some of them contemplating taking actions against employees, after studying this book (especially the hundreds of case summaries in the back of it) might try to find other, quieter ways to settle personnel or *personal* beefs before third parties get involved.

In an ideal world workplace disputes would be handled informally. Since all of us in this perfect world would be good workers and model employees, the mere mention of our perceived shortcomings would prompt us to behave. There would be no hard feelings because, after all, our bosses have the mission of the agency and our best interests in mind. Besides, once we improved no disciplinary action would be necessary; so everybody would win.

But alas, as thousands of federal employees over the years can attest, too often seemingly petty squabbles turn into administrative nightmares with the endurance of long distance runners. What begins as a misunderstanding in the office becomes a running case that can take—literally—years to settle.

But happily most situations don't call for drastic measures. They are best left to informal discussions between reasonable men and women. If you don't believe that, just read on and you might be surprised to discover that the right to appeal carries risk for both sides of any dispute, including the risk of being tied up in a costly war of attrition.

It is not our intention to discourage people with legitimate complaints from sticking up for their rights or seeking redress to the full extent of the law. It is, however, our desire that you know not only the procedures for protecting your rights but the lay of the land, as well.

The Odds

What are the chances that you'll prevail in a workplace dispute? This depends upon how you define "prevail." Many cases never reach the formal stage. How many is impossible to determine because agencies generally don't keep track of them and the majority of them are settled without formal steps being taken. Of those that do go to the "bench," the majority are won by the government. For example, at the Merit Systems Protection Board, which hears most federal employee appeals, the large majority of cases that reach a hearing are decided in favor of the agency. In a typical year the board's hearing officers uphold the agency decision about 80 percent of the time. Generally the percentage holds true at the board level and in federal court. And these figures do not include the large number of cases that are settled or dismissed as groundless.

The Book

To that end this book takes you through a discussion of the pros and cons of appeals in the federal sector.

We include explanations of which agencies handle your appeals and what procedures they require you to follow. Included are the General Accounting Office, Equal Employment Opportunity Commission, Federal Labor Relations Authority, Merit Systems Protection Board, Office of Personnel Management and Office of Special Counsel. And we walk you through the administrative and negotiated (union) grievance processes, as well.

The "heart" of the book, we believe, is the large section in the back that contains short summaries of hundreds of decisions in cases brought by employees and unions that originated at the local level—perhaps right where you work. The listings are rich with information. You usually can obtain the full text of these rulings by contacting the agencies or courts that decided them. We have even included a handy table on how to order them and what copies usually cost, information we know is hard to come by through normal channels.

Use the book as a guide for yourself, or for people who are helping you but may not know the "ropes." After all, you have one of the most extensive list of job protections in the working world, a comprehensive list unknown to most outsiders, including the majority of private practice attorneys.

Chapter 2

Settlements — Can't We Just Work This Out?

Almost any federal personnel dispute can be settled at any stage. All it takes is a willingness by the two sides to listen to the other and to compromise. That willingness is often in short supply in such disputes but settlement nonetheless is becoming an increasingly attractive option to both the individual employees and the agencies involved.

Going through a full-blown appeal is costly in terms of time and money for both sides. There are legal and other fees involved, which easily can run into the tens of thousands of dollars, depending on how far the case is pursued. Many employees who go through the entire process and win find they've achieved a costly victory in terms of their own finances. And while agencies can afford the costs better than an individual, budgets will be upset—and a manager who was the cause of it may find his stock falling with high officials.

Time is lost as the employee prepares his or her case and management officials prepare the agency's response. And cases can drag on for years through the various levels of hearings and appeals, with decisions often being sent back for reconsideration because of some overlooked legal point. Personnel disputes have been known to last ten or more years—often long after the people involved have retired or moved on to other jobs.

Settlements Are Encouraged

No one sees this drain more often than the agencies that hear employment cases. They say that many of the disputes they see should never have reached the formal stage. And they have active programs to encourage settlements.

An example of this trend is the Merit Systems Protection Board, where half of all initial appeals that are not dismissed on technical grounds are settled. That's up from just 6 percent in the early 1980s.

Similarly, the Equal Employment Opportunity Commission has been training agency counselors in ways to resolve disputes before the

---

going gets formal. The counselors are being trained in negotiation and mediation techniques to help management and employees resolve complaints at the earliest possible stage.

And the Federal Labor Relations Authority provides training in problem solving strategies to labor and management representatives. And many contracts in the federal workplace now allow for labor-management dispute resolution teams. These teams typically have equal numbers of representatives from the agency and the union, plus a mediator. The team reaches a consensus decision and if the employee accepts the proposed resolution, a settlement agreement is reached.

Settlements as Contracts

Settlement agreements can be reached either in writing or orally, and are enforceable either way. But even an oral agreement eventually will be put in writing, becoming a contract.

Settlements obligate each side to do certain things. For example, an employee whose firing was proposed might accept a transfer to a different office while the agency purges his personnel files of the derogatory information that was used as the basis of the proposed discipline.

Those obligations are enforced the same way as any other contract, and are governed by contract law. For this reason, it may be wise to have an attorney involved in the drafting of the agreement, or at least have an attorney review a proposed settlement before signing it. While this involves some expense, it likely will be much less than the cost of formally pursuing an appeal to its end.

Of course it is up to both sides to judge whether to settle. Either might feel strongly that its position ultimately will prevail, and will be unwilling to accept less than the full loaf. Also, personnel disputes tend to take on a momentum of their own; once the formal process starts rolling, the parties often find it hard to apply the brakes.

However, the growing numbers of settlements in the government show that satisfactory compromises can be reached—even "late in the game" after formal hearings have been held and a first-level decision issued. These settlements no doubt have saved many an employee and management official the shock of learning that their supposedly iron-clad cases were in fact weak enough that the final decision would go against them.

A settlement also has the advantage of being less poisonous to a work atmosphere. Many employees who win appeals find themselves back at the same desk, still working for the same person who proposed the action that was overturned. While perhaps a legal point has been made, relations between the two sides can be tense (or worse), probably permanently. Again, you might find yourself with a costly victory, reinstated in your job but with less chance of advancement. A settlement, while stressful, may not produce the same level of ill feelings.

'Alternative Dispute Resolution' Channels

Settlements are available through routes other than the formal appeals agencies such as MSPB, EEOC and FLRA. Individual employing agencies, too, are increasingly turning to "alternative dispute resolution" strategies. One or several of them may be available to you, depending on your agency and worksite. These include:

Arbitration. Arbitration provides for a neutral, third party to hear arguments and evidence and resolve a dispute. It can be binding or not, voluntary or (in the case of arbitration created by labor-management contracts) compulsory.

Several agencies have set up expedited arbitration processes with strict time limits, no formal transcript produced, the number of witnesses limited, no legal briefs filed, and other time and cost saving steps used. Often there is a strict time limit on the hearing itself, a length limit on the arbitrator's report and early deadlines on all stages of the process.

These less formal arbitration processes are considered especially useful for less serious grievances.

Fact-Finding. In fact-finding, individuals or groups with expertise in the subject matter of the dispute are called in to prepare a report on a dispute (in some cases they come from other agencies, or are private contractors). They conduct personal and telephone interviews and use informal investigative techniques.

The fact-finder typically makes no formal recommendations or binding decisions. However, the report can then be used as the basis for a negotiation leading to a binding settlement agreement.

The advantage of invoking this process is that it can be done more quickly than more formal hearing procedures, which often don't even begin until months after a complaint is filed. Early on, the facts of the dispute are still fresh in everyone's mind, and the positions of the parties might not yet have hardened. And less formal techniques often produce information more useful to understanding and settling a dispute than do the affidavits and other documents filed by parties in a formal appeal.

Peer Review. Peer review panels give co-workers a role in resolving disputes. Typically these panels consist of colleagues and disinterested agency officials who collectively act in much the same way as an arbitrator. After investigating and considering the matter, the panel may issue a recommendation by a simple majority vote.

This is another potentially rapid means of settling disputes, as these panels often are given strict time limits to conduct their work.

Ombudsmen. Ombudsmen are points of contact within an agency where employees may seek answers to questions about work-related activities. They also may serve as designated neutral officials who serve as informal counselors, mediators or fact-finders, providing a means of resolving work disputes.

Typically, an ombudsman might review the employee's situation and give advice about his options. He might try to resolve conflicts, although he or she has no formal decision-making authority.

If you decide to use any of these alternative dispute resolution techniques, examine first the effect it might have on your other appeal rights. In some cases, using one of these channels might close off other routes that otherwise would be open.

Chapter 3

Discipline — When Push Comes To Shove

Adverse Actions
(Chapter 75 of Title V, U.S. Code)

An "adverse action" is a removal, suspension of more than 14 days, reduction in pay or grade, or furlough of 30 days or fewer. These are actions in which the agency is claiming that the "efficiency of the service" demands the personnel action be taken. Although most often taken because of misconduct, adverse actions may also be taken for performance reasons or for other reasons related to the "efficiency of the service." For example, short-term furloughs may be imposed for budgetary reasons.

Some of the most common grounds for misconduct charges are: insubordination or other disrespectful behavior toward supervisors; habitual tardiness; abuse of leave (particularly sick leave); absence without leave; physical altercations or threats; falsifying documents such as an employment application, time and attendance card or travel records; disrupting the workplace; misuse of government property; conflicts of interest; sexual harassment and other discriminatory acts; nepotism, and criminal behavior.

An adverse action also may be taken for off-duty conduct so long as there is a connection between the conduct and the efficiency of the service. This is most commonly used for criminal acts away from work—such as illegal drug use.

It should be noted that a person's relative rank and type of job can influence the disciplinary action. For example, supervisors and law enforcement personnel are held to a higher standard of conduct than are most other employees. (See "Douglas Factors" in this chapter.)

When taking an adverse action an agency must comply with certain requirements in personnel laws and rules. These requirements include 30 days of advance notice in writing of the charges that must explain the charges and be specific enough to permit a detailed reply. The employee must be told of his or her right to review the material on which the action is based.

The Douglas Factors

The Douglas factors act as a set of standards to be considered when deciding whether a penalty is appropriate in an adverse action. Generally, an agency will have to show that it considered such factors and why it chose a particular penalty. It is not required that every standard be weighed in every case, however.

- The nature and seriousness of the offense. Actions taken intentionally, or repeatedly, or maliciously, or for personal reasons are considered the most serious.
- The employee's job level and the type of employment. The higher an employee's level of trust, the more serious misconduct is taken.
- Past discipline taken against the employee. Particularly important is discipline for the same or similar violations.
- The employee's previous work record. A long and previously unblemished record will be seen in the employee's favor.
- How the offense affected the employee's ability to work at a satisfactory level. Considerations include the supervisor's ability to maintain confidence in the employee, especially in positions of trust.
- Consistency of the penalty with other employees in similar situations. The other employees to which the decision is being compared must have been in the same organization and in positions of similar responsibility, however.
- Whether the discipline met the agency's table of penalties. If the agency has such a table, a deviation from it must be supported by strong evidence.
- How well known was the offense. Conduct that causes a public scandal or other embarrassment to the agency can merit a more severe penalty.
- How well the agency informed employees of rules that were violated. Breaking an obscure rule will be viewed less harshly than breaking one that is well publicized, and particularly one on which the employee was given specific notice.
- The potential for rehabilitating the employee. An employee can help here by being willing to accept responsibility for misconduct, rather than blaming others.
- Other mitigating circumstances. These can include personal problems, unusual tension in the workplace, provocation and many others.
- Whether alternative penalties would prevent the same from happening again. This consideration especially applies to relatively minor offenses in which an apology or other less serious step can be taken.

Adverse action cases often involve investigations. The employee generally is obligated to cooperate unless there is a possibility that criminal charges will result. Often a union representative is allowed to be present at interviews to help protect the rights of a bargaining unit employee.

An agency generally may not suspend an employee or put him or her on annual leave during a notice period. However, an agency may shorten the notice period or indefinitely suspend an employee if it has reason to believe he has committed a crime, so long as there is a connection between the crime and the efficiency of the service.

After receiving notice of a proposed action, the employee has the right to a reasonable period (not less than seven days) to respond either orally or in writing. He or she has the right to representation and the right to review pertinent material.

The reply must be heard by an official with high enough rank to make the final decision or to make a recommendation to the final decision maker.

Appeals of final agency actions may be filed either with the Merit Systems Protection Board or through grievance procedures—either administrative or those negotiated under union contracts. *The employee may use the MSPB or the grievance channel, but not both*. Also, the employee must meet eligibility requirements—for example, completion of a mandatory probationary period.

MSPB and arbitrators have the authority to impose lesser penalties in adverse action cases. The penalty will be reviewed under a set of standards that MSPB outlined in a 1981 decision (*Douglas v. Veterans Administration*). These standards are used to weigh whether the penalty is appropriate for the offense and whether it is consistent with past disciplinary actions in similar situations. The idea is to ensure equal treatment for all.

The factors also serve as a guide for supervisors who might be considering a personnel sanction. If the decision is appealed, the agency must show how a penalty promotes the efficiency of the service. The agency will have to show that the supervisor considered the "Douglas factors" (see box this chapter) and why the choice of penalty was reasonable in light of them.

All of the factors won't necessarily be considered in each case— for example, not all agencies have tables of discipline. However, the "Douglas factors" serve as the best single indicator of which side is likely to prevail in an adverse action case.

An employee also can successfully challenge an adverse action by showing that it was the result of a prohibited personnel practice. Prohibited personnel practices include reprisal for whistleblowing, discrimination, political coercion, retaliation for filing an appeal and others (see Office of Special Counsel chapter).

If this claim is raised the agency must show that its decision was taken for legitimate reasons. If a prohibited practice is proved, the Office of Special Counsel may seek discipline against the supervisor who took it by filing a complaint with MSPB.

Also, an agency's failure to meet procedural requirements in taking an adverse action, if it is judged a "harmful error" to the employee's case, can be grounds for overturning the decision.

Performance Actions
(Chapter 43 of Title V, U.S. Code)

Disciplinary actions taken against federal employees on grounds of poor performance, if taken under Chapter 43, *must be based on formal performance appraisal systems.* These systems not only are used to periodically rate employees, but also can be used as the basis for decisions on training, rewarding, reassigning, promoting, demoting or firing employees.

Individual agencies draw up their own performance rating systems depending on the nature of work being done. But to be valid, these systems must have been approved by the Office of Personnel Management. Each must identify "critical elements" of a position, describe how performance will be weighed against the standards, and explain how personnel decisions will be made based on an appraisal. The standards must be based as much as possible on "objective" criteria, although not necessarily on strictly numerical measures. And it is not necessary that standards for employees having the same job description be identical.

In general, standards must be reasonable, sufficient to permit adequate measurement and adequate to inform employees of what is needed to get a satisfactory rating. They must be described in positive terms—that is, tell the employee what he must do, not what he must not do. (Tip: An employee can successfully challenge a disciplinary action based on poor performance if he can prove that the standards were invalid.)

An agency may take action against an employee for poor performance under one of two chapters found in Title 5 of the U.S. Code.

"Chapter 43" requires that the agency prove its case by "substantial evidence" and that it meet certain requirements, such as giving the employee the chance to improve. "Chapter 75" has a higher standard of proof—"a preponderance of the evidence"—and the agency must prove a connection between the employee's performance and the efficiency of the service.

Employees disciplined under Chapter 43 have the right to 30 days' advance notice, which must include specific examples of unacceptable performance and the critical elements that are involved. The employee may respond orally or in writing or both, may be represented by counsel, and is entitled to a decision by an official higher than that of the one proposing the action.

An employee can be removed or reduced in grade on performance grounds only within 12 months of the notice of the proposed action. In such cases the employee must be given an opportunity to demonstrate acceptable performance. During that period he is entitled to normal assistance from the agency to correct his deficiencies. This is sometimes called a "performance improvement plan" or an "opportunity period."

An employee disciplined for performance under either Chapter 43 or Chapter 75 has the right to appeal to the Merit Systems Protection Board, so long as he has completed one year of employment. Violations of the agency obligations or employee rights mentioned above can be grounds for overturning the action. When an agency uses the Chapter 75 disciplinary system, MSPB will weigh the "Douglas factors," standards used for assessing penalties for misconduct (see box this chapter).

Performance appraisals also can be used to deny within-grade pay increases. These increases are given for longevity, so long as the employee is performing at an acceptable level. An agency can consider an employee as not performing up to snuff if his or her performance is not satisfactory in any "critical" element of the job.

This determination must be based on performance throughout the entire waiting period for the within-grade raise. These waiting periods vary.

An employee must be told in writing that he or she is not performing acceptably and what he or she must do to improve. Unlike other actions based on performance, a within-grade raise can be denied without giving the employee a chance to improve.

An employee denied a within-grade increase may request reconsideration, where he or she may have a representative present and may review pertinent documents. From there he or she may appeal to MSPB.

Chapter 4

Miscellaneous Appeals

Sexual Harassment

W ell publicized incidents of alleged sexual harassment in recent years are in the forefront of workplace issues, both inside the government and outside. While this is a still-developing area of the law that is especially open to subjective judgment, sexual harassment is wrong and clearly illegal—it is a violation of trust and the Civil Rights Act.

Federal agencies increasingly have turned to prevention as the best tool against sexual harassment. They are publicizing the law, providing training and counseling, expressing strong disapproval of the practice, threatening discipline for violations and informing employees of their rights under the law. Yet sexual harassment still occurs in the government workplace and it has created intolerable working conditions for its victims.

The law defines sexual harassment as unwelcome sexual advances, requests for sexual favors, and other verbal or physical conduct of a sexual nature. It becomes a matter for legal action when: submission to such conduct is made either explicitly or implicitly a term or condition of an individual's employment; or submission to or rejection of such conduct by an individual is used as the basis for employment decisions; or the conduct has the purpose or effect of unreasonably interfering with an individual's work performance or creating an intimidating, hostile, or offensive working environment.

Harassment that becomes a condition of employment or is used as the basis of employment decisions is commonly called quid pro quo harassment. Harassment that interferes with an individual's work or creates an intimidating situation is called hostile environment harassment.

Employees who believe they are the victims of sexual harassment should use the appeals procedures of the Equal Employment Opportunity Commission, which enforces the Civil Rights Act (see EEOC chapter), unless they can settle the matter informally. As with many other job-related appeals it's often a good idea to work things out. If you do not wish to confront the alleged culprit in person, you might consider contacting your personnel office. Because agencies are attuned to sexual harassment as a workplace issue, the personnel office may be able to solve the problem with counseling.

Sexual harassment cases often involve difficult decisions regarding whether the conduct was harassing in nature. EEOC will look at the record as a whole and the circumstances, such as the nature of the sexual advances and the context in which the alleged incidents occurred. Legal decisions are made on the facts of each case.

An employer, including a federal agency is responsible for its acts and those of its agents and supervisory employees in quid pro quo sexual harassment. This applies regardless of whether the specific acts complained of were authorized or even forbidden by the employer and regardless of whether the employer knew or should have known they were happening.

The employer is liable for hostile environment harassment by its agents and supervisory employees depending upon whether principles of agency law would impose liability under the circumstances (Supreme Court decision in *Meritor Savings Bank v. Vinson, 477 U.S. 57, 72 (1986)*).

Regarding conduct between co-workers, an agency is responsible for acts of sexual harassment in the workplace where the employer (or its agents or supervisory employees) knows or should have known of the conduct, unless it can show that it took immediate and appropriate action to correct it.

An agency may also be responsible for acts of non-employees, with respect to sexual harassment of employees in the workplace, where the employer (or its agents or supervisory employees) knows or should have known of the conduct and fails to take immediate and appropriate corrective action. In reviewing these cases, EEOC will consider the extent of the employer's control and any other legal responsibility which the employer may have with respect to the conduct of non-employees.

RIF (Reduction-In-Force) Appeals

Some people love the acronym "RIF" because being under a reduction-in-force can improve their chances of being offered earlier than normal retirement. But to the folks who aren't ready to leave federal service, RIF can be a frightening and an ugly word.

No one seems prepared for a RIF once its possibility becomes a probability, or a sure bet. A sinking feeling of helplessness often is the first response to the dreaded reduction in force. But this need not be so—not to an employee armed with facts.

Knowing about the rules that protect you in RIFs alone can be a comfort. The exercise of these protections can be tricky but considering that most people in the private sector have virtually no recourse in similar situations, what's a bit of complexity when weighed against the alternative?

Generally, during a reorganization the government can't separate you, demote you, furlough you for more than 30 days or displace you by reassignment without employing formal RIF procedures.

You should not be surprised by a RIF, either, because the government is required to give you at least 60 days written notice of an impending RIF. (An exception to this rule is where the agency has to institute a RIF for reasons it could not reasonably foresee, in which case the Office of Personnel Management could approve a shorter period but not fewer than 30 days.) If your agency decides it has to take more severe RIF actions after it has issued the initial notice, then it has to furnish you with another specific RIF notice reflecting the new scope with at least 60 days notice, as well.

And, once you receive a notice your rights kick in automatically. Your agency is required to consider your type of appointment, veterans status, how long you've been working for Uncle Sam and your performance record. If you believe that any of your rights have been trampled you may appeal to the Merit Systems Protection Board (see MSPB chapter). An exception is where you are a member of a union's bargaining unit that has a negotiated grievance procedure that includes RIFs. You must follow that procedure and can't appeal the RIF to MSPB.

Even people in the excepted service, those with no protections against adverse and performance-based actions, can appeal alleged RIF improprieties to MSPB.

To properly follow RIF procedures, your agency must establish a "retention register," which groups employees by their civil service status: Here are the tenure classifications listed in descending order of retention standing:

Tenure Group	Sub-group	Tenure	Who is Covered
I	AD	Career >3 or more years	30% or more disabled vets
I	A	Career >3 or more years	5-10 point vets
I	B	Career >3 or more years	No vets preference
II	AD	Career Conditional	other 5-10 point vets
II	B	Career Conditional	non-vets
III		comprised of temporary and indefinite workers.	

Generally, the lower on the list the lower the retention standing and the most likely to go out first.

RIF Procedures

RIF procedures are required when your agency releases you from a competitive level by, among other reasons, separation, demotion, furlough (for more than 30 days), reassignment that displaces you, when you're released for lack of work or funds, reorganization and reclassification resulting from a change in duties.

Your agency must consider your tenure and, if applicable, your veterans status (see table above), how long you've been employed by Uncle Sam and your job performance ratings. (A relatively new rule entitles you to additional service retention credit based on your three most recent annual ratings "of record" during the four-year period before the date of the RIF notice, or other appropriate date.)

Another procedural requirement is the formal retention register that classifies you and other employees on the basis of retention standings.

If you're released from a competitive level your agency must assign you—with or without your consent—to a position that will last for a minimum of three months, or furlough you or separate you. Under some circumstances you may be assigned to a temporary position if it will save you from separation. You don't have a right to be assigned to a vacant position unless your agency decides to fill it during the RIF, in which case it has to follow RIF procedures to the letter.

Take a look around while the slot is being filled by your agency. Generally, it must go to you if your retention ranking is higher than others in your competitive level.

If the agency opposes your RIF appeal, it has the burden of proving that it followed the RIF procedures correctly in your case. To support your claim, the agency should furnish you with a current file containing proof of your qualifications, if you need it.

Any RIF notice must state the actions to be taken, their effective date, your competitive area and level, where you may review regs and records, any existing exceptions to retention standing rules and your appeal rights.

RIF Appeals

Your appeal must be filed during a 20-day period beginning the day after the effective date of the RIF action. MSPB doesn't have blanket authority in these matters, however. Its review of your agency's action is limited to the written record unless MSPB decides that the facts are in dispute. If it rules in your favor, your agency must restore you to the job you held before separation or to which you should have been assigned.

And, your agency may owe you back pay, as well.

If, on the other hand, you are covered by a union contract that does not exclude RIF appeals, then you must follow the negotiated procedures. You can't go your own way unless you allege that the removal action was based on discrimination. Time limits in negotiated grievances are governed by the labor agreement in force (see Grievances chapter). Your agency also is required to notify your union of an impending RIF if the negotiated grievance procedure is applicable.

Other Help

Your agency also must give you information on RIF help, including your re-employment rights, employment assistance from OPM, and how you may apply for unemployment insurance payments. The *Federal Employees Almanac* has detailed information on what help is available for employees displaced in RIFs. Also, if your agency issues RIF separation notices to 50 or more employees, it has to notify appropriate state and local government officials and OPM.

Injury Claims and Appeals

If you are injured on the job, or suffer a work-related illness, you are entitled to protections under the Federal Employees' Compensation Act (FECA). The Act provides death benefits, as well.

The law covers all civilian officers and employees of all branches of the federal government, and certain volunteer civilian members of the Civil Air Patrol and of the Reserve Officers' Training Corps. The Act also covers a number of other groups, including Peace Corps and VISTA volunteers; Job Corps and Youth Conservation Corps enrollees and the U.S. Postal Service.

The Act provides benefits for disability or death resulting from an injury sustained in the performance of duty. Coverage also extends to employees who suffer a non-work injury as a result of a war-risk hazard while employed outside the continental United States. The term "injury" includes any disease proximately caused by the employment. No benefits may be authorized if the injury or death is caused by willful misconduct of the employee, or by the employee's intention to injure himself or herself, or another, or if the employee's intoxication is the proximate cause.

If you sustain a disabling traumatic injury you are entitled to continuation of regular pay for a period not to exceed 45 calendar days. Monetary compensation is based on your monthly pay at the time of injury, or at the time disability begins or compensable disability recurs, if such recurrence begins more than six months after you resume regular, full-time employment with the United States, whichever is greater.

If you recover from your disability within one year from the time compensation payments begin, you have the right to return to your former job or an equivalent position. Even if the disability extends beyond one year, you would receive priority placement in the former position or an equivalent.

You must report your injury to your immediate superior within 30 days, and claim for disability or death compensation must be filed within three years. (The time limitations don't apply to (1) a minor until he or she reaches the age of 21 or has had a legal representative appointed and (2) a person while he or she is incompetent and has no duly appointed legal representative.) In cases of latent disability, the time limitations don't begin to run until you have a compensable disability and/or should have been aware that the disability is causally related to your employment. A claim for disability or death compensation filed after the three-year period may not be allowed, unless your superior had actual knowledge of the injury or death within 30 days, or written notice of the injury or death was properly given within 30 days. Failure to timely file a claim may be excused where notice could not be given because of exceptional circumstances.

Appeal Rights

If your injury occurred on or after July 4, 1966 and you have not requested reconsideration as described below, you may, within 30 days after the date of the decision, ask for a hearing before an Office of Workers' Compensation Programs (OWCP) representative. At the hearing, you will be afforded an opportunity to present evidence, either oral or written, in further support of your claim. The hearing will be informal and will be held at a convenient location. You may be represented at the hearing by any person authorized by you in writing. (Injury compensation claims under this Act can be extremely contentious. The government often tries its best to deny claims. Thus, it might be a good idea for you to hire a professional or seek help from a union or other employee group to assist you *every step of the way*. Even small mistakes along the line can hurt your case or possibly have it thrown out.)

As soon as possible after the hearing, a copy of the OWCP representative's decision will be mailed to you. You will have the right to appeal this decision. The request for hearing should be addressed to the Office of Workers' Compensation Programs, Branch of Hearings and Review, P.O. Box 37117, Washington, D.C. 20013-7117. Section 8124(b)(1) of the Act provides entitlement to a hearing only before reconsideration.

In lieu of an oral hearing, you may request a review of the written record by an OWCP representative. You may submit additional written evidence or argument in further support of your claim. You may not have an oral hearing and a review of the written record on the same issue. The request for review of the written record should be addressed to the Branch of Hearings and Review at the address shown above.

If you have other evidence which you believe to be pertinent, you may ask the OWCP to reconsider the decision. No special form is required, but the request must be in writing and state clearly the grounds upon which reconsideration is requested. Also, the request must be accompanied by evidence not previously submitted, such as medical reports, affidavits or statements. In order to insure that you receive a new and independent evaluation of the evidence, your case will be reconsidered by persons other than those who made the original determination. Request for reconsideration, along with new evidence, should be addressed to the office handling your case. Reconsideration may be requested within one year of the most recent decision on the merits of the claim, whether or not a hearing has been held. Where reconsideration is initially requested, you are not entitled to a hearing.

If you believe that all available evidence has been submitted, you have the right to appeal to the Employees' Compensation Appeals Board for review of the decision. Review by the appeals board is limited to the evidence of record. No new evidence may be submitted to the board. Request for review by the board should be made within 90 days from the date of the decision and should be addressed to the Employees' Compensation Appeals Board, 300 Reporters' Building, 7th & D Streets, S. W., Washington, D.C. 20210. If you request a hearing or reconsideration by OWCP as indicated above, the 90-day period within which you may request review by the board will run from the date of any later decision by the OWCP. For good cause shown, the board may waive the filing time limit if application is made within one year from the date of the decision.

Mixed Cases

A "mixed case" is one of the more complicated situations that a federal employee might encounter, reflecting the complex nature of many personnel disputes. Such cases arise when some form of job discrimination and another personnel action are intertwined—for example, a disciplinary action based on poor performance that the employee believes is motivated by bias.

A mixed case thus involves an action appealable to the Merit Systems Protection Board that includes one or more allegations of discrimination. Where a discrimination issue arises in connection with an action that is *not* appealable to the Board, the employee may pursue a remedy through internal agency procedures and the Equal Employment Opportunity Commission's regulations.

When an appealable action has been taken against an employee and the employee raises an issue of discrimination, the employee may file a discrimination complaint with the agency or may file an appeal with the Board. If the employee files a discrimination complaint with the agency, he or she then may appeal to the Board within 20 days after receipt of the agency's decision. If the employee chooses to appeal to the Board without filing a discrimination complaint with the agency, the appeal must be filed no later than 20 days after the effective date of the agency action.

Where the employee has filed a grievance with the agency under a negotiated grievance procedure, he or she may request the Board to review the final decision of the arbitrator within 25 days after receipt of that decision. The discrimination issue need not have been raised before the arbitrator; it can be raised first at the Board level.

An agency has 120 days to resolve a discrimination complaint that has been timely filed. If the agency fails to meet this time limit, the employee may file an appeal with the Board at any time after the expiration of 120 days. If the agency issues a decision before the 120-day time limit expires, and the employee is dissatisfied with the decision, he or she may file an appeal with the Board not later than 20 days after receipt of the agency decision.

When discrimination is an issue in an appeal, the Board must decide both the discrimination issue and the appealable action within 120 days. If discrimination was not an issue when the appeal was filed with the Board, but became an issue after the proceedings began, the Board must decide both the issue of discrimination and the appealable action within 120 days after the issue was raised.

If an employee raises an issue of discrimination after filing an appeal with the Board, and if the parties file an agreement with the administrative judge that the issue should be remanded to the agency for further consideration, the judge will remand the issue only if he or she determines that it will be in the interest of justice. The remand order will specify the time within which the agency action is to be completed, which can be no longer than 120 days. When an issue of discrimination has been returned to an agency for action, the Board's processing of the appeal must be completed within 120 days after the agency action is completed and the case is returned to the Board.

Following a final decision by the Board in a mixed case, the appellant may: (1) accept the decision of the Board, (2) file a civil action in the appropriate U.S. District Court within 30 days of receipt of the Board's final decision, or (3) file a petition for review with the Equal Employment Opportunity Commission within 30 days of receipt of the Board's final decision.

If the person petitions the EEOC to review the Board's decision on the discrimination issue, the EEOC must determine whether it will consider the case within 30 days, or the Board's decision becomes final. If the EEOC determines that it will review the decision of the Board, it must complete the process and, within 60 days, either concur in the decision of the Board or report to the Board the reasons why it disagrees with the Board's decision.

If the EEOC disagrees with the Board's decision on the discrimination issue, the Board has 30 days in which to concur in and adopt the decision of the EEOC, reaffirm its original decision or reaffirm its original decision with whatever revisions are considered necessary. If the Board concurs in the decision of the EEOC, that decision becomes administratively final. However, the decision still may be appealed to the appropriate U.S. District Court.

If the Board does not concur with the decision of the EEOC, the matter must immediately be referred to the special panel. The special panel must issue a final decision in mixed cases no later than 45 days after the matter was referred by the Board. The decision of the special panel is administratively final and may then be appealed to the appropriate U.S. District Court.

Security Clearances

Holding a security clearance is required for many federal positions, especially in agencies such as Defense, Energy and State, where the large majority of federal employees holding clearances work. Denial of a security clearance can be the difference between being accepted or rejected when applying for a position; revocation of one can be the difference between being able to continue a job and being forced out of it.

Yet the appeals rights of federal employees in security clearance disputes are very limited—much more so than in other situations that can cause the loss of a job. There is no formal right to appeal to the Merit Systems Protection Board or through a grievance procedure negotiated between labor and management. Only internal agency channels exist, and they often are called inadequate and stacked against the employee.

This has led to calls on Congress to revise the system to give employees the same types of rights they would enjoy in "adverse action" situations. But so far Congress has not acted.

The first thing to know about holding a security clearance is that the government and the courts consider access to restricted information a privilege for the employee, not a right. The government has a great deal of latitude when acting in the interests of national security—but not unlimited latitude.

Security clearances are granted after investigations that get ever more intensive at each level of clearance being requested. Periodic reinvestigations of employees already holding clearances also are performed, varying in frequency and intensity with the level of the clearance. Thus, there is no guarantee that an individual will be able to get—or keep—a clearance even at the lowest levels.

When an investigation brings to light information or actions that make the granting or continuance of a clearance questionable, an agency may move to deny or revoke it. For those already holding a clearance, the first step usually is to suspend access to classified information until the unfavorable information is resolved. This may involve further investigation and an evaluation by the agency's central security office. At that point a clearance can be formally denied or revoked.

When this happens, the individual has a right only to "fair treatment." This includes notification and a chance to challenge a proposed action, provided that classified information is not disclosed to unauthorized persons in the process. The employee generally is told the reasons for the decision and given a chance to respond and appeal to a higher authority.

This is commonly known as "administrative due process." Details of such processes vary greatly among agencies, however. There is no legislative requirement or executive order that spells out mandatory procedures for agencies to use. They have set up their own systems, some with extensive protections, some without. For example, some give employees the right to a hearing of the type held by arbitrators or MSPB, while other agencies don't. And some that give the opportunity to a hearing allow the agency to waive that right.

Because of this discretion, the system is sometimes abused, according to critics who say employees are put in a "Kafkaesque" situation. Some clearances have been suspended for long periods with no explanation to the employee. Also, individuals often are not told why a decision went against them or how to get access to investigative records about themselves.

And the appeals process is widely seen as lacking independence. Generally, these appeals are heard by panels of officials the agency chooses—sometimes the same officials involved in making the unfavorable determination or in the same chain of command.

In some cases the panel's decision is final while in others it is considered advisory and the final decision is made by the agency head or a designated official.

Only procedural questions in such situations are subject to review by MSPB. Such questions include whether the agency met its obligation to give the employee the minimum due process protections of advance notice and an opportunity to respond. Also, when the clearance decision resulted in a loss of a job, an agency must show that it considered the employee for appointment to a non-sensitive position that did not require a clearance.

The rationale behind the grant or denial of a security clearance rests solely with the executive branch agencies, however. A U.S. Supreme Court decision in 1988 (*Department of Navy v. Egan)* held that MSPB cannot review the merits of a removal "for cause" based on national security considerations. The rationale was that an appeals agency such as MSPB doesn't have the knowledge needed to make decisions involving national security.

Whistleblowing

Blowing the whistle carries a great potential for bringing about change as well as getting you in deep trouble with your agency. However, the government may not take or fail to take any personnel action, or even threaten to take or not take an action, in retaliation for whistleblowing.

Whistleblowing is not something to be done on the spur of the moment, or to be taken lightly. Many whistleblowers' careers have been ruined despite the legal protections. People who have pursued this process often say they wouldn't do it again, even at the cost of allowing the waste or abuse that they disclosed to continue.

Possibly no type of personnel dispute takes so much out of a person as a whistleblowing case. They tend to be emotionally charged, complicated affairs that can consume years of a life and in extreme cases ruin a person's health.

Legally, whistleblowing is disclosing information that you reasonably believe is evidence of a violation of a law, rule or regulation, or gross mismanagement, a gross waste of funds, an abuse of authority or a substantial and specific danger to public health or safety. While "whistleblowing" is most commonly associated with providing information to the news media, the protections of whistleblower law also apply to disclosures to Congress, agency inspectors general, the Office of the Special Counsel or an agency official designated to receive such complaints (see Inspector General chart in Chapter 4).

This is a broad definition, but not so broad as many employees seem to think. Calling a reporter and complaining about your boss will not provide you with the cloak of whistleblower protection—unless your boss is involved in one of the types of misconduct listed above.

Many whistleblowers act from noble motives. Major cost overruns in Defense Department programs, deficiencies in meat and poultry inspection, lax enforcement of environmental protections and many more such matters have been brought to the public's attention by whistleblowers who believed their agencies were not serving the taxpayer well.

If you are considering taking information outside channels, you should look first at your own motives. Are you doing it out of a desire to do the public good, or a desire to get even with someone in your organization? Are you trying to protect the taxpayer by disclosing waste or trying to protect yourself by invoking whistleblower status?

Most whistleblowing situations feature some of both motives, although in varying proportions. It can become a chicken-and-egg situation: the employee is in trouble with his agency because of his disclosures and is making disclosures because he is in trouble with his agency. But in general, the more noble the motives, the more likely the experience will be satisfactory to the whistleblower.

You also should weigh your feelings about publicity. It can easily become common knowledge soon in your organization that someone has blown a whistle. The process of verifying such tips, regardless of who is doing the investigating, requires that inquiries be made. Eyes naturally will turn to an employee who is disgruntled for some reason, such as a personnel dispute or personal beef. This is especially true if the information being disclosed is tightly restricted.

A whistleblower may not be able to maintain anonymity, even if the news operation, inspector general or other office to which the disclosure was made never releases his or her name. Of course, many whistleblowers do not wish to remain anonymous, especially those who are trying to shield themselves from a personnel action. To gain that appeals shield, they must be identified as the whistleblower.

If you believe you have been retaliated against for whistleblowing, your first step must be to contact the Office of Special Counsel (see OSC chapter) and ask it to seek corrective action before the Merit Systems Protection Board. The Special Counsel has authority to seek either remedial action—overturning a personnel action already taken—or preventive action—asking for a stay of a proposed action. OSC also has authority to seek disciplinary action against officials who have committed prohibited personnel practices, of which retaliation for whistleblowing is one.

If the Special Counsel ends its investigation of your complaint without seeking corrective action, you may file an appeal called an "individual right of action" with MSPB. You may also file such an appeal if 120 days pass after you file a complaint with the Special Counsel and you receive no indication that it will seek corrective action.

The appeal must be filed at the MSPB regional office covering your location (see MSPB chapter for addresses). It must contain a description of your whistleblowing disclosure, a chronology of the facts and evidence of retaliation. MSPB will order corrective action if you show that your whistleblowing was a contributing factor in a personnel action threatened, proposed, taken or not taken against you. You bear the burden of proving that with decisive evidence.

MSPB will not order corrective action if the agency shows by clear and convincing evidence that it would have taken the same action regardless of your whistleblowing.

Another possible avenue of appeal to MSPB in a whistleblower case exists apart from the OSC/individual right of action route. This involves a personnel action that is normally appealable to MSPB, where the individual contends the action was taken because of whistleblowing. MSPB refers to such cases as "otherwise appealable actions."

In such cases, eligibility to appeal to MSPB depends on the laws and rules applying to that particular action. In general, competitive service and veterans preference-eligible employees have MSPB appeal rights to most actions while most excepted service employees may appeal adverse actions and performance-based actions.

If there is a question regarding whether you come under the jurisdiction of the Special Counsel regarding prohibited personnel practices or under the jurisdiction of MSPB regarding appealable actions, it is wise to file with both in order to preserve your appeal rights.

Whistleblowers Hotlines

Most federal departments and agencies have established whistleblower hotlines to serve federal employees who have complaints or information about fraud, waste or mismanagement. The calls will be to the offices of the inspectors general who were appointed to the various department, and agencies to help wipe out waste and corruption in government.

The General Accounting Office, the investigative arm of Congress, has also set up a toll-free line which federal employees may call to report waste, fraud, corruption and mismanagement in their department or agency. The number is 800-424-5454 or, in Washington D.C., (202) 272-5557.

Whistleblower Contact Information

Department of Agriculture
Room 117W
Administration Building
12th Street and Independence Avenue, S.W.
Washington, D.C. 20250
(202) 690-1622/(800) 424-9121
Leon Snead
Inspector General
(202) 720-8001

Agency for International Development
320 21st Street, N.W., Room 5756
Washington D.C. 20523-0060
(703) 875-4999
Herbert L. Beckington
Inspector General
(202) 647-7844

Central Intelligence Agency
Room 2X30
New Headquarters Building
Washington, D.C. 20505
Frederick P. Hitz
Inspector General
(703) 874-2553

Department of Commerce
14th and Constitution Avenue, N.W.
Room 7898-C
Washington, D.C. 20230
Francis D. DeGeorge
Inspector General
(202) 377-4661
(800) 424-5197/(202) 377-2495

Department of Defense
400 Army-Navy Drive
Room 1000
Arlington, VA 22202-2884
Derek J. Van der Schaaf
Deputy Inspector General
(703) 695-4249
(800) 424-9098/(703) 693-5080

Department of Education
330 C Street, S.W.
Room 4006 Switzer Building
Washington, D.C. 20202-1510
James B. Thomas, Jr.
Inspector General
(202) 205-5439
(202) 205-5770

Department of Energy
1000 Independence Avenue, S.W.
Room 5D039, Forrestal Building
Washington, D.C. 20585
(202) 586-4073/(800) 541-1625
John C. Layton
Inspector General
(202) 586-4393

Department of Health & Human Services
330 Independence Avenue, S.W.
Room 5246, Cohen Building
Washington, D.C. 20201
(800) 368-5779
Richard P. Kusserow
Inspector General
(202) 619-3148

Department of Interior
1849 C Street, N.W.
Room 5359
Mail Stop 5341
Washington, D.C. 20240
(800) 424-5081
FTS 235-9399 or (703) 235-9399
James R. Richards
Inspector General
(202) 208-5745

Department of Justice
Room 4706
10th Street and Pennsylvania Avenue, N.W.
Washington, D.C. 20530
(800) 869-4499
Richard J. Hankinson
Inspector General
(202) 514-3435

Department of Labor
200 Constitution Avenue, N.W.
Room S-1303
Washington, D.C. 20210
(800) 347-3756/(202) 357-0227
Julian W. De La Rosa
Inspector General
(202) 523-7296

Department of State
2201 C Street, N.W.
Washington, D.C. 20520-7310
(202) 647-3320, collect calls
accepted
Sherman M. Funk
Inspector General
(202) 647-9450

Department of Transportation
400 7th Street, S.W.
Room 9210, J-1
Washington, D.C. 20590
(800) 424-9071/(202) 366-1461
A. Mary Schiavo
Inspector General
(202) 366-1959

Department of the Treasury
1500 Pennsylvania Avenue, N.W.
Room, 2412—Main Treasury
Washington, D.C. 20220
(800) 359-3898
Donald E. Kirkendall
Inspector General
(202) 622-1090

Dept. of Veterans Affairs
810 Vermont Avenue, N.W. (50)
Room 1200, McPherson Building
Washington, D.C. 20420
(800) 488-8244/(202) 233-5394/
FTS 233-5394
Stephen A. Trodden
Inspector General
(202) 233-2636

Environmental Protection Agency
401 M Street, S.W.
Room 301 N.E. Mall (A109)
Washington, D.C. 20460
(800) 424-4000/(202) 260-4977
FTS 260-4977
John C. Martin
Inspector General
(202) 260-3137

Federal Bureau of Investigation
Room 7116
9th Street and Pennsylvania
Avenue, N.W.
Washington D.C. 20535
(202) 324-3333
W. Douglas Gow
Assoc. Deputy
Director-Investigations

Federal Emergency Management
Agency
500 C Street, S.W.
Room 825
Washington D.C. 20472
(800) 323-8603
Russell F. Miller
Inspector General
(202) 646-3910

General Services Administration
18th and F Streets, N.W.
Room 5340
Washington, D.C. 20405
(800) 424-5210/(202) 501-1780
William R. Barton
(202) 501-0450

Housing and Urban Development
451 7th Street, S.W.
Room 8256
Washington, D.C. 20410-4500
John Connors
Deputy Inspector General
(202) 708-0430
(202) 708-4200

National Aeronautics and Space
Administration
400 Maryland Avenue, S.W.
Room 6075 (Code W)
Washington, D.C. 20546
(800) 424-9183/(202) 755-3402
Bill D. Colvin
Inspector General
(202) 453-1220

Nuclear Regulatory Commission
Mail Stop EWW 542
Washington, D.C. 20555
(800) 233-3497
David C. Williams
Inspector General
(301) 492-9093

Office of Government Ethics
1201 New York Avenue, N.W.
Suite 500
Washington, D.C. 20005
Stephen D. Potts, Director
(202) 523-5757

Office of Management and
Budget
Old Executive Office Building
17th Street and Pennsylvania
Avenue, N.W.
Washington D.C. 20503
Frank Hodsoll
Deputy Dir. for Management
(202) 395-6190

Office of Personnel Management
1900 E Street, N.W.
Room 6400
Washington, D.C. 20415-0001
FTS 266-2423/(202) 606-2423
Patrick E. McFarland
Inspector General
(202) 606-1200
(Vacant)
Deputy Director
(202) 606-1001

Office of Special Counsel
1730 M Street, N.W.
Suite 300
Washington, D.C. 20036
(202) 653-9125
Kathleen Day Koch
Special Counsel
(202) 653-7122

Railroad Retirement Board
844 North Rush Street
Room 450
Chicago, IL 60611
(800) 772-4258/FTS 386-4336/
(312) 751-4336
William J. Doyle III
Inspector General
(312) 751-4690

Resolution Trust Corporation
1725 North Lynn Street
Room 1125
Rosslyn, VA 22209
(800) 833-3310
John Jay Adair
Inspector General
(703) 908-7800

Securities and Exchange
Commission
450 5th Street, N.W.
Stop 7-9
Washington, D.C. 20549
Walter Stachnik
Inspector General
(202) 272-3157

Small Business Administration
409 3rd Street, S.W.
Room 7150
Washington, D.C. 20416
(202) 376-6766
James F. Hoobler
Inspector General
(202) 205-6586

United States Information Agency
400 6th Street, S.W.
Room 1100
Washington, D.C. 20547
FTS 441-7202/(202) 401-7202
George F. Murphy, Jr.
Inspector General
(202) 401-7931

ACTION
1100 Vermont Avenue, N.W.
12th Floor
Washington, D.C. 20525
Judith A. Denny
Inspector General
(202) 606-4804

The Office of the Special Counsel investigates charges or reprisals against federal employees for lawful disclosure of information relating to fraud, illegalities, corruption or mismanagement in government. (See chapter on Special Counsel.) The number is 202-653-7188, toll-free 800-872-9855.

Chapter 5

What Do I Do Now?

The Freedom of Information Act and the Privacy Act

Federal employees preparing to appeal a personnel action may need to gather numerous documents. Prominent among these are their own personnel files: records of dates of hire, promotions, awards, prior discipline if any, transfers, pay increases and many more. And the employee also may need to see other documents that were not personal in nature but that also affected the personnel action.

Most of these documents are held by the employing agency—the very agency that made the decision that is being appealed. While the employee appeal channels guarantee rights to certain documents, employees often find it difficult to gain access to some records that they believe they need.

Two laws that can help in such situations are the Privacy Act and the Freedom of Information Act (FOIA). The laws work hand-in-hand: the Privacy Act generally controls release of personal records while the FOIA law controls access to other types of agency documents.

The Privacy Act

The Privacy Act of 1974 generally allows federal employees to inspect and receive copies of their files and protects them from having those files disclosed to outside parties (apart from the exceptions described below).

Employees wishing to see or amend their personnel records should contact their personnel office or their agency's designated Privacy Act officer. Requests from former federal employees regarding their official personnel folders should be directed to the Work Force Information Division, Office of Personnel Management, 1900 E St., NW, Washington, D.C. 20415.

Employees can request the agency to correct or amend any Privacy Act-covered information about them that is in error. If the agency does not correct the record, the employee can appeal the agency's denial to a person whose name and address should be provided in the denial letter. If the employee loses the appeal, he or she has the right to file a brief statement giving reasons for disputing the record, which will accompany the record if it is sent somewhere else by the agency.

When making a Privacy Act request, an employee should be sure to give enough identifying information to enable the agency to find his or her record, and assure the agency of his or her identity. Giving your full name and date of birth, and having your signature notarized would help.

There is no set time limit for an agency to respond to a Privacy Act request. General policy, though, is to acknowledge receipt of a request within 10 days and to provide access to the records within 30 days. The law does not permit an agency to charge for the time it takes to search for the records requested. Copying fees may be charged, however.

An employee may sue an agency for refusing to release or amend his or her records. The employee can also sue if he or she is adversely affected by an agency's failure to comply with any of the other provisions of the Act. An employee could obtain money damages in certain circumstances if it is proven, among other things, that he or she has been adversely affected as a result of the agency's intentional and willful disregard of the Act's provisions. Court costs and attorney fees might also be awarded.

The Act provides criminal penalties for the knowing and willful disclosure of records to those not entitled to receive them, for willfully maintaining a record that is not in accordance with the Privacy Act, and for the knowing and willful attempt to gain access to an individual's records under false pretenses.

The law also requires agencies to obtain an employee's written permission before disclosing information concerning him, unless disclosure is specifically authorized under the Act. Information can be disclosed without an individual's consent when the disclosure is: required under the Freedom of Information Act; made to an employee or officer of the agency which maintains the record who has a need for the information in order to perform his or her duties; made under a "routine use" of the documents; made to a law enforcement agency in response to the written request of the agency head; made to individuals acting in behalf of the health or safety of the subject of the record; or required by a court order.

Agencies must keep an accurate accounting of all disclosures of their employees' records, except when the disclosure was required by the Freedom of Information Act, or was made within the agency. With the exception of disclosures requested by law enforcement agencies, a list of all recipients of an employee's records must be given to the employee upon request.

The Freedom of Information Act

The Freedom of Information Act of 1966 gives federal employees, and other Americans, access to government documents that otherwise might not be disclosed or published. While some documents and information are protected from disclosure by the exceptions listed below, millions of other reports, correspondence and regulations may be released.

The law covers executive agencies (except for the immediate office of the President) but not the Congress or courts.

Each agency has a designated FOIA officer responsible for handling such requests. Larger agencies have separate officers for their subdivisions and regional offices. If you are sure which lower-level office would handle your request, send it there; otherwise, send it to the top agency FOIA officer, who will forward it to the appropriate office.

The law specifies only two requirements for requesting information: that a request "reasonably describe" the document sought and that it meet an agency's published FOIA procedures. Clearly mark the envelope and letter as an FOIA request and send it via registered mail, return receipt requested.

FOIA requests also can be made informally. Often information that can be disclosed will be released after a simple contact in person or by phone, saving both parties the trouble of filing and processing a formal request. Many agencies have a policy of dealing with such informal contacts as if they were formal requests. When making such a personal contact it may be wise to mention that a formal request will be filed if releasable information is not provided.

Agencies are obliged to make a reasonable effort to search for and turn over copies of records that are releasable. Agencies have up to 10 working days to answer an FOIA request and must "promptly" provide information deemed releasable. They may charge reasonable search fees, copying fees and, in some cases, fees for the review of records.

You have the right to inspect the documents in person if you believe that the time or expense involved in having the documents copied by the agency would be excessive.

If your request is denied, the agency must state the reason and give the point of contact for an appeal. If your appeal is denied, or if the agency fails to respond to your appeal within 20 working days, you may file suit in the U.S. district court in your area (see district court listings in chapter 14 for addresses and jurisdictions). These appeal and legal rights apply only to formal written requests, not to oral requests.

The categories of information that can't be disclosed under FOIA are government records on: national security; internal agency personnel rules; information specifically exempted by other federal laws; trade secrets; internal agency memos and policy decisions; personal privacy; law enforcement investigations; federally regulated banks; oil and gas wells.

The law provides that if portions of a document are exempt from release, the remainder must be segregated and disclosed. The law also provides that an "arbitrary or capricious" withholding of information requested under the Act can subject the responsible official to discipline.

The Justice Department publishes two books, the *Freedom of Information Case List*, which contains an alphabetical listing of FOIA judicial decisions, and the *Freedom of Information Act Guide & Privacy Overview*, which contains the "Justice Department Guide to the FOIA," as well as an overview discussion of the provisions of the Privacy Act. Copies are available by writing to the Superintendent of Documents, U.S. Government Printing Office, Washington, D.C. 20402, or by calling (202) 783-3238.

Where to Challenge an Agency Action

The following table describes where actions should first be appealed. Where more than one channel is available, an employee may choose only one. However, some provide for an appeal from one agency to another—for example, to the Merit Systems Protection Board after a request for reconsideration at the Office of Personnel Management. Also, many of these matters can be appealed into federal courts once the internal government appeals have been exhausted. See the chapters on the appeals agencies and on administrative and negotiated grievances for further information including addresses, procedures, limits on jurisdiction and court appeal rights.

Agency Action	*Where to Appeal*
• Adverse actions for misconduct • Performance-based actions • Denials of within-grade salary increases • Reduction-in-force actions • Involuntary reassignment • Coerced resignation • Violation of restoration rights following military service or recovery from compensable injury	• Merit Systems Protection Board • Negotiated grievance procedures may be available—depends on existence of local union contract, its provisions and whether an individual is in the bargaining unit
• Equal employment opportunity violation—discrimination based on race, color, religion, gender or national origin • Age Discrimination in Employment Act violation—discrimination based on age (over 40) • Equal Pay Act violation—wage discrimination based on gender • Rehabilitation Act violation—discrimination based on disabling condition	• Agency EEO complaints procedure, then Equal Employment Opportunity Commission if dissatisfied • Negotiated grievance procedure (if applicable)

Agency Action	*Where to Appeal*
• "Mixed" cases—involving both alleged discrimination and other actions that are appealable to the Merit Systems Protection Board	• Merit Systems Protection Board • Agency EEO complaints procedure • Negotiated grievance procedure (if applicable)
• Prohibited personnel practices (see Office of Special Counsel chapter for list)	• Office of Special Counsel (adjudicates before Merit Systems Protection Board) • Negotiated grievance procedure (if applicable)
• Unfair labor practices (see Federal Labor Relations Authority chapter for list) • Negotiability appeals • Exceptions to arbitration awards	• Federal Labor Relations Authority (only agency or union may take matters to arbitration or to FLRA)
• Position classification appeals • Life insurance eligibility determinations • Health insurance eligibility determinations and claims disputes • Examination ratings • Retirement eligibility and other determinations • Fair Labor Standards Act (FLSA) violations • Termination of grade or pay retention after reduction in force	• Office of Personnel Management
• Monetary claims arising out of official duties • Requests for waiver of collection of erroneous payments of pay or allowances	• Internal agency channels, then Office of the Comptroller General if dissatisfied

Agency Action	Where to Appeal
• Retaliation for whistleblowing	• Office of Special Counsel • Merit Systems Protection Board (if OSC hasn't sought corrective action within 120 days of the employee filing a complaint there)
• Minor discipline (reprimands, ordered counseling, suspensions of less than 14 days, etc.) • Challenges to performance ratings not involving claims of prohibited personnel practices • Transfer or reassignment not causing reduction of pay or grade • Disputes over work assignments or tour of duty • Denial of request for training • Similar disputes not involving issues appealable to the Merit Systems Protection Board or other appeals agencies	• Agency administrative grievance procedure • Negotiated grievance procedure (if applicable)
• Final retirement decisions of the Office of Personnel Management: eligibility for annuity, survivor annuity or early retirement (including determination of law enforcement officer or firefighter status); determination of disability, restoration to earning capacity or recovery from disability; entitlement to discontinued service annuity; division of annuity after divorce	• Merit Systems Protection Board
• Security clearance denials or revocations	• Internal agency channels

How to Research Decisions of Federal Appeals Agencies and Federal Courts

Agency Name	Resource	View	Ordering Info
Merit Systems Protection Board	*Merit Systems Protection Reporter (Volumes 1-54)*	MSPB library (open to public), law libraries, or agency libraries; volumes may be purchased through West Publishing Co., Eagon, Minnesota	If purchase is government funded, call (612) 687-6858; if individual is purchasing, call 1-800-328-9352; both numbers have pricing information
Equal Employment Opportunity Commission	Personnet Plus - CD-ROM product; decisions back to 1984	Available on a subscription basis; can search by plaintiff name, agency name, appeal number, date, subject term, or any word or phrase	Personnet Plus Information Handling Services, P.O. Box 1154, Englewood, CO 80150-1154 (1-800-241-7824)
	EEOC Case Decisions, Information Handling Services - microfiche product; decisions back to 1983	Microfiche indexes available by appeal number, plaintiff name, and agency name; subscription includes a printed subject index	Available for use at EEOC Library and other federal government agency libraries
	Federal Equal Opportunity Reporter (bound volumes of selected decisions back to 1980, plus selected court cases)	Indexing available by plaintiff name, agency name, appeal number, and subject term Available for use at	EEOC Library and other federal government agency libraries
	Decisions on microfiche	Selected depository libraries all over the U.S.; indexing available by plaintiff name, agency name, and appeal number	Contact local depository library; inquire for decisions in the depository collection

Agency Name	Resource	View	Ordering Info
Equal Employment Opportunity Commission (continued)	Decisions	Copies - 15 cents/page; Research for decisions on particular subjects - $12/hour. NOTE: All charges waived if caller's total bill is less than $15.	Call 1-800-241-7824
Federal Labor Relations Authority	*Decisions of the Federal Labor Relations Authority (Volumes 1- 43)* (22 volumes are no longer printed)	Maintained in depository libraries around the U.S., regional and sub-regional offices, or at headquarters in Washington D.C.	In Washington D.C., copies will be provided to the public upon request; call (202) 482-6600
	Reports of Case Decisions (current decisions as they issue)	Subscriptions come out twice a month; price is $207/year	Call (202) 482-6600
Federal District Courts	*Federal Supplement*	Subscriptions through West Publishing Co., Eagon, Minnesota (not all decisions are listed; judge decides whether or not the case should appear in this publication)	The file and copy desk at the clerk's office will help the public find specific decisions; OR Call West Publishing Co. (see numbers listed above for MSPB)
Federal Appeals Courts and United States Court of Federal Claims	*Federal Reporter 2nd Series*	Includes decisions of: the U.S. Circuit Court (1880-1912); the Commerce Court (1911-1913); the District Court of the U.S. (1880-1932); the U.S. Court of Appeals from 1891; the U.S. Court of Customs and Patent Appeals from 1929; the U.S. Emergency Court of Appeals from 1943	Call West Publishing Co. (see numbers listed above for MSPB)

Agency Name	Resource	View	Ordering Info
U.S. Supreme Court	*United States Reports*	Law libraries and other places legal resources are kept	Contact superintendent of Documents, U.S. Government Printing Office, Mail Stop SSOP, Washington, D.C. 20402
Other Court Decisons	*Federal Rules Decisions*	Opinions of the U.S. District Courts that are not designated for the *Federal Supplement*; involve the Federal Rules of Civil Procedure since 1939 and the Federal Rules of Criminal Procedure since 1946	Call West Publishing Co. (see number listed above for MSPB)
Arbitration	*Labor Agreement Information Retrieval Service (LAIRS)*	Indexing system of arbitration decisions operated by the Office of Personnel Management	Call or write LAIRS Section Office of Personnel Management Room 7429 1900 E St., N.W. Washington, D.C. 20415 (202) 606-2940
Comptroller General	*Decisions of the Comptroller General of the U.S. (Volumes 1-71)*	Federal employees may order any volume for free	Call (202) 512-6000; give name, address, and case number

General Questions and Answers about Appeals

Q. *Are all federal employees covered by all the appeals agencies?*

A. No. Each has its own eligibility rules. Employees may be excluded from some routes based on their employer, probationary status, part-time status, excepted service status, bargaining unit membership and other factors.

Q. *What happens when an employee is eligible to challenge an action through more than one channel?*

A. The employee must choose one or the other. The employee may not use both channels, nor change the choice in mid-stream.

Q. *What type of relief is available for an employee successfully challenging a personnel action?*

A. All appeals channels have the authority to order some type of corrective action. Relief depends on the facts and outcome of each case, as well as the authority of the agency issuing the decision. An employee might be put back in the *status quo*, the situation existing before the personnel action, or may get partial relief—such as the reduction of the length of a suspension, the substitution of a suspension for a firing, and so on.

Q. *Is an employee who wins a personnel appeal eligible for back pay?*

A. Yes, if he or she meets the criteria set out in the Back Pay Act. That law allows reimbursement for lost pay, allowances and differentials if the victim of an "unjustified or unwarranted" personnel action—for example, wrongful withholding of a within-grade raise, wrongful reduction in grade or wrongful firing.

The award can include interest on the back pay, calculated from the date the pay was first affected. The interest rates are set by the Treasury Department.

The authority doesn't cover other expenses that occurred as a result of the personnel action. Nor are punitive damages available.

Earnings from outside employment while an employee was away from an agency can be deducted from the back pay award. Unemployment compensation, however, is not deducted.

Q. *Is it required that an attorney be used in processing a personnel appeal?*

A. No. The various appeals routes allow the employee to hire an attorney, to have a representative who is not a lawyer, or to represent himself. The choice is up to the individual.

Q. *Are attorney's fees granted in federal personnel appeals?*

A. They can be. The employee must be the "prevailing party" and the award must be in the "interests of justice."

To be a prevailing party, the employee must win all, or a substantial part, of the relief he originally sought. He must show that the relief was the result of his appeal. This can be proved even if the case was settled in the employee's favor before a final judgment of an administrative body or court, so long as it's clear that the settlement was the result of the appeal.

An award is considered in the "interests of justice" in situations including: where the agency engaged in a prohibited personnel practice; where the agency's action was clearly without merit, wholly unfounded or the employee was substantially innocent; where the agency acted in bad faith; where the agency committed gross procedural error, or where the agency knew or should have known it wouldn't prevail on the merits.

Legal fees reimbursement is calculated according to standard rates of payment known as the "Lodestar."

Q. *Can action be taken against a supervisor found to be in the wrong?*

A. If a personnel action is ruled to have been a prohibited personnel practice, discipline on those grounds may be taken against the official who ordered the action.

Q. *Does a supervisor who is found to be in the wrong have to pay money?*

A. Employee suits against supervisors for money damages are relatively common. However, most are dismissed for lack of jurisdiction. In general, managers or supervisors are immune from suit if they acted within the scope of their official duties.

Q. *How long does an agency keep records on grievances, adverse actions and appeals?*

A. Generally four to seven years.

Chapter 6

Where to Find Help

A personnel dispute is essentially a personal dispute because it's personal to the people involved, especially to those facing discipline or another type of setback. The choices of the individual will determine the outcome. But there is outside help available: some of it free, some of it expensive, some of it reliable, some of it less so.

Unions and Other Groups

Many federal employees don't give a second thought to federal unions until they are in trouble. Often they will freely admit that they don't know if they belong to a union or to its bargaining unit, or even if one exists at their worksite. Some are surprised to hear that unions exist at all in the government.

But a union often will be the first place they turn when trouble comes. Often they are surprised to learn that a union isn't available to help them, or if available, might not provide the help they were expecting.

The first lesson they learn is that not all federal employees are covered by union protections—they apply only to those in positions included in union bargaining units. This amounts to about sixty percent of federal executive branch positions—both white collar and blue collar—and about 90 percent in the U.S. Postal Service. (These figures must not be confused with actual dues-paying membership, however. Almost all postal employees in bargaining units are dues-paying union members, while the percentage in the executive branch is much lower, probably less than a third.)

A bargaining unit is a group of employees for whom the union is entitled to act. Bargaining units may or may not be limited to one site or to a certain category of employees or to a certain agency function; it depends on how the unit was organized for the union's representation. Thus, employees can be members of a bargaining unit without knowing it, or believe they are members when in fact they are not. The local union office or agency labor relations office keeps this information.

Eligibility for membership in a bargaining unit depends largely on job responsibility, not on grade. Thus, most managers are not in bargaining units at a worksite, even though the unit may include other white collar employees at the same or higher grades there who have no managerial or supervisory duties.

To enjoy union representation the employee must be a member of a collective bargaining unit.

They can be members of a bargaining unit without being dues-paying union members. Law prohibits unions from imposing dues, representation fees and the like on bargaining unit members—there is no "closed shop" in either the executive branch or the postal service. Unions are required to represent the interests of all bargaining unit members equally, regardless of whether they are dues-paying union members. Thus, in theory at least, union membership (as opposed to bargaining unit membership) makes no difference in whether a union will choose to pursue a grievance.

However, unions naturally are somewhat reluctant to spend time and money representing non-dues paying members. At the very least, a non-member employee might find the union more eager to settle a grievance at a lower level, rather than take the matter to binding arbitration.

On the other hand, some union locals are very aggressive and have a policy of pushing to the limit any perceived violation by management. They may view an action taken against a non-member that goes unchallenged as a potential precedent for future actions against dues-paying members. Thus, they may decide to bring a grievance out of self-preservation.

Even in unionized workplaces, grievances can be filed by individual employees, not just by the union. Thus, should the union local decline to file such a complaint, an employee may bring it himself or herself. But he or she would not have the right to go to arbitration if the decision on the grievance is unacceptable. Only the union—or the agency—can invoke arbitration.

Besides the filing of formal complaints, unions can be of value in other ways, as well. Perhaps most important is their expertise and experience, which an individual otherwise might have to pay an attorney to get, if he or she could find it at all. A talk with an experienced unionist might help a person decide whether it is worthwhile to start a formal appeals process or to try to solve things in another way.

Union officials by definition are more involved with the personnel situation in a workplace than is the typical employee. They tend to be "old hands" who know not only how the agency and the site operate, but also much of its history, as well as the personalities involved. All of these factors may be important in understanding what is really happening in a personnel dispute, and the steps that might be taken to correct it.

Also, unionists often have received formal training from their national offices and can call on those offices for help—for legal advice, for information and for political backing.

They also have the advantage of having been "down this road before." While a dispute may seem unique to the individual, chances are that a veteran union official has seen similar situations many times before and is able to cut to the heart of the matter. This can be invaluable in settings such as grievance hearings where clear-headed thinking is vital.

Most important, employees should be willing to recognize words of wisdom when they are being spoken, and to act accordingly.

In personnel disputes emotions and personal feelings are never far from the surface. In fact, they are a prime cause of many of these disputes. While union officials naturally are inclined to back the employee, they can act as an important buffer between the feelings on the two sides. For example, in most cases, they will advise that they do the talking at a grievance rather than the employee. This can prevent hot words that will only make matters worse.

Unions take pride in helping employees since that is their role in the federal workplace; if they didn't, there would be no real reason to have them at all. However an employee must not consider a union a blank check on which he or she can draw.

Unions have their limits, the foremost of which is financial resources. Many union locals—and also national offices—operate on tight budgets. Partly, this is because there is no requirement that bargaining unit employees pay dues. Those who do pay in effect are underwriting the services for those who don't.

Another factor the employee should bear in mind when approaching a union might be summed up in one word: manners. Employees angered with a personnel situation, or possibly facing discipline or even firing, naturally are upset. This, however, is no excuse to pound desks, throw papers, slam doors and so on—all behavior that has been seen over and over again in these situations. Such outbursts don't help the situation and very often worsen it.

When dealing with a union office employees should remember that while they may have certain rights, they are, after all, asking for help. Demanding that help is not much more likely to make it come about—and if it does come about, it could very well be grudging.

Good behavior when approaching a union for help includes accepting several facts: that the unionist has other responsibilities; that the union doesn't have limitless time and money to devote; that not every dispute in a federal office is grounds for a formal complaint, and that there might be no way to win a certain case.

When confronted with an aggrieved employee, a unionist has to perform an investigation much like that of a hearing officer: try to gather the facts, put them together in sequence, see pertinent documents, speak to witnesses, try to sort out the important from the unimportant—in other words, make a judgment on whether the matter should be pursued.

Naturally the unionist's conclusion in some cases will be to drop the grievance. The employee who finds this unacceptable is free to file a formal grievance without the union's involvement, and may file an unfair labor practice complaint against the union for failure to carry out its representation duty.

However, this is another situation where good judgment must be exercised. Filing such a complaint will not correct the personnel action that is at the heart of the matter. Instead, the best that could happen is that after a series of formal steps the union might be compelled to take up the case. The union officials naturally might feel resentful after this process; they would be acting on a case that they had concluded was hopeless. This would not do much to improve the employee's ultimate chances of prevailing in the dispute.

Many of the considerations that apply to seeking help from unions apply equally as well to professional and other groups. They have generally the same advantages: experience, resources, contacts, a willingness to help. As with unions, of course, they are most eager to help their own members, but membership status might not necessarily close out one of these groups as a source of help. Again, it depends partly on how the employee approaches them and the facts of the case.

But also remember that professional organizations depend greatly on good will to get things done. Unlike unions, they have no direct authority with the agency—no right to bargain, to create a grievance process, and so on. However, if for no reason other than expertise, contacting a professional organization is generally good strategy in any personnel dispute.

Attorneys

Like union representatives, a lawyer well versed in federal personnel law can be a valuable shortcut. An hour or two spent in his or her office could give you a good idea of what to do: if you have grounds to file a formal appeal, what that would involve and your options for settling matters less formally.

But even if you are going to file a formal appeal, you don't have to use a lawyer. You could do everything yourself, from the first complaint form all the way up to an appeal to the U.S. Supreme Court. The question is whether you believe in the adage that "he who represents himself has a fool for a client."

For some people there is no choice. Hiring a lawyer costs money, possibly more than they may be able to afford—especially when all the other costs involved in a personnel appeal are considered. In addition to the lawyer's time, for which he or she may charge $100 an hour or more, there are many other potential costs: filing fees, copying costs, notary fees, delivery fees, travel, research materials, and on and on. (It should be noted that many of these costs will be incurred regardless of whether a lawyer is handling your case or not).

It is difficult, if not impossible, to estimate the cost of pursuing a formal appeal. This depends on how much time the lawyer and any of his or her colleagues has to spend on the case.

Under the various laws that govern federal personnel matters, legal fees can be reimbursed. Generally, the standard is that the employee must be the prevailing party and that reimbursement must be "in the interests of justice." Awards of attorney's fees are thus not automatic. Therefore, it is quite possible to win a case and still come out behind financially after all the costs have been subtracted from any monetary award you might have been granted.

The "right to representation" that personnel law gives you doesn't include the right to free representation—unlike, for example, indigent people involved in criminal cases. An appeals agency will not provide you with a lawyer no matter what your financial situation—their willingness to do it aside, they have no authority to do it. You must pay for your own legal representative and hope to gain reimbursement.

But the right to representation does include the right to be represented by someone who is not a lawyer. This is another way to reduce the costs, but it's up to you to decide whether to put your career in the hands of a co-worker or a brother-in-law who "knows a little about the law."

Nearly half of those who appeal to the Merit Systems Protection Board represent themselves. However, you should remember that this (called *pro se* representation) does not relieve you of the many and often baffling procedural requirements that administrative agencies and the courts impose. They expect you to follow their rules—filing the right papers at the right time, citing previous precedent to back up arguments, stating claims on which they have authority to grant relief, and so on.

The rules of each of these bodies are available to anyone wishing to bring a complaint before them, but these rules often are not models of clarity. Yet failure to meet any of these requirements can—and usually does—lead to a dismissal of the case even without a hearing. And once that has happened, it is too late to go back with a lawyer and ask for another shot.

Another consideration in choosing representation is how much of your time and emotional energy you want to devote to your case. Personnel disputes tend to draw people in deeply. You could easily find yourself spending a great deal of your off-duty time absorbed in the case—giving depositions, producing legal briefs, scheduling hearings, and so on. Many employees become totally consumed by such efforts, often to the detriment of their personal lives and their health. Hiring a lawyer will relieve some—but not all—of this burden.

You also should remember that on the other side usually will be attorneys who are skilled and experienced in personnel law. Federal agencies have not only in-house legal staffs but also the resources of the U.S. Justice Department and contract attorneys on which to call. It is well to think twice before taking on by yourself such formidable opponents on their own ground—even when you are convinced that justice is on your side.

Those with the financial ability to hire legal help have to decide whether it is worth spending the money. This of course is an individual decision, but it should be remembered that attorneys spend three years in law school and much time afterward studying the law for a very good reason: law is complicated and full of potential traps for those unfamiliar with it. This is especially true of federal personnel law, with its numerous and overlapping routes available, and its delicate balancing between the rights of the individual and the rights of the government as an employer.

Should you decide to hire legal help, an attorney with a background in federal personnel law obviously is the best bet. Attorneys tend to specialize in certain areas of law because there is so much to know in any one field that it is impossible to stay current and effective in all. However, it certainly is possible for a lawyer to take up a case in a field outside his or her normal practice.

A local bar association might be able to provide a list of attorneys in your area who practice federal employment law. Other employees at your worksite who have been through legal challenges might be able to recommend someone. Also try some research into cases similar to your own; the decisions often carry the names of the attorneys who handled those cases for the employee side. (Review some of the hundreds of cases in the back of this book for ideas.)

The choice of an attorney is a highly personal one. Beyond expertise and cost considerations, it is important that you be able to work well together, since a formal appeal will require spending a substantial amount of time together. Trust and rapport either will build up or it won't. If it doesn't, find out why and try to correct it immediately. Working effectively as a team will greatly improve your odds of success.

Finally, you must be aware that ultimately, you are responsible for keeping the case on track. It's a well-settled legal principle in federal employment law that an employee is responsible for his or her representative's actions or failures to act. It is rare that an employee who lost a case receives a new hearing on grounds that the attorney failed to represent him or her properly.

Elected Representatives

As an American, you have a constitutional right to petition the government to "seek redress of grievances," a right that isn't changed by working for the government. Many federal employees who lack confidence in their own agencies, the various specialty appeals agencies and even the federal courts, turn to their members of Congress. This doesn't solve their problems overnight, and in some cases unintentionally makes them worse. But in some cases it can be effective.

House and Senate members don't have to be reminded that they hold their jobs because their constituents voted them in. All members of Congress try to serve their constituents in myriad ways, from getting federal grants and spending projects to tracking down lost Social Security checks. Each has a personal staff, numbering in the dozens, assigned to take care of such matters.

By far your best ally will be the representative from your district and the senators from your home state—you are their constituent, their potential voter. Behind them in effectiveness in personnel matters are the two committees that handle federal and postal employee and retiree matters, the House Post Office and Civil Service Committee and the Senate Governmental Affairs Committee. Writing letters to every member of Congress hoping that one will take up your cause is a waste of postage; at best, your letter will be simply routed to your own representatives.

A first rule in contacting Congress is write, don't call. A phone call won't get results any faster than a letter. Should you call your congressman's office, your chances of getting through directly to him or her are slim; doubtless, you will be routed to one of the staff members. And while that staff member will listen to you, he or she almost certainly will ask you to put the facts in writing.

Members of Congress may be addressed at The Capitol, Washington, DC. The House zip code is 20515. The Senate zip code is 20510. The main telephone number for Congress is (202) 224-3121.

Keep your letter to the point and as brief as possible. State what the problem is, what you have tried to do to get it corrected and what you would like to see done. Give your name and phone number for follow-up contacts. Don't threaten, and don't try to pull strings that you don't hold. Remember, they receive hundreds of letters each day.

A letter complaining of federal personnel actions will be treated in the same way as any other constituent complaint—it will start with a junior staff member (probably the same person you would reach if you called) who handles routine inquiries. Since your situation probably will defy quick solution, it likely will be sent to a more senior staff member and eventually might be seen by, or at least summarized to, the congressperson or senator.

The course from there depends much on the personality of the member of Congress. Some might see the matter as outside their authority and simply write back to you suggesting you go through the normal appeals channels. Others put absolute top priority on constituent service, and may call or write a letter to the head of your agency, or to a lower level official who has authority over the matter.

Federal agency officials take contacts from Congress very seriously—and especially so if the member is a leader or sits on a committee that oversees the agency. Congress's ultimate power is the power of the purse, and no official wants to be known as one who angered a member of Congress enough to get the purse strings tightened. A simple letter or phone call from Capitol Hill has been known to get quick results.

But agency officials do not work for the congressman; they take their orders from agency management. Because of this, writing to a member of Congress can backfire.

Sometimes letters from constituents are simply passed on to a responsible agency official with a request for comment or action. Personality can come into play here. An official might resent an employee who is seen as going "outside the chain of command" and set out to make life more difficult for that employee. And sometimes they succeed.

The Media

The power of the "press"—these days called the "media"—has long been a point of debate in America. It's undeniable that the media do influence government decisions and policies. And the media have relied heavily on information from government sources. It's also undeniable that many of these whistleblowers have been motivated in part by disagreements with their agencies that became intertwined with personnel disputes.

The power of the press is the power to bring attention. A few days of following the news will provide examples of government decisions being changed because of unfavorable publicity. These decisions can include federal personnel matters. Moreover, by making disclosures to the media a federal employee can gain whistleblower protections under civil service law that could make the difference between keeping a job and losing it.

However, the power of the media is indirect. As numerous are the cases of the government changing its mind after bad publicity are instances of the government staying its course. A news story, even a very harsh one, doesn't guarantee change.

Simply presenting information to a news organization doesn't guarantee that a story will be published or broadcast. It will have to pass the test of news worthiness. News judgment varies from place to place and individual to individual; there are no written standards for what becomes a story. But personnel disputes in a government office will be low on just about every reporter's and editor's list. They are not likely to find a fight between two federal employees very newsworthy—unless some type of misconduct or national issue is involved.

Not every publication or broadcast station is interested in doing whistleblower stories. They require a long time, and often high costs, to develop. And most news operations are very careful about publishing anything derogatory about someone who is not a public figure in the legal sense of the term. Numerous libel suits that have resulted in huge dollar awards have put them on guard.

Also, the subject may be far afield from what they normally cover. In these days of specialization a problem in a federal office may seem hopelessly arcane to them and no story will be done. Story ideas are rejected in newsrooms all the time regardless of the enthusiasm of the person who first provided the information.

Thus, you may take the whistleblowing risk and possibly be found out in your office without any published or broadcast story having resulted.

Whether anonymity is desired or not, there is another career-risking consideration. The reporter will want to see personnel or other files that may be restricted from public view, or to which you would not ordinarily have access. (An investigator from an inspector general office would want to see similar information but he or she would have official authority to do so.) Providing such information means taking a risk. Making a charge of misconduct against your agency or against someone else does not shield you from punishment for misconduct of your own.

Organizations that May Be Able to Help or Provide Information

Federal Employee Unions

AMERICAN FEDERATION OF GOVERNMENT EMPLOYEES, AFL-CIO. 80 F Street, NW, Washington, D.C. 20001. John Sturdivant, nat. pres.; Bobby L. Harnage, sec.-treas. Phone (202) 737-8700.

AMERICAN FEDERATION OF STATE, COUNTY AND MUNICIPAL EMPLOYEES. 1625 L. Street, NW, Washington, D.C. 20036. Gerald W. McEntee, pres.; William Lucy, sec-treas. Phone (202) 429-1000.

NATIONAL AIR TRAFFIC CONTROLLERS ASSOCIATION, MEBA-AFL-CIO. Suite 845, 444 North Capitol Street, NW, Washington, D.C. 20001. Barry Krasner, pres. Phone (202) 347-4572.

NATIONAL ASSOCIATION OF AGRICULTURE EMPLOYEES. 1270 Woolman Place, Atlanta Perishables Building, Atlanta, GA 30354. Stan Freehoffer, nat. pres. Phone (404) 763-7716.

NATIONAL ASSOCIATION OF GOVERNMENT EMPLOYEES. 159 Burgin Parkway, Quincy, MA 02169. Kenneth Lyons, pres. Phone (617) 376-0220.

NATIONAL FEDERATION OF FEDERAL EMPLOYEES. 1016-16th Street, NW, Washington, D.C. 20036. Robert Keener, pres.; Phone (202) 862-4448.

NATIONAL TREASURY EMPLOYEES UNION. 901 E. Street, NW, Suite 600, Washington, D.C. 20004. Robert M. Tobias, nat. pres.; Bobby Hooten, nat. exec. v-pres. Phone (202) 783-4444.

NATIONAL WEATHER SERVICE EMPLOYEES ORGANIZATION. 400 North Capitol St., Suite 326, Washington, D.C. 20001-1151.

Postal Employee Unions and Professional Groups

AMERICAN POSTAL WORKERS UNION, AFL-CIO. 1300 L Street, NW, Washington D.C. 20005. Moe Biller, pres.; William Burrus, exec. v.-pres.; Douglas Holbrook, sec.treas.; Patrick J. Nilan, legis. dir.; Tom Neill, dir. of industrial relations; Frank A. Romero, dir. of org.; Kenneth Wilson, clerk director; Thomas Freeman, maintenance director; George N. McKeithen, SDM director; Donald A. Ross, MVS director. Phone (202) 842-4200.

NATIONAL ALLIANCE OF POSTAL AND FEDERAL EMPLOYEES. 1628 11th Street, NW, Washington, D.C. 20001. James McGee, pres.; Wilbur L. Duncan, sec. Phone (202) 939-6325.

NATIONAL ASSOCIATION OF LETTER CARRIERS, AFL-CIO. 100 Indiana Avenue, NW, Washington, D.C. 20001. Vincent R. Sombrotto, pres.; Francis J. Conners, exec. v-pres.; Lawrence Hutchins, v-pres.; Richard P. O'Connell, sec.-treas. Phone (202) 393-4695.

NATIONAL ASSOCIATION OF POSTAL SUPERVISORS. 490 L'Enfant Plaza, SW, Suite 3200, Washington D.C. 20024-2120. Vince Palladino, pres.; Margarete A. Grant, exec. v-pres., Adolph Ruiz, natl. sec., Bob McLean, editor/legislative counsel. Phone (202) 484-6070.

NATIONAL ASSOCIATION OF POSTMASTERS. 8 Herbert Street, Alexandria, VA 22305-2600. James Miller, nat. pres.; Ken Vlietstra, exec. dir. Phone (703) 683-9027.

NATIONAL POSTAL MAIL HANDLERS UNION, LIUNA, AFL-CIO. 1 Thomas Circle, NW, Suite 525, Washington, D.C. 20005. William Quinn, pres.; Mark Gardner, sec.-treas; Phone (202) 833-9095, FAX (202) 833-0008.

NATIONAL LEAGUE OF POSTMASTERS. 1023 North Royal Street, Alexandria, VA 22314-1569. Armando Olvera, pres. Phone (703) 548-5922.

NATIONAL RURAL LETTER CARRIERS ASSOCIATION. 1630 Duke Street, 4th Floor, Alexandria, VA 22314-3465, William R. Brown, Jr., pres., Scottie B. Hicks, vice pres., (703) 684-5545.

Skilled Trades, Professional, Retirement and Miscellaneous Groups

AFL-CIO PUBLIC EMPLOYEE DEPARTMENT. (Composed of 33 AFL-CIO federal, state and local public employee unions). 815 16th Street, NW, Suite 308, Washington, D.C. 20006. Al Bilik, pres., John F. Leyden, sec. treas. Phone (202) 393-2820. Fax (202) 347-1825.

AFL-CIO METAL TRADES DEPARTMENT. 815 16th Street, NW, Washington, D.C. 20006. Paul J. Burnsky, pres. Phone (202) 347-7255.

AFFILIATED GOVERNMENT ORGANIZATIONS. Rhoda A. Ruff, pres.; 160 Beach 137th Street, Belle Harbor, NY 11694.

AIR TRAFFIC CONTROL ASSOCIATION, INC. 2300 Clarendon Boulevard, Suite 711, Arlington, VA 22201 Gabriel A. Hartl, pres. Phone (703) 522-5717.

ALLIANCE OF GOVERNMENT MANAGERS. 1331-A Pennsylvania Ave., NW, Suite 159, Washington D.C. 20004, Bun B. Bray Jr., exec. dir.; John M. Ellis, pres. Phone (202) 310-3021.

AMERICAN FEDERATION OF TEACHERS, AFL-CIO. 555 New Jersey Avenue, NW, Washington, D. C. 20001. Albert Shanker, pres.;Edward J. McElroy, sec.-treas.; Gregory Humphrey, director-legis. Phone (202) 879-4400.

AMERICAN FOREIGN SERVICE ASSOCIATION. 2101 E. Street, NW, Washington, D.C. 20037. William Kirby, pres. Phone (202) 338-4045.

AMERICAN NURSES' ASSOCIATION. 600 Maryland Ave., SW, Washington, D.C. 20024-2571. Sandra L. Houglan, M.S., RN, dir. labor relations.and workplace advocacy. Phone (202) 554-4444, ext. 310.

ASSOCIATION OF CIVILIAN TECHNICIANS. 12510-B Lake Ridge Drive, Lake Ridge, VA 22192. John T. Hunter, pres. Phone (703) 690-1330.

ASSOCIATION OF GOVERNMENT ACCOUNTANTS. 2200 Mount Vernon Avenue, Alexandria, VA 22301. Thomas L Woods, exec. dir., Phone (703) 684-6931.

ASSOCIATION OF PART-TIME PROFESSIONALS. 7700 Leesburg Pike, Suite 216, Falls Church, VA 22043. Phone (703) 734-7975.

FEDERAL BUREAU OF INVESTIGATION AGENTS ASSOCIATION. P.O. Box 250, New Rochelle, NY 10801. Phone (914) 235-7580. Larry W. Langberg, pres., James T. Burnett, exec. v-pres.

FEDERAL INVESTIGATORS ASSOCIATION . Ernest J. Alexander, natl. pres., P.O. Box 65864, Washington, D.C. 20035-5864.

FEDERAL FIREFIGHTERS ASSOCIATION. 1095 Blaine Avenue, Idaho Falls, Idaho 83402. Phone (208) 529-5383.

FEDERAL LAW ENFORCEMENT OFFICERS ASSOCIATION. 192 Oak Street, Amityville, NY 11701-3028. John B. Knowles, admin. dir., Phone (516) 264-0260.

FEDERAL MANAGERS ASSOCIATION. 1000 16th Street, NW, Suite 701, Washington, D.C. 20036. Bruce L. Moyer, ex. dir. (202) 778-1500.

FEDERAL PHYSICIANS ASSOCIATION, THE,P.O. Box 45150, Washington, D.C. 20026, Dennis W. Boyd, exec, dir., (703)455-5947.

FEDERALLY EMPLOYED WOMEN. 1400 Eye Street, NW, Suite 425, Washington, D.C. 20005. Carolyn Kroon, pres.; Karen Scott, exec. dir. Phone (202) 898-0994, FAX (202) 898-0998.

FEDERATION OF ORGANIZATIONS FOR PROFESSIONAL WOMEN. 2001 S St., NW, Suite 500, Washington D.C. 20009. Viola M. Young-Horvath, Ph.D. Phone (202) 328-1415.

FORUM OF UNITED STATES ADMINISTRATIVE LAW JUDGES, THE. Michael O. Miller, pres; P.O. Box 14076, Washington, D.C. 20044-4076. Phone (703) 235-2110.

GRAPHIC COMMUNICATIONS INTERNATIONAL UNION. 1900 L Street, NW, Washington, D.C. 20036. James J. Norton, pres. Phone (202) 462-1400.

INTERNATIONAL ASSOCIATION OF FIRE FIGHTERS. 1750 New York Avenue, NW, Washington, D.C. 20006. Alfred K. Whitehead, pres.; Vincent J. Bollon, sec-treas. Phone (202) 737-8484

INTERNATIONAL ASSOCIATION OF MACHINISTS AND AEROSPACE WORKERS—GOVERNMENT EMPLOYEES DEPARTMENT. 9000 Machinists Place, Upper Marlboro, MD 20772-2687. John F. Meese, Director. Phone (202) 857-5235.

INTERNATIONAL BROTHERHOOD OF BOILERMAKERS, IRON SHIP BUILDERS, BLACKSMITHS, FORGERS AND HELPERS. Ande Abbott, dir. Ship Building & Marine Div., 2722 Merrilee Drive, Suite 360, Fairfax, VA 22031. Phone (703) 560-1493.

INTERNATIONAL BROTHERHOOD OF ELECTRICAL WORKERS. 1125 15th Street, NW, Washington, D.C. 20005. Gil Bateman, dir, govt employees dept. Phone (202) 728-6042.

INTERNATIONAL BROTHERHOOD OF FIREMEN AND OILERS. 1100 Circle 75 Parkway, Suite 350, Atlanta, Ga. 30339. Jimmy L Walker, Intl. pres., Michael A. Matz, Intl. sec.-treas. Phone (404) 933-9104.

INTERNATIONAL BROTHERHOOD OF TEAMSTERS. 25 Louisiana Avenue, NW, Washington, D.C, 20001. Ron Carey, general pres., Tom Sever, general sec-treas..Phone (202) 624-6800.

INTERNATIONAL FEDERATION OF PROFESSIONAL AND TECH-NICAL ENGINEERS. 8701 Georgia Avenue, Suite 701, Silver Spring, MD 20910. James E. Sommerhauser, pres. Phone (301) 565-9016.

INTERNATIONAL UNION OF OPERATING ENGINEERS. 1125 17th Street, NW, Washington, D.C. 20036. Frank Hanley., gen. pres. Phone (202) 429-9100.

NATIONAL ASSOCIATION OF AERONAUTICAL EXAMINERS. 640 Iowa Street, San Diego, CA 92154-1146. George P. Major, pres. Phone (619) 545-7031, Autovon 735-7031/7037.

NATIONAL AIR TRAFFIC CONTROLLERS ASSOCIATION. 444 N. Capitol Street, NW, Washington, D.C. 20001. Phone (202) 347-4572.

NATIONAL ASSOCIATION OF AIR TRAFFIC SPECIALISTS. 4740 Corridor Place, Suite C, Beltsville, MD 20705. Marsha J. Brown, pres. Phone (301) 595-2012.

NATIONAL ASSOCIATION OF ASCS COUNTY OFFICE EMPLOY-EES. Wayne Perryman, pres., P.O. Box 318, Lonoke, Ark. 72086. (501) 676-6660. ; Leo Osborne, sec. treas., 740 South Main, Nephi, UT 84648. Phone (801) 623-2182.

NATIONAL ASSOCIATION OF FEDERAL INJURED WORKERS. P.O. Box 73578, Puyallup, WA 98373.Wil Clow, dir., Phone (206) 848-7442.

NATIONAL ASSOCIATION OF FEDERAL VETERINARIANS. 1101 Vermont Avenue, NW, Suite 710, Washington, D.C. 20005. Dr. Owen W. Hester, pres.; Dr. Edward L. Menning, exec. v.-pres. Phone (202) 289-6334.

NATIONAL ASSOCIATION OF PLANNERS/ESTIMATORS AND PROGRESSMEN (IFPTE Affiliate). Don Smith, pres., P.O. Box 5112, Bear Creek Station, Belfair, WA 98528, (206) 275-5744. Terry Taylor, vice pres., P.O. Box 31921, Jacksonville, FL. 32230, (904) 772-5629; Howard Wilcox, sec. treas., 3079 Rocky Point Road, NW, Bremerton, WA 98312. Phone (206) 479-4740.

NATIONAL ASSOCIATION OF RETIRED FEDERAL EMPLOYEES. 1533 New Hampshire Avenue, NW, Washington, D.C. 20036. Charles Carter, pres.; Carolyn LeeDecker, chief, op. off. Phone (202) 234-0832.

NATIONAL COUNCIL OF INDUSTRIAL NAVAL AIR STATIONS. 12345 Peach Orchard Drive, Jacksonville, FL 32223. Dennis A. Wood, pres. Phone (904) 260-9101.

NATIONAL COUNCIL OF JEWISH GOVERNMENT EMPLOYEE ORGANIZATIONS. 45 E. 33rd Street, Suite 604, New York, NY 10016. Louis Weiser, pres. Phone (212) 689-2015.

NATIONAL MARINE ENGINEERS BENEFICIAL ASSOCIATION. Alexander Cullison, natl. pres., 444 North Capitol Street, Suite 800, Washington, DC. 20001, Phone (202) 347-8585.

NATIONAL SOCIETY OF PROFESSIONAL ENGINEERS. 1420 King Street, Alexandria, VA 22314 Donald G. Weinert, exec. dir. Phone (703) 684-2800.

ORGANIZATION OF PROFESSIONAL EMPLOYEES (OPEDA), (Agriculture Dept.) P.O. Box 381, Washington, D.C. 20044. Phone (202) 720-4898, FAX (202) 720-2799.

OVERSEAS EDUCATION ASSOCIATION. 1201 16th Street, NW, Washington, D.C. 20036. Jackie Rollins, pres.; Ronald Austin, exec. dir. & gen. counsel; Sandra Vickstrom, dir.of programs; Connie Shanaghan, dir. of admin. Phone (202) 822-7850.

OVERSEAS FEDERATION OF TEACHERS, AFT, AFL/CIO. Dr. Marie Sainz-Funaro, pres.; CMR 426 - Box 541, APO AE 09613. Phone 0039-586-503418 (Italy). Ernest J. Lehmann, European Director, CMR 428 - Box 1276, APO AE 09628 Phone (0039-45-8034943 (Italy). Mel Cann, vice pres., CMR 427 - Box 1174, APO AE, phone 0039-444-597196 (Italy).

PATENT OFFICE PROFESSIONAL ASSOCIATION. P.O. Box 2745, Arlington, VA 22202. Ronald J. Stern, pres. Phone (703) 308-0818.

POLICE ASSOCIATION OF THE DISTRICT OF COLUMBIA. 1441 Pennsylvania Avenue, SE, Washington D.C. 20003. Ralph T. Pfister, pres.; Bruce Nixon, exec. dir. (202) 543-9557.

PROFESSIONAL AIRWAYS SYSTEMS SPECIALISTS. District No. 1-MEBA/NMU PASS Division, 305 S. Andrews Avenue, Suite 840, Ft. Lauderdale, FL 33301. Howard E. Johannssen, div. chairman, Phone (305) 779-7277.

PROFESSIONAL ENGINEERS IN GOVERNMENT (A division of NSPE). 1420 King Street, Alexandria, VA 22314. Karen Lambert, dir. Phone (703) 684-2833.

PROFESSIONAL MANAGERS ASSOCIATION. Helene Benson, pres. P.O. Box 895, Washington, D.C. 20044. Phone (202) 927-3990.

SERVICE EMPLOYEES INTERNATIONAL UNION (AFL-CIO-CLC). 1313 L. Street, NW, Washington, D.C. 20005. John Sweeney, pres. Phone (202) 898-3200.

SOCIAL SECURITY MANAGEMENT ASSOCIATIONS NATIONAL COUNCIL, P.O. Box 749, Rockville, MD 20848-0749. Daniel M. Smith, pres. Phone (706) 731-0667: Janet M. Garry, Washington rep., Phone (301) 770-1850.

SOCIETY OF FEDERAL LABOR RELATIONS PROFESSIONALS. 1730 Rhode Island Avenue, NW, Suite 512, Washington, D.C. 20036-3169. Joyce K. Blackwell, Exec. sec., (202) 785-8529.

UNITED POWER TRADES ORGANIZATION. PO Box 428, Dallesport, WA. 98617. Phone/FAX (509)767-4773. Richard Fadness, pres., Tom Gjovik, sec., Phone (503)451-1217, FAX (503)451-1309, P.O. Box 306, Lebanon, OR 97355.

Chapter 7

The Comptroller General (General Accounting Office)

The Comptroller General, who is head of the General Accounting Office, has the authority to decide various types of claims brought against and by the government. This includes matters of compensation, leave, travel, relocation and other monetary issues that may arise between a federal employee and his or her agency.

The Comptroller General's authority over such matters rests in his power to determine the legality of the spending of appropriated money. It is exercised when the legality of an expense is questioned by either an agency or another "interested party," such as an individual employee.

In general, such claims are subject to a six-year statute of limitations, starting from the date the claim accrued. Other statutes of limitations may apply under laws governing certain claims. The burden of proving timeliness lies with the claimant.

Hypothetical questions generally are not accepted since they do not present questions of law that can be decided under the Comptroller General's authority over claims.

The Comptroller General also generally will not consider "minimal" claims, which it defines as matters involving $25 or less. In such cases, agency disbursing and certifying officers are to rely on written advice from the agency official designated to interpret previous Comptroller General rulings.

Certain claims involving erroneous payments to employees may be waived in whole or in part if collection "would be against equity and good conscience and not in the best interests of the United States." If the amount involved is not more than $1,500, the debt may be waived by the agency head; amounts over $1,500 may only be waived by the Comptroller General (PL 102-190, December 5, 1991). Also, there must be no indication of fraud, misrepresentation, fault or lack of good faith on the part of the employee. Any significant unexplained increase in pay or allowances which would require a reasonable person to make inquiries about the correctness of the amount ordinarily would not be waived if the employee failed to bring the matter to the attention of appropriate officials.

Any incorrect payments made on the basis of erroneous advice or actions of government officials are recoverable by the government. The fact that agency personnel may have certified an erroneous voucher does not relieve an employee from the obligation to refund any amount overpaid. This rule cannot be circumvented by invoking principles of contract law, since federal employees are appointed and serve under personnel laws and rules, not under contractual relationships with the government.

Generally the government is not responsible for paying interest on accounts or claims that the Comptroller General orders to be paid, except when interest is stipulated by contract or by law. One law that does allow such payment is the Back Pay Act, covering many federal employment matters.

Who May File a Claim

An individual employee who has exhausted the administrative channels available to him by getting a final decision from his agency may file a claim with the Comptroller General's Claims Group.

A disbursing official or the head of an agency may apply to the Comptroller General for a decision upon any question involving a payment to be made. Also, certifying officers are granted the same right to obtain a decision on any question of law involved in a payment on any vouchers submitted to them for certification. Thus, when a certifying officer has doubts about the legality of an expenditure which he has been asked to certify, he should request a decision from the Comptroller General.

Also, claims that cannot be resolved by a department or agency can be taken directly to the Comptroller General.

What May Be the Subject of a Claim

Matters of payment of pay and allowances and of travel, transportation and relocation expenses and allowances make up the majority of claims brought to the Comptroller General. Claims are subject to the following limits on the office's authority:

• It is the policy of the Comptroller General not to question the constitutionality of a statute enacted by the Congress.

• The Comptroller General has no authority to issue formal opinions concerning the application of criminal conflict of interest statutes.

- Final decisions of the Merit Systems Protection Board will not be reviewed, nor will allegations of unfair labor practices (since the Federal Labor Relations Authority has exclusive jurisdiction to decide such complaints).

Other matters generally not reviewable by the Comptroller General include: civil service retirement annuity claims; federal income tax consequences of claims settlements; matters pending before other forums such as federal courts; matters related to a grievance; claims involving the Federal Tort Claims Act; claims involving the U.S. Postal Service; compensation for work injuries sustained by employees; claims for civilian disability retirement; position classification issues; discrimination complaints, and matters already adjudicated by a federal court.

Filing a Claim

A claimant should first file his or her claim with the administrative department or agency out of whose activities the claim arose. The agency will initially decide the claim.

If the claimant is not satisfied with the agency's determination, he or she may appeal to the Claims Group, General Accounting Office, Washington, D.C. 20548. Generally no particular form is required for filing a claim, but it must be in writing over the signature and address of the claimant or an attorney or other agent acting on his or her behalf.

Claims are settled on the basis of the facts as established by the government agency involved and by evidence submitted by the claimant. Settlements are founded on a determination of the legal liability of the United States under the factual situation that is established by the record. The burden is on claimants to establish the liability of the United States and their own rights to payment.

Settlement of claims is based on a written record only. The agency has no authority to conduct adversarial hearings or to interview witnesses. When questions of fact are disputed, the policy is to accept the position of the administrative officers, in the absence of convincing evidence to the contrary.

The Claims Group will certify claims for payment either through a certificate of settlement or by certificate of allowance placed on a voucher. Totally disallowed claims will be announced through a settlement certificate. Partially disallowed claims will be explained in a settlement certificate or voucher.

A claimant or the head of an agency dissatisfied with a decision may petition the Comptroller General to reconsider the ruling, or the Comptroller General may reopen a case on his own accord. Applications for reconsideration should state the errors which the applicant believes occurred. In order for a decision to be reversed, a material mistake of fact or law must be proved; an application that merely repeats previous statements and allegations or simply questions the previous ruling ordinarily is not considered a valid basis for reconsidering a claim.

Independent of the Comptroller General's authority, the United States Court of Federal Claims and the U.S. district courts have jurisdiction to consider certain claims against the government if suit is filed within six years after the claim first accrued. The courts ordinarily will not require the employee to first exhaust his or her right to file a claim with the Comptroller General.

For More Information

The Civilian Personnel Law Manual provides an overview of the Comptroller General's role and its decisions in the area of civilian personnel law, including citations to both published and unpublished decisions. The manual, updated periodically, comes in five parts: an introduction and four individual titles on compensation, leave, travel and relocation. Parts can be purchased individually or as a set from the Superintendent of Documents, U.S. Government Printing Office, Washington, D.C. 20402, phone (202) 783-3238.

Another helpful reference is Title 4, Code of Federal Regulations, "Accounts," available from the same address.

To obtain copies of Comptroller General decisions, call (202) 275-6241 or write or visit Room 1000, GAO Headquarters, 441 G St., N.W., Washington, D.C. 20548.

GAO also operates a research service at (202) 512-6000 and maintains an indexing and research section at Room 6536 of its headquarters, same address, which keeps a digest and citation system for decisions of the Comptroller General.

Questions and Answers

Q. *Who is the Comptroller General?*

A. The head of the General Accounting Office, an arm of Congress.

Q. *What authority does he have over decisions about appropriated funds?*

A. The authority to settle public accounts and approve or disapprove payments made by the government.

Q. *Who may apply to the CG for decisions about payments?*

A. A disbursing official or the head of an agency may apply to the CG. Also, an individual employee may request a decision of the CG after a final decision by his own agency.

An individual also may ask for a waiver of collection of an erroneous payment of travel, transportation or relocation expenses and allowances. Collection may be waived in whole or in part when the claim is in an amount totaling $500 or less and the collection would be against equity and good conscience and not in the best interest of the U.S.

Q. *Is there a certain form that must be used?*

A. No. But the request must be in writing and should be accompanied by an original voucher, properly certified and approved, and other supporting documents.

Q. *What is the standard for reversing a prior decision?*

A. A mistake of law or fact must be proved. Mere disagreement with the previous decision is not a proper basis for reversal of a decision upon reconsideration.

Q. *What happens when a claimant is given erroneous advice and authorization regarding a payment?*

A. The government may repudiate erroneous advice and authorizations of its officials, and any payments made on the basis of such erroneous advice or authorizations are recoverable by the government.

Q. *What are the time limitations for claims against the United States?*

A. The claim must be received by the CG within six years from the date it first accrued. The starting date of a claim for compensation is the day the services were first performed.

Q. *Who has the burden of proof in these claims?*

A. The burden of proof is on the claimants to establish the liability of the United States and the claimants' right to payment. The burden is on the claimant to prove every element of the claim. In the absence of government records—or any other documentation substantiating the claim—the claim is disallowed. The CG generally accepts the statement of facts furnished by the administrative officers if there is no convincing evidence to the contrary.

Q. *Are hearings conducted?*

A. No. All claims are considered on the basis of the written record only.

Q. *Will GAO make a ruling in advance where an expense might be questionable?*

A. The GAO generally will not consider hypothetical questions. Such questions are usually deferred for future consideration in the context of a specific claim. But the CG will answer requests for advanced rulings on specific cases if asked by competent authority, such as an agency disbursing officer without questioning the propriety of a payment. This is on a case-by-case basis, however.

Q. *Does the CG ever review or reconsider claims settlements?*

A. Claims settlements will be reviewed:

• At the discretion of the CG upon the written application of 1) a person whose claim has been settled, or 2) the head of the department or government establishment to which the claim or account relates; or

• for the CG's own reasons.

Q. *What are the limits on the CG's authority?*

A. The CG has no jurisdiction over: the constitutionality of a statue enacted by the Congress; criminal conflict of interest statutes; a final decision of the MSPB; allegations concerning unfair labor practices; matters in litigation; claims from other than GAO employees for damages in a tort action; claims and litigation involving the U.S. Postal Service; claims for the loss of, or damage to, personal property; medical expense claims; disability retirement; annuity entitlement; classification appeals, and claims of discrimination.

Q. *Will the CG issue a decision or comment on the merits of a matter which is subject to a negotiated grievance procedure?*

A. Only upon the request of an agency and labor organization.

Q. *Does the government pay interest on its unpaid accounts or claims?*

A. Only when interest is stipulated for in legal and proper contracts, or when allowance of interest is specifically directed by statute.

Q. *Can decisions of the CG be appealed into federal court?*

A. Some claims may fall under the jurisdiction of the U.S. Court of Federal Claims or a federal district court.

Chapter 8

Equal Employment Opportunity Commission

E ditors' Note As this book went to print Congress was considering an overhaul of federal equal employment opportunity complaint processing procedures. Some duties would be transferred from individual agencies to the EEOC, with new filing and processing time limits imposed. If you are involved in a matter likely to go to EEOC double check the procedures you must follow.

The Equal Employment Opportunity Commission enforces anti-discrimination law in both the federal and private sectors.

EEOC was created in 1964 by the Civil Rights Act to enforce that law's prohibition on employment discrimination based on race, color, sex, religion or national origin. It later took on responsibility for enforcing the Age Discrimination in Employment Act of 1967, the Equal Pay Act of 1963, parts of the Rehabilitation Act of 1973, and the Americans with Disabilities Act of 1990.

The agency, led by a five-member commission, also coordinates federal equal employment opportunity rules and policies.

EEOC oversees agencies' affirmative action efforts and their administrative complaints process, administers the complaints hearings program and reviews final agency decisions on complaints. If that review demonstrates that discrimination has occurred which has not been fully remedied, EEOC may order the agency to provide complete relief.

EEOC also provides technical assistance and information to complainants, agency heads, senior management officials of federal agencies and employee groups and organizations on EEOC procedures and rules. It also sponsors periodic seminars on the appeals process and the resolution of federal sector disputes.

Who May File a Discrimination Complaint

A federal government employee or applicant who believes that he or she has been discriminated against because of race, color, religion, sex, national origin, disability or age may file a discrimination

---

complaint with the agency concerned, under the procedures outlined below.

In cases where the employee alleges violations that would otherwise be appealable to the Merit Systems Protection Board, the complaint of discrimination will be processed under special "mixed case" rules.

If an employee is covered by an agency grievance procedure (or one produced through bargaining with a union) that allows discrimination complaints to be raised through that channel, he or she may choose to file either a complaint through EEO procedures or a grievance, *but not both*. The employee is considered to have made this choice when the initial written complaint or grievance is filed and may not later switch to the other process.

Complaints may also be brought on behalf of a class of employees, former employees or applicants who believe they suffered discrimination. Such a complaint may be brought by an individual acting in the interests of the group. An action certified as a class complaint proceeds through the appeals process, and members of the class may come forward to claim relief if the employing agency or the EEOC finds that discrimination has occurred.

Regulations governing the complaint process are found in 29 CFR 1614.

Discrimination Prohibited

EEOC's federal sector responsibilities include oversight of: Title VII of the Civil Rights Act of 1964, prohibiting employment discrimination based on race, color, sex, religion or national origin; the Age Discrimination in Employment Act of 1967, which protects employees and applicants 40 years of age and older from age-based discrimination; the Equal Pay Act of 1963, which protects men and women who perform substantially equal work in the same establishment from sex-based wage discrimination; and Section 501 of the Rehabilitation Act of 1973, which prohibits federal sector discrimination against persons with disabilities. Retaliation against a person who participates in a discrimination complaint process or opposes a discriminatory employment practice also is illegal. A complaint of reprisal is filed and processed in the same manner as other complaints of discrimination.

The Civil Rights Act— Title VII of the 1964 Civil Rights Act prohibits discrimination on the basis of race, color, religion, national origin and sex. The act did not include federal employees when passed but it was amended in 1972 to cover them. An employee who believes he or she suffered from a loss of employment opportunity because of unlawful discrimination or in retaliation for filing a discrimination complaint, participating in the EEO process or opposing a discriminatory employment practice may bring a complaint under Title VII.

Sexual harassment is a violation of Section 703 of Title VII. Sexual harassment is unwelcome sexual advances, requests for sexual favors and other verbal or physical conduct of a sexual nature, when submission to such conduct is made a term or condition of the employment or of employment decisions affecting the individual, or when it interferes with the individual's work performance or creates an intimidating, hostile or offensive work environment.

Age Discrimination in Employment Act (ADEA) — Discrimination in federal employment on account of age is prohibited and agencies are required to assure that all personnel actions are free from age discrimination. Enforcement responsibility is assigned to the EEOC. The administrative complaint procedures are available to federal employees and applicants who are at least age 40 who believe they have been discriminated against on account of age. The ADEA provides the right to go to court but is not specific as to time limits or conditions for filing civil actions after a complaint has been filed under administrative procedures. In addition, the ADEA provides direct access to the courts after a 30-day notice of intent to sue is filed with the EEOC, if the notice is filed within 180 days of the discriminatory act.

Equal Pay Act — The Equal Pay Act prohibits sex discrimination in the payment of wages to men and women employed in the same establishment performing jobs requiring equal skill, effort and responsibility which are performed under similar working conditions. Equal pay complainants employed by the federal government should also be aware that relief for sex discrimination in wages may be pursued under Title VII of the Civil Rights Act.

Rehabilitation Act — The Rehabilitation Act requires each federal agency to develop an affirmative action plan for the hiring, placement and advancement of individuals with disabilities. It not only prohibits discrimination against "qualified" individuals with disabilities but also requires agencies to make reasonable accommodations where appropriate, unless doing so would be an undue hardship. Federal employees or applicants believing they are the victims of discrimination on the basis of disability may use the administrative processes available to all complainants, including discrimination complaints, mixed case appeals, grievances under negotiated contracts, or civil actions.

Complaint and Appeal Procedures

Individual Discrimination Complaints — If you, as a federal employee, applicant or former employee believe you have been subjected to discrimination because of race, color, religion, sex, national origin, disability or age, you must, as a first step, discuss the problem with an equal employment opportunity counselor—who is an employee of your agency—within 45 days of the alleged discriminatory act or the effective date of a personnel action. Ordinarily, counseling must be completed within 30 days. If the matter is not resolved, the EEO counselor will notify you in writing of your right to file a formal discrimination complaint.

You must file a formal complaint with an appropriate agency official within 15 days of the notice of the right to file. You may also file a formal complaint if the matter has not been resolved within 30 calendar days from the date you first contacted the EEO counselor. The agency must acknowledge or reject the complaint. If the agency dismisses all or part of the complaint, you will be notified in writing of your right to appeal to EEOC's Office of Federal Operations within 30 days of receipt of the agency's dismissal. The EEOC may determine that the dismissal was improper, reverse the dismissal, and send the matter back to the agency for completion of the investigation. If the agency does not dismiss the complaint, it must conduct a complete and fair investigation within 180 days of the filing of the complaint, unless the parties agree in writing to extend the period.

You have the right to request a hearing or a final decision by the agency 180 days after filing the complaint. If the agency fails to complete its investigation within 180 days, it must notify you of your right to request a hearing within 30 days. In the absence of the required notice, you may request a hearing at any time after 180 days has elapsed from the filing of the complaint. If a hearing is requested, an EEOC administrative judge must issue findings and conclusions within 180 days from the request. If you request a final decision, the agency must issue its decision within 60 days. If you are not satisfied with the agency's decision, you may appeal either to the EEOC within 30 days after you receive the final decision or file a civil action in a U.S. district court within 90 days of receiving the final decision. If you appeal and are dissatisfied with the decision on appeal, you may still file a civil action.

You may also file a civil action after 180 days from the date on which the complaint was filed if the agency has not issued its final decision.

And, you may file suit after 180 days from appeal to the EEOC when no decision has been made. You have the right to be represented at any stage of the complaint process, including the counseling stage, by a representative of your own choosing.

Class Complaints—The class complaint procedure permits a group of employees, former employees or applicants to file a complaint when it believes that they and other members of the class have been adversely affected by an agency personnel management policy or practice because of race, color, religion, sex, national origin, disability or age. Before filing a class complaint, an aggrieved party must contact a designated counselor of his or her agency within 45 days of a specific alleged discriminatory act. If counseling is unsuccessful, after 15 days of receipt of the notice of right to file the aggrieved party may, as an agent of the class, file a complaint showing that the class is so numerous that a consolidated complaint of the members of the class is impractical, that questions of fact are common to the class, that his or her claims are typical of the claims of the class and that he or she, or a representative, if any, will fairly and adequately protect the interests of the class. An initial determination is made on the satisfaction of these requirements.

If the complaint is accepted as a class action, the second phase of the procedure provides for a right to hearing, a recommended decision by an EEOC administrative judge and a final agency decision which is appealable to the EEOC. In addition, an agent may file a civil action after 180 calendar days from the date in which the complaint was filed if the agency has not issued its final decision. If an agency or the EEOC finds discrimination, members of the class may come forward to claim relief. If the agency fails to resolve such claims within 60 days, a claimant may request a hearing on his or her claim for final decision. An EEOC administrative judge drafts a recommended decision on the claim (whether or not a hearing is held) and returns the file to the agency. The agency's final decision is appealable to the EEOC. A claimant has the same rights to file a civil action as an agent.

Remedies are tailored to the circumstances. They may include making the employee whole through awards of back pay or lost benefits, recovery of attorney's fees and costs, placement in the position the victim would have occupied had the discrimination not occurred, and action to correct the source of the discrimination.

For More Information

More information about the EEOC or the laws it enforces can be obtained by calling (800) 669-EEOC. The agency's TDD phone number for the hearing impaired is (800) 800-3302.

Helpful pamphlets include "Information for the Federal Sector" and "Laws Enforced by EEOC."

For a copy of an EEOC decision, contact Information Handling Services, Attention: Telemanagement, 15 Inverness Way, Englewood, CO 80150, phone (800) 525-7052. EEOC decisions also are republished by two private concerns, the Commerce Clearing House, 600 13th Street, N.W., Suite 700 South, Washington, D.C. 20005, phone (202) 626-2200 and the Bureau of National Affairs, 1231 25th St., N.W., Washington, D.C. 20037, phone (202) 452-4200.

Questions and Answers

Q. *What is the commission's role?*

A. To ensure equality of opportunity by enforcing federal laws prohibiting employment discrimination through investigation, conciliation, litigation, coordination, education and technical assistance. EEOC has 23 district, one field, 16 area and 10 local offices. District offices are full service units which investigate charges and conduct litigation. Area offices investigate charges including those involving potential litigation. Local offices investigate charges but forward cases to district offices for litigation.

Q. *What is an EEO violation?*

A. Treating an employee or job applicant differently (discriminating) due to race, color, religion, sex, national origin, age, disability, or for EEO complaint activity.

Q. *Does an employee who believes he or she is the victim of discrimination have to decide between filing a complaint or a grievance?*

A. Yes. The employee may choose to file either a complaint or a grievance, but not both. The employee cannot subsequently switch to the other process.

Q. *Does the employee file a complaint directly with the EEOC?*

A. No. The employee must first consult with an equal employment opportunity officer at the agency. Only complaints of sex-based wage discrimination in violation of the Equal Pay Act are filed directly with EEOC.

Q. *How soon after an alleged discriminatory act must an employee consult with an equal employment opportunity officer at the agency?*
A. Within 45 days.

Q. *What does the employee do after receiving a written notice of final interview with the EEO counselor?*
A. He or she has 15 days to file a formal complaint in writing with the employing agency.

Q. *Can the case be settled even after a formal complaint is filed?*
A. Yes.

Q. *What happens if the complaint is rejected by the employing agency?*
A. The complainant is notified in writing of the right to appeal to EEOC's Office of Review and Appeals.

Q. *What happens if the complaint is accepted by the employing agency?*
A. An investigator is assigned. This investigation must be completed within 180 days of the filing of the complaint. An extension of not more than 90 days can be granted, but only by written agreement of the complainant.

Agencies are allowed to use a variety of investigative techniques and dispute resolution methods. This may include exchanges of letters or memos, written questions, fact-finding and other techniques.

The complainant and the agency are expected to cooperate with this investigation. The investigator may draw an "adverse inference" from a refusal to cooperate.

Once the investigation is complete, the complainant must be provided with a copy of the investigative file. He or she has 30 days from receipt of the file to request a hearing before an EEOC administrative judge or to seek a final decision from the agency.

If no hearing is requested, the agency must make its final decision within 60 days from the end of the investigation. If a hearing is requested, up to 180 more days may pass before findings and conclusions must be issued, and the agency must make its final decision within 60 days of those findings. If the agency doesn't reject or modify the administrative judge's decision within 60 days, that decision becomes final.

Q. *Can a complainant appeal the employing agency's final decision?*
A. Yes. Complainants may appeal to EEOC's Office of Review and Appeals within 30 days of receiving the dismissal or final decision. Employees may appeal to that office once the agency has rendered a

decision on the complainant and 1) the agency rejects the complaint, fully or partially, or 2) the agency cancels the complaint because the complainant failed to prosecute the complaint, or 3) the agency decision does not resolve an allegation of breach of settlement agreement to the complainant's satisfaction, or 4) the agency decision on the merits or the award of attorneys' fees is unsatisfactory to the complainant.

Q. *What are some remedies issued by the EEOC?*

A. 1) Posting a notice to all employees advising them of their rights under the laws EEOC enforces and their rights to be free from retaliation, 2) corrective, curative or preventative actions taken to cure or correct the source of the discrimination and minimize the chance of its happening again, 3) nondiscriminatory placement to the position the victim would have occupied if the discrimination had not occurred or to a substantially equivalent position, 4) back pay or lost benefits or both, 5) stopping the specific discriminatory practices involved in the case, 6) recovery of reasonable attorneys' fees and costs, except in age discrimination complaints.

Q. *What can the EEOC do if it finds that an agency has not complied with its decision of corrective action?*

A. It can: issue a notice to the head of the agency to show cause for lack of compliance; refer the matter to the Office of Special Counsel for action; notify the complainant of the right to file a private lawsuit for judicial review of the agency's refusal to comply with the EEOC's decision.

Q. *Can cases be reopened and decisions reconsidered?*

A. The commissioners may, under rare circumstances, reopen and reconsider previous EEOC decisions. The commission will consider a case on a request to reopen only once.

Q. *When can a complainant file a lawsuit?*

A. A civil suit may be filed in the appropriate U.S. district court within 90 days after receiving notice of final action taken by the employing agency. A suit also may be filed if there has been no final agency decision within 180 days after filing a complaint with the employing agency.

A suit also may be filed within 90 days after receiving notice of final action taken by EEOC on the complainant's appeal or after 180 days from filing an appeal with EEOC when there has been no EEOC decision.

EEOC District Offices

LOCATION	ADDRESS	JURISDICTION
Atlanta	Citizens Trust Bank Building 75 Piedmont Avenue, N.E., Suite 1100 Atlanta, GA 30335 (404) 331-6408 (FTS) 841-6093	Georgia
Baltimore	111 Market Place, Suite 4000 Baltimore, MD 21202 (301) 962-3932 (FTS) 922-3932	Maryland, Virginia
Birmingham	1900 3rd Avenue, N., Suite 101 Birmingham, AL 35203-2397 (205) 731-0082 (FTS) 229-0082	Alabama, Mississippi
Charlotte	5500 Central Avenue Charlotte, NC 28212 (704) 567-7100 (FTS) 628-7100	North Carolina, South Carolina
Chicago	Federal Building, Room 930-A 536 South Clark Street Chicago, IL 60605 (312) 353-2713 (FTS) 353-2713	Illinois
Cleveland	1375 Euclid Avenue, Room 600 Cleveland, OH 44115 (216) 522-2001 (FTS) 942-2001	Ohio
Dallas	8303 Elmbrook Drive Dallas, TX 75247 (214) 767-7015 (FTS) 729-7015	Oklahoma, Texas

LOCATION	ADDRESS	JURISDICTION
Denver	1845 Sherman Street, 2nd Floor Denver, CO 80203 (303) 866-1300 (FTS) 564-1300	Colorado, Montana, Nebraska, North Dakota, South Dakota, Wyoming
Detroit	Patrick V. McNamara Federal Building 477 Michigan Avenue, Room 1540 Detroit, MI 48226-9704 (313) 226-7636 (FTS) 226-7636	Michigan
Houston	1919 Smith Street, 7th Floor Houston, TX 77002 (713) 653-3320 (FTS) 653-3381	Texas
Indianapolis	46 East Ohio Street, Room 456 Indianapolis, IN 46204 (317) 226-7212 (FTS) 331-7212	Indiana, Kentucky
Los Angeles	3660 Wilshire Boulevard, 5th Floor Los Angeles, CA 90010 (213) 251-7278 (FTS) 983-7278	California, Nevada
Memphis	1407 Union Avenue, Suite 621 Memphis, TN 38104 (901) 722-2617 (FTS) 222-2617	Arkansas, Tennessee
Miami	Metro Mall 1 Northeast 1st Street, 6th Floor Miami, FL 33132-2491 (305) 536-4491 (FTS) 350-4491	Florida, Panama Canal Zone

LOCATION	ADDRESS	JURISDICTION
Milwaukee	310 West Wisconsin Avenue Suite 800 Milwaukee, WI 53203-2292 (414) 297-1111 (FTS) 362-1111	Iowa, Minnesota, Wisconsin
New Orleans	701 Loyola Avenue, Suite 600 New Orleans, LA 70113 (504) 589-2329 (FTS) 682-2329	Louisiana
New York	90 Church Street, Room 1501 New York, NY 10007 (212) 264-7161 (FTS) 264-7161	Connecticut, Maine, Massachusetts, New Hampshire, New York, Rhode Island, Vermont, Puerto Rico, U.S. Virgin Islands
Philadelphia	1421 Cherry Street, 10th Floor Philadelphia, PA 19102 (215) 597-9350 (FTS) 597-9350	Delaware, New Jersey, Pennsylvania, West Virginia
Phoenix	4520 North Central Avenue Suite 300 Phoenix, AZ 85102-1848 (602) 640-5000 (FTS) 261-5000	Arizona, New Mexico, Utah
San Antonio	5410 Fredericksberg Road, Suite 200 San Antonio, TX 78229-3555 (512) 229-4810 (FTS) 730-4810	Texas
San Francisco	901 Market Street, Suite 500 Fifth and Market Streets San Francisco, CA 94103 (415) 744-6500 (FTS) 484-6500	California, Hawaii, American Samoa, Guam, Northern Mariana Islands, Wake Island

LOCATION	ADDRESS	JURISDICTION
Seattle	2815 Second Avenue, Suite 500 Seattle, WA 98121 (206) 553-0968 (FTS) 399-0968	Alaska, Idaho, Oregon, Washington
St. Louis	625 N. Euclid Street, 5th Floor St. Louis, MO 63108 (314) 425-6585 (FTS) 279-6585	Kansas, Missouri
Main Office Equal Employment Opportunity Commission	1801 L Street, N.W. Washington, D.C. 20507 (202) 663-4264 (FTS) 989-4264 (TDD) 663-4399	District of Columbia

EEO Complaint Processing

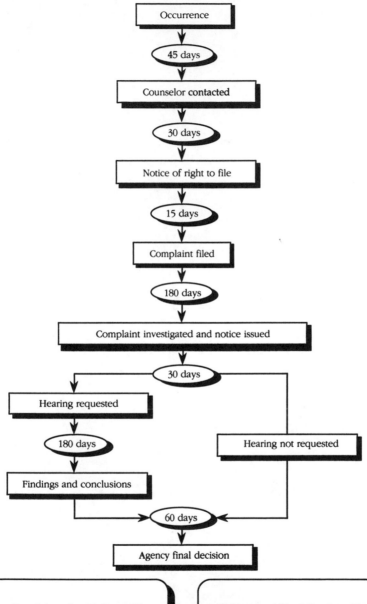

Chapter 9

Federal Labor Relations Authority

The Federal Labor Relations Authority interprets and enforces the federal service labor-management relations statute (Title VII of the 1978 Civil Service Reform Act) which protects the rights of employees of the federal government to organize, bargain collectively and participate through their labor organizations in decisions affecting them.

The Authority also ensures compliance with the rights and obligations of federal employees and the labor organizations that represent them before agency management.

FLRA consists of a three-member body, not more than two of whom can be members of the same political party and one who serves as chair. It operates a nationwide network of regional offices where unfair labor practice and representation cases are filed and processed.

Employees covered by the statute have a protected right to form, join or assist a labor organization or to refrain from such activity without fear of penalty or reprisal. The right includes acting for a labor organization in the capacity of a representative, and presenting the views of that organization before Executive branch officials, the Congress or other authorities.

Covered employees also have the right to engage in collective bargaining with respect to conditions of employment—meaning personnel policies and practices affecting their working conditions. Topics of such disputes can range from smoking and telephone use policies to use of alternate work schedules, from the availability of office amenities, to issues of promotions and reassignments.

For employees, FLRA's primary roles is its power to resolve negotiability disputes, unfair labor practice complaints and exceptions to arbitration awards. Unions commonly use those routes to challenge agency policies and decisions as they affect the group of represented employees or individuals.

Other FLRA responsibilities include determining the appropriateness of bargaining units, supervising representation elections and resolving issues relating to unions' consultation rights with regard to internal agency policies and government-wide rules.

Entities within the FLRA are the Federal Service Impasses Panel, which provides assistance in resolving deadlocks reached in negotiations between labor and management, the Foreign Service Labor Relations Board, which oversees the labor-management program for foreign service employees of the State Department, and the Foreign Service Impasse Disputes Panel, which resolves bargaining deadlocks for those employees.

Who May Bring Appeals

Unlike other forms of federal employee appeals where the individual acts on his or her own behalf, complaints under the labor-management statute primarily are brought by labor organizations that have won the right to represent a group of employees before management.

Federal union membership is generally available to employees of the Executive branch, as well as the Library of Congress and the Government Printing Office. Excluded are non citizens of the United States, members of the armed services, supervisors and management officials, and anyone who participates in a strike against the government. Also excluded are employees of the General Accounting Office, the Federal Bureau of Investigation, Central Intelligence Agency, National Security Agency, Tennessee Valley Authority, FLRA itself and the Federal Service Impasses Panel.

However, a union local must have representation rights for a position in order for the employee to be represented by the union. There are many sites within the government eligible to be organized into a bargaining unit, but for one reason or another, no unit has been formed. Employees in such situations lack rights of representation that would be available to them under the statute if they were in a bargaining unit.

Once a labor organization is recognized as the representative for a group of employees, it becomes entitled to act for and negotiate collective bargaining agreements for them. Such agreements must contain a negotiated procedure for resolving grievances and provide that binding arbitration may be invoked if the grievance proceeding fails to resolve the dispute. Such grievances can be brought by a union—acting on its own behalf or on behalf of an employee—by an individual employee, or by management.

The rights of a union under the law do not preclude an individual employee from being represented by an attorney or other person of his or her own choosing in any grievance or appeal action, except in the case of grievance or appeal procedures negotiated under the statute. Nor do they prohibit the employee from exercising any grievance or appeal right established by law or rule, except in the case of grievance or appeal procedures negotiated between the union and management. In such cases union representation must be used.

An aggrieved employee generally has an option of using either an appeals procedure set by statute or a grievance procedure set in negotiations, but not both. This applies to claims of discrimination, demotions or removals for unacceptable performance, and disciplinary actions based on misconduct.

What May Be Appealed

The most common type of appeal filed under the labor-management statute involves the unfair labor practice complaint. Most of these are filed by unions to protect their interest in representing employees or to seek reversal of management decisions affecting individuals. Management may also file such complaints against the union.

In general, management may not:

• Interfere with any employee's exercise of rights under the statute, including the rights to form, join or assist any labor organization.

• Discipline or otherwise discriminate against an employee because the employee has filed a complaint, affidavit or petition, or has given any information or testimony under the statute.

• Refuse to consult or negotiate in good faith with a labor organization.

• Enforce any rule or regulation that conflicts with a collective bargaining agreement.

• Refuse to honor other union rights, such as the right to have a representative present during an employee interview with management when such a meeting could lead to disciplinary action.

In general, unions may not:

• Attempt to coerce an employee into joining the organization.

• Discriminate in its representation of an employee on grounds of membership in the labor organization or on the basis of race, color, creed, national origin, sex, age, preferential or non-preferential civil service status, political affiliation, marital status, or handicapping condition.

• Call, participate in, or condone a strike, work stoppage or slowdown, or picketing of an agency in a labor-management dispute if such picketing interferes with the agency's operations.

There are several other common forms of appeals. One concerns disputes over negotiability, where the union and management disagree over a matter proposed to be bargained. In most cases such disputes arise because a union has proposed to bargain on a subject over which management believes it has sole discretion.

Another common appeal is the exception to an arbitration award, in which one side—and sometimes both—feel that the award is inconsistent with law or appropriate regulations.

Filing an Appeal

Unfair labor practice charges must be filed with the appropriate FLRA regional office within six months from the date the alleged unfair practice occurred. The regional office investigates the allegations and passes its recommendation to FLRA's Office of the General Counsel, which may bring a complaint before an administrative law judge. The law judge's decision may be appealed to the three-member FLRA governing board. The Authority has the power to order that any employee victimized by the improper practice be made whole and order other corrective steps.

A negotiability appeal must be filed with the FLRA's national office within 15 days after the agency notifies the union of its position that a matter raised in bargaining is not negotiable.

Exceptions to arbitration awards must be filed with FLRA's national office within 30 days after the award is served on the parties.

Parties wishing to challenge FLRA's final orders generally can appeal in the U.S. court of appeals for the circuit in which the party resides or in the U.S. Court of Appeals for the District of Columbia. Exceptions to this include determinations of bargaining units and arbitrator's awards, unless the award involves an unfair labor practice. Arbitration awards under civil service law governing discipline for poor performance or misconduct may be appealed to the U.S. Court of Appeals for the Federal Circuit on the same basis as if the award were the final decision of the Merit Systems Protection Board.

For More Information

FLRA is headquartered at 607 14th Street, N.W., Washington, D.C. 20424, phone (202) or (FTS) 482-6600. A useful pamphlet is "A Guide to the Federal Service Labor-Management Relations Statute." The FSIP can be reached at the same address, phone (202) or (FTS) 482-6670.

For decisions of the FLRA and the FSIP, contact the Office of Information Resources and Research Services, same address, phone (202) 482-6550 for FLRA cases and (202) 482-6670 for FSIP cases.

Unfair Labor Practices

The underlying concept of unfair labor practices is that unions and management must refrain from infringing upon each other's basic rights as well as from violating the basic rights of employees.

It is an *unfair labor practice for management:*
- to interfere with, restrain, or coerce any employee in the exercise by the employee of any right under 5 U.S.C. Chapter 71 (prohibited interference by an agency with the rights of federal employees to organize, form, join, or assist a labor organization, to bargain collectively, or to refrain from any of these activities constitutes a violation of this subsection);
- to encourage or discourage membership in any labor organization by discrimination in connection with hiring, tenure, promotion, or other conditions of employment;
- to sponsor, control, or otherwise assist any labor organization other than to furnish, upon request, customary and routine services and facilities if the services and facilities are also furnished on an impartial basis to other labor organizations having equivalent status;
- to discipline or otherwise discriminate against an employee because the employee has filed a complaint, affidavit, or petition, or has given any information or testimony under Chapter 71;
- to refuse to consult or negotiate in good faith with a labor organization as required by the Chapter (This section protects many of the different rights of an exclusive representative, such as the right to bargain collectively and in good faith over conditions of employment, the right to be the sole representative for its appropriate unit of employees, and the right to be notified of proposed changes in conditions of employment.);
- to fail or refuse to cooperate in impasse procedures and impasse decisions as required by the Chapter;
- to enforce any rule or regulation (other than a rule or regulation implementing 5 U.S.C. section 2302) which is in conflict with any applicable collective bargaining agreement if the agreement was in effect before the date the rule or regulation was prescribed; or
- to otherwise fail or refuse to comply with any provision of the Chapter (5 U.S.C. 7116(a)).

(continued on following page)

(continued from previous page)

It is an *unfair labor practice for unions:*
• to interfere with, restrain or coerce any employee in the exercise by the employee of any right under 5 U.S.C. Chapter 71;
• to cause or attempt to cause an agency to discriminate against any employee in the exercise by the employee of any right under 5 U.S.C. Chapter 71;
• to coerce, discipline, fine or attempt to coerce a member of the labor organization as punishment, reprisal, or for the purpose of hindering or impeding the member's work performance or productivity as an employee or the discharge of the member's duties as an employee;
• to discriminate against an employee with regard to the terms or conditions of membership in the labor organization on the basis of race, color, creed, national origin, sex, age, preferential or non-preferential civil service status, political affiliation, marital status, or disability;
• to refuse to consult or negotiate in good faith with an agency as required under 5 U.S.C. Chapter 71 (This includes, among others, the union's responsibility to approach negotiations with a sincere resolve to reach agreement, and to be represented by duly authorized representatives.);
• to fail or refuse to cooperate in impasse procedures and impasse decisions as required under 5 U.S.C. Chapter 71 (This is identical to the agency requirement.);
• a. to call, or participate in, a strike, work stoppage, or slowdown, or picketing of an agency in a labor-management dispute if such picketing interferes with an agency's operations, or
b. to condone any activity described in subparagraph (a) of this paragraph by failing to take action to prevent or stop such activity; or
• to otherwise fail or refuse to comply with any provision of 5 U.S.C. Chapter 71 (5 U.S.C. 7116(b)).

Questions and Answers

Q. *What does the Federal Labor Relations Authority do?*
A. It sets policies governing relations between management and organized labor in the executive branch (FLRA has no authority over

the U.S. Postal Service; the National Labor Relations Board performs that role for postal employees). This includes overseeing representation elections called to form union locals, resolving issues relating to the duty to bargain, conducting hearings and resolving complaints of unfair labor practices and considering exceptions to arbitrators' awards.

Q. *How can FLRA help an individual employee in a personnel dispute?*

A. Through its power to review arbitrators' awards that are made under negotiated grievance procedures.

Q. *Are all federal employees eligible to use those grievance procedures?*

A. No. Only employees in a union bargaining unit are eligible to use the grievance route set by that unit's contract. About 60 percent of executive branch employees are covered by bargaining units. A bargaining unit is the group of employees covered by a contract.

Q. *Does it matter if I'm a dues-paying union member?*

A. No. The coverage of the contract applies on the basis of bargaining unit membership, not dues-paying status. So does the union's duty to represent you.

Q. *I'm not in the bargaining unit but would like to join. Can I?*

A. Not unless you move to a job that is covered by the unit.

Q. *Do all contracts provide for a negotiated grievance procedure?*

A. By law they must.

Q. *Do negotiated grievance procedures cover all personnel actions?*

A. No. There is considerable variation from site to site regarding what types of disputes may be settled in this process. And certain subjects are prohibited from coverage by law. These include political activities violations, retirement, life insurance, health insurance, suspension for national security reasons, any examination, certification or appointment and any position classification that doesn't result in the reduction in grade or pay of an employee

Q. *Who brings the grievance, the union or the individual?*

A. Either. As a practical matter, most are brought by the union because of the union's expertise and its interest in seeing compliance with the grievance procedure it has negotiated. Generally the union representative does most of the talking at a grievance hearing.

Q. *What happens in a grievance hearing?*

A. Grievances can proceed through several steps, each more formal than the last. At first there might be a simple oral or written presentation to the employee's immediate supervisor. From there the matter might be referred to a management official at a higher level than the one who made the original decision—a second-level supervisor, for example. For this second-level decision, written material usually is required. A possible third step is to raise the issue with a still higher official—for example, a senior manager or executive.

Q. *How long does this take?*

A. Depending on how many levels are available, from several weeks to several months.

Q. *Can the dispute be settled even after the grievance process is invoked?*

A. Yes.

Q. *The decision of the grievance went against me. What happens now?*

A. The union may invoke arbitration. An arbitrator is an impartial third party hired from outside the agency. He or she will hear witnesses, examine documents and so on. The decision could fall in favor of one or the other sides, or could strike a compromise. Arbitrators typically take six months or more to issue decisions, although sometimes they move faster.

Q. *Can the arbitrator's decision be appealed?*

A. Yes, to FLRA. Either of the parties to the arbitration (the agency or the union) may file "exceptions" within 30 days. This must contain a statement of the facts and legal arguments for why the arbitrator erred. FLRA examines whether the award is contrary to law or rule. This process can last a number of months.

Q. *Can FLRA decisions be appealed?*

A. Yes, to a U.S. court of appeals—but only if an unfair labor practice is involved.

Q. *I've discussed my case with the local union but they refuse to bring a grievance. What can I do?*

A. You may bring the grievance yourself. However, you may not invoke arbitration if you are dissatisfied with the decision. Only the union (or the agency) can do that. Also, the union has the right to send an observer to any grievance at which you represent yourself or have a non-union representative.

Q. *The union backed me at the grievance hearing but refuses to go to arbitration. What can I do?*

A. You can bring an unfair labor practice complaint at the Federal Labor Relations Authority against the union for failure to represent you. You will have to prove the union's decision was arbitrary, discriminatory or in bad faith.

FLRA Regional Offices

(Note: Sub-Regional Offices assist in the jurisdiction of their Regional Offices)

LOCATION	ADDRESS	JURISDICTION
Boston Regional Office	99 Summer Street Suite 1500 Boston, MA 02110-1200 (617) 424-5730	Connecticut, Delaware, Maine, Massachusetts, New Hampshire, New Jersey, New York, Pennsylvania, Puerto Rico, Rhode Island, Vermont, Virgin Islands
Philadelphia Sub-Regional Office	105 South 7th Street 5th Floor Philadelphia, PA 19106 (215) 597-1527	
New York Sub-Regional Office	26 Federal Plaza Room 3700 New York, NY 10278 (212) 264-4934	
Washington Regional Office	1255 22nd Street, NW Suite 400 Washington, D.C. 20037 (202) 653-8500	District of Columbia, Maryland, Virginia, West Virginia
Atlanta Regional Office	1371 Peachtree Street, NE Suite 122 Atlanta, GA 30367 (404) 347-2324	Alabama, Florida, Georgia, Kentucky, Mississippi, North Carolina, South Carolina, Tennessee
Chicago Regional Office	55 West Monroe Suite 1150 Chicago, IL 60603 (312) 353-6306	Illinois, Indiana, Michigan, Minnesota, Ohio, Wisconsin
Cleveland Sub-Regional Office	Renaissance Building Suite 420 1350 Euclid Avenue Cleveland, OH 04415 (216) 522-2114	

LOCATION	ADDRESS	JURISDICTION
Dallas Regional Office	525 Griffin Street Suite 926, LB107 Dallas, TX 75202-1906 (214) 767-4996	Arkansas, Louisiana, New Mexico, Oklahoma, Texas, Panama (Limited FLRA jurisdiction)
Denver Regional Office	1244 Speer Boulevard Suite 100 Denver, CO 80204 (303) 844-5224	Colorado, Iowa, Kansas, Missouri, Montana, Nebraska, North Dakota, South Dakota, Utah, Wyoming
San Francisco Regional Office	901 Market Street Suite 220 San Francisco, CA 94103 (415) 744-4000	Alaska, Arizona, California, Hawaii, Idaho, Nevada, Oregon, Washington, All land and water areas west of the continents of North and South America (except coastal lands) to longitude 90 1/4E
Los Angeles Sub-Regional Office	350 South Figueroa Street Room 370 World Trade Center Los Angeles, CA 90071 (213) 894-3805	

Appeals to FLRA of Arbitration Awards

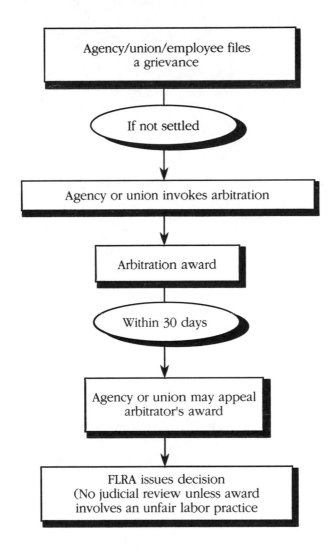

Agency/union/employee files a grievance

If not settled

Agency or union invokes arbitration

Arbitration award

Within 30 days

Agency or union may appeal arbitrator's award

FLRA issues decision
(No judicial review unless award involves an unfair labor practice

Chapter 10

Merit Systems Protection Board

The Merit Systems Protection Board hears appeals of personnel actions brought by individual federal employees. It is an independent, quasi-judicial agency that was designed to be the guardian of the federal merit system.

MSPB was created by the 1978 Civil Service Reform Act to take over the personnel appeals role that formerly rested in the old Civil Service Commission. The Board's mission is to ensure that employees are protected against abuses by agency management, that employment decisions are made in accordance with law, and that the personnel system is kept free of prohibited personnel practices.

The Board hears and decides employee appeals from agency actions, as well as cases brought by the Office of Special Counsel involving alleged abuses of the merit system. MSPB also has jurisdiction over certain other matters, such as the Hatch Act, and it issues studies of the federal merit systems and reviews certain actions of the Office of Personnel Management.

The Board itself is a three-member body based in Washington, D.C., that consists of a chairman, a vice-chairman and a member, with no more than two of the three from the same political party. They oversee an agency with 11 regional offices across the country, and a network of hearing officials—called administrative judges—who issue some 7000 decisions on appeals yearly.

For the Board to decide any appeal of a personnel action, it must have jurisdiction over both the action and the employee filing the appeal. Due to the overlapping nature of civil service law, there are several situations where the test of jurisdiction can be confusing.

One such situation involves employees who are members of union bargaining units that have negotiated grievance procedures covering matters that can be appealed to MSPB. They normally must use the grievance route. If the agreement covers adverse actions and/or performance based actions, however, an employee may choose to go through the grievance procedure or MSPB—but not both. The employee also has a choice when the grievance procedure covers an action appealable to the Board and the employee raises an issue of prohibited discrimination.

Merit System Principles Governing the Federal Personnel System

The civil service law [5 U. S. C. 2301(b)] requires that federal personnel management be implemented consistent with the following merit system principles:

• Recruitment should be from qualified individuals from appropriate sources in an endeavor to achieve a work force from all segments of society, and selection and advancement should be determined solely on the basis of relative ability, knowledge, and skills, after fair and open competition which assures that all receive equal opportunity.

• All employees and applicants for employment should receive fair and equitable treatment in all aspects of personnel management without regard to political affiliation, race, color, religion, national origin, sex, marital status, age, or disability, and with proper regard for their privacy and constitutional rights.

• Equal pay should be provided for work of equal value, with appropriate consideration of both national and local rates paid by employers in the private sector, and appropriate incentives and recognition should be provided for excellence in performance.

• All employees should maintain high standards of integrity, conduct, and concern for the public interest.

• The federal work force should be used efficiently and effectively.

• Employees should be retained on the basis of the adequacy of their performance, inadequate performance should be corrected, and employees should be separated who cannot or will not improve their performance to meet required standards.

• Employees should receive effective education and training in cases in which such education and training would result in better organizational and individual performance.

• Employees should be —
(a) protected against arbitrary action, personal favoritism or coercion for partisan political purposes, and
(b) prohibited from using their official authority or influence for the purpose of interfering with or affecting the result of an election or a nomination for election.

• Employees should be protected against reprisal for the lawful disclosure of information which the employees reasonably believe evidences —
(a) a violation of any law, rule, or regulation, or
(b) mismanagement, a gross waste of funds, an abuse of authority, or a substantial and specific danger to public health or safety.

It is a prohibited personnel practice to take or fail to take any personnel action if the taking of or failure to take the action violates any law, rule or regulation implementing or directly concerning these merit system principles.

The Merit Systems Protection Board is directed by law to conduct special studies of the civil service and other federal merit systems to determine whether these statutory mandates are being met, and to report to the Congress and the President on whether the public interest in a civil service free of prohibited personnel practices is being adequately protected.

Another involves cases in which the employee alleges discrimination in a case that is appealable to MSPB. The Board will hear such cases, but if the employee is dissatisfied with its decision, he or she may ask the Equal Employment Opportunity Commission to review it. If the EEOC and the Board cannot reach agreement, the case is referred to a special panel made up of one member from each agency plus a chairperson who is appointed by the President and confirmed by the Senate. A discrimination complaint in connection with an action that is not appealable to the Board may be pursued through internal agency procedures and the EEOC.

Who May Bring Appeals

About two million federal employees, or about two-thirds of the full-time civilian work force, currently have appeal rights to the Board. Generally, this group comprises employees in the competitive service who have completed a probationary period and those in the excepted service (other than the postal service and a number of other agencies) with at least two years of service.

Probationary employees have only limited appeal rights. They may appeal a termination based on political affiliation or marital status. They also may appeal a termination based on conditions that arose before employment if the dismissal is not in accordance with regulations.

The right to appeal sometimes depends on the agency, the employee's position, or the type of action involved. In some cases, certain classes of employees, such as political appointees, are excluded. Employees of specific agencies such as the intelligence agencies and the General Accounting Office are excluded with respect to certain actions.

Generally, employees who may appeal adverse actions are:

• Those in the competitive service who have completed a one-year probationary or trial period.

• Veterans-preference eligible employees with at least one year of continuous employment in the same or similar positions outside the competitive service.

• Postal service supervisors and managers and postal service employees engaged in personnel work (other than those in non confidential clerical positions) who have completed one year of current continuous service in the same or similar positions.

• Excepted service employees, other than preference-eligibles, who are not serving a probationary or trial period and who have competed two years current continuous service in the same or similar positions in an Executive agency (excluding the postal service and a number of other agencies).

What Types of Actions May Be Appealed

About half of cases brought to MSPB involve adverse actions against employees. These include removals, suspensions of more than 14 days, reductions in grade or pay and furloughs of 30 days or fewer.

The other half of MSPB's workload includes appeals regarding: performance-based removals or reductions in grade; denials of within-grade salary increases; reduction-in-force actions; determinations of suitability for a position by the Office of Personnel Management; OPM employment practices; OPM determinations in retirement matters; denial of restoration or reemployment rights; terminations of probationary employees under the circumstances described above, and removal from the Senior Executive Service for failure to be recertified in the SES.

Under the Whistleblower Protection Act of 1989, individual employees gained the right to appeal additional actions to MSPB in certain circumstances. They include actions that may be the subject of a prohibited personnel practice complaint to the Office of Special Counsel, such as appointments, promotions, details, transfers, reassignments and decisions concerning pay, benefits, awards, education or training. To appeal such actions to MSPB, the employee must allege that the action was taken because of his or her whistleblowing; he or she must have filed a complaint with the Office of Special Counsel, and the Special Counsel must not have asked MSPB to order corrective action.

Filing an Appeal

When an agency takes an appealable action against an employee, it must provide him or her with a notice of the time limits for appealing to the Board, the address of the appropriate Board regional office for filing the appeal, a copy or access to a copy of the Board's regulations, a copy of the Board's appeal form, and a notice of any rights concerning an agency or negotiated grievance procedure.

An appeal must be filed in writing with the Board regional office serving the employee's area within 20 days of the effective date of the action, if the notice sets an effective date. For actions with no effective date, the employee must file the appeal within 25 days of the date that appears on the notice of the action.

In the case of whistleblower appeals where the employee has first filed a complaint with the Special Counsel, an appeal to the Board must be filed within 65 days of the date of notice from the Special Counsel that that office does not intend to seek corrective action. If 120 days have passed since the employee filed the complaint, and the Special Counsel has not advised the employee that office will seek corrective action, the employee may appeal to the Board anytime thereafter.

Those who miss their deadline for any type of appeal may apply for a waiver by showing good reason for the delay and including supporting evidence. Granting such a waiver is up to the discretion of the administrative judge, however.

The appeal may be in any format, including letter form, as long as it is in writing and contains all of the information required by Board regulations. Employees should use the Board's appeal form to meet filing requirements. An appeal must bear the signature of the employee or a representative, if one is designated.

An employee may represent himself or herself or may hire a private attorney or make use of union attorneys and union representatives, if available.

When the Board regional office receives an appeal, it issues an order acknowledging receipt and raising any questions of timeliness or jurisdiction. The appeal is then assigned to an administrative judge. The agency has the right to respond within 20 days of the regional office's order. If no response is received by the Board within that limit, the case may be decided on the basis of the information available.

Once jurisdiction and timeliness are established, the employee has the right to a hearing on the merits of the complaint, but may waive that right and ask that the case be decided on the basis of the written record. A prehearing conference may be held in which issues are defined and narrowed, stipulations to undisputed facts are obtained, and the possibility of settlement is discussed. If a hearing is conducted, each party has the opportunity to call and cross-examine witnesses, present evidence and make arguments to the administrative judge. Hearings are open to the public and recorded by a court reporter, with copies of the record later available to the parties.

The agency bears the burden of proving that it was justified in taking its action. If that burden is met, in order to prevail the employee must show that there was "harmful error" in the agency's procedures, that the agency decision was based on a prohibited personnel practice, or that the decision was not in accordance with the law. The employee bears the burden of proving any "affirmative defenses" such as contentions that the personnel action was motivated by discrimination or retaliation for whistleblowing.

Once the record is closed, the administrative judge issues an initial decision. That decision may dismiss the appeal on various grounds, accept a settlement that has been agreed to by the parties or affirm or reverse the agency's action. In some instances the initial decision may reduce the penalty imposed by the agency.

The initial decision becomes final unless a party petitions the three-member Board for review within 35 days or the Board reopens the case on its own motion. Petitions for review must be filed with the Office of the Clerk at MSPB headquarters.

The Board does not automatically grant review. It accepts appeals only when it is established that the initial decision was based on an erroneous interpretation of law or regulation, or that new and material evidence is available that was not available when the record was closed. The Board may affirm, reverse or modify the initial decision, or send the case back to the administrative judge for further consideration.

If the employee wins an initial decision that is appealed to the Board, he or she normally will be granted the relief that the decision specifies while the case is on review. This does not apply, however, if the administrative judge deems it inappropriate or if the decision requires that the employee be returned to the workplace and the agency determines that this would be "unduly disruptive."

An employee may seek review of a final MSPB decision—either an initial decision that has become final or a final decision of the three-member Board—by the U.S. Court of Appeals for the Federal Circuit, or in cases involving certain types of discrimination, by a U.S. district court or the Equal Employment Opportunity Commission. In addition, the Office of Personnel Management may seek judicial review of a Board decision that it believes will have a substantial impact on civil service law, rule or policy. No other agency may seek judicial review of a Board decision.

Certain types of cases are processed initially at Board headquarters rather than in a regional office. These include appeals from MSPB employees, appeals involving classified national security information and petitions to review an arbitrator's award.

For More Information

For more information about MSPB, contact the Board regional office in your area or MSPB headquarters at 1120 Vermont Ave., N.W., Washington, D.C. 20419, phone (202) 653-8898. Helpful MSPB booklets include "An Introduction to the MSPB," "Questions & Answers About Appeals" and "Questions and Answers About Whistleblower Appeals."

For decisions of the MSPB or its regional officials or for information on filing a petition for review before the Board, contact the Office of the Clerk, same address, phone (202) 653-7200. MSPB officials are prohibited from discussing the possible merits of any appeal that an employee or another party may bring. However, they are free to answer questions about Board procedures and the processing of appeals.

Questions and Answers

Q. *What is the U.S. Merit Systems Protection Board?*

A. It's an independent agency in the executive branch that seeks to protect the federal merit systems. The Board is a three-member panel overseeing a network of hearing officers, called administrative judges.

Q. *What is the mission of the Merit Systems Protection Board?*

A. To ensure that federal employees are protected against abuses by agency management, that executive branch agencies make employment decisions in accordance with the merit system principles and that federal merit systems are kept free of prohibited personnel practices.

Q. *How does the MSPB accomplish its mission?*

A. Hearing and deciding employee appeals from agency actions; hearing and deciding cases brought by the Special Counsel involving alleged abuses of the merit systems, and other cases arising under the Board's original jurisdiction; conducting studies of the civil service and other merit systems, and overseeing the significant actions and regulations of the Office of Personnel Management.

Q. *What type of appeals does MSPB hear?*

A. Major categories are:

• Adverse actions for misconduct (removal, suspension for more than 14 days, reduction in grade, reduction in pay, or a furlough of 30 days or fewer).

• Performance-related actions (actions taken against an employee for not meeting the standards of the agency's performance appraisal system).

- Within-grade increase denials (based on the performance appraisal system, the determination of whether an employee is performing at an acceptable level of competence during the waiting period for the next step increase).

- Reduction-in-force actions (when an agency releases a competing employee from his/her competitive level by separation, demotion, furlough for more than 30 days, or reassignment requiring displacement, when the release is required because of lack of work, shortage of funds, reorganization, reclassification due to change of duties, or the exercise of reemployment rights or restoration rights).

- Retirement-related actions (eligibility for disability retirement, restoration to earning capacity, determination of recovery from disability, eligibility for retirement based on status as a federal employee, eligibility for survivor annuity, entitlement to discontinued service annuity, apportionment of civil service annuity pursuant to a divorce decree, determination of law enforcement officer and firefighter status for purposes of early retirement, and adjudications of agency-filed disability retirement applications).

- Various Office of Personnel Management actions (suitability for employment determinations, OPM employment practices, the development and use of examinations, qualification standards, tests, and other measurement instruments, denials of restoration or reemployment rights, and terminations of probationary employees under certain circumstances).

MSPB also has jurisdiction over actions brought by the Office of Special Counsel, certain proposed disciplinary actions against administrative law judges and cases involving proposed removal from the Senior Executive Service on performance grounds.

Q. *Does the MSPB ever handle discrimination cases?*

A. Yes, in "mixed" cases where the complainant alleges discrimination in connection with an action that is otherwise appealable to the Board. The complainant may ask the EEOC to review the Board's final decision on the discrimination issue. If the EEOC disagrees with the Board's decision on that issue, the case is returned to the Board. If the Board does not adopt the EEOC decision, the case is referred to a special panel for final resolution. The panel is made up of a chair appointed by the President, one member of the Board and one EEOC commissioner. Its decisions may be appealed to the appropriate U.S. district court.

Q. *Must employees be advised of their right to appeal to the Board?*

A. When an agency takes an appealable action against an employee, the agency must provide the employee with 1) a notice of the time limits for appealing to the Board, 2) the address of the appropriate Board regional office for filing the appeal, 3) a copy or access to a copy of the Board's regulations, 4) a copy of the Board's appeal form and 5) a notice of any rights concerning an agency or negotiated grievance procedure.

Q. *What are the guidelines for filing an appeal with MSPB?*

A. A notice of appeal must be filed within 20 days of receipt of the agency's notice of final decision. If the case does not set an effective date, the appeal must be filed within 25 days of the date of issuance of the decision. If an appeal is filed after the deadline, a good reason and supporting evidence must be provided. An appeal may be in any written format, containing all information specified in the Board's regulations.

Q. *How can I research the rules governing MSPB procedures?*

A. The rules are published in 5 Code of Federal Regulations parts 1201 and 1209. The rules also may be obtained by contacting the Office of the Clerk, Merit Systems Protection Board, 1120 Vermont Ave. N.W., Washington, D.C. 20419.

Q. *Where should the appeal be filed?*

A. With the appropriate Board regional office. (See list in this chapter.) Letters to MSPB headquarters, members of Congress, etc. are not considered formal notices of appeal and may result in a case's dismissal as untimely.

Q. *How long does the employing agency have to respond to the appeal to MSPB?*

A. Twenty calendar days from the date of the Board's order acknowledging receipt of the appeal.

Q. *What rights do employees have in MSPB appeals?*

A. The right to a hearing if the appeal is timely and within the Board's jurisdiction; the right to representation by an attorney or other person; the right to present witnesses at a hearing, if one is held, and access to relevant documents.

Q. *Are hearings held on all appeals?*

A. No. The complainant may waive the right to a hearing and choose to have the decision made on the basis of the written record (including all pleadings, documents, and other materials filed in the proceeding).

Q. *Can disputes be settled even after a formal appeal is filed?*

A. Yes; the Board encourages such settlements. The Board's administrative judges are trained in dispute resolution, and may initiate an attempt to settle an appeal informally at any time. In general, such agreements become the final resolution of the matter and the employee loses further appeal rights—except the right to ask the Board to order compliance with the agreement.

Q. *What happens if the hearing process is allowed to proceed?*

A. The process involves many of the same steps as a court case—the filing of responses, discovery, the making of motions, testimony from witnesses and so on. The administrative judge bases the decision on that record; that ruling is called an "initial decision." It becomes final and takes effect 35 days after issuance unless it is appealed within that time.

Q. *How are initial decisions appealed?*

A. Either party may appeal the written decision by filing a notice with the Office of the Clerk (address above). The Board may deny a petition for review and simply allow the initial decision to stand. In order to convince the Board to review an initial decision, it generally must be shown that new evidence has arisen since the hearing or that the administrative judge erred in interpreting a law or rule.

The Board also has broad powers to reopen cases on its own initiative.

Q. *What happens when the Board reviews an initial decision?*

A. The Board acts as an appeals court, reviewing the record and the legal motions, and occasionally hearing oral arguments. The Board may send the case back to the administrative judge if it decides more evidence is needed.

Q. *How long does this process take?*

A. MSPB's goal is to have initial decisions issued within 120 days from the filing of the appeal; the goal for a full Board decision is 110 days after receiving the request to review the initial ruling. MSPB meets these goals in most cases.

Q. *Can Board decisions be appealed?*

A. The Board's decision cannot be further reviewed administratively except in cases involving discrimination that may be appealed to the EEOC. The individual bringing the case to MSPB may appeal to the U.S. Court of Appeals for the Federal Circuit within 30 days of MSPB's decision. Only OPM may appeal on behalf of agencies.

Q. *What's the relationship between the Office of Special Counsel and the Board?*

A. The relationship of the Special Counsel to the Board is like that of a prosecutor to a judge; the Special Counsel prosecutes cases before the Board.

Q. *What types of corrective action can MSPB take?*

A. MSPB has the authority to modify or overturn agency decisions, including putting the employee back in the *status quo* before the action was taken, with back pay and other benefits. It also can order stays of personnel actions before they become final, for example in whistleblower cases.

Q. *Are MSPB decisions legally binding on agencies?*

A. Yes, subject to potential appeal to federal court. MSPB has the authority to dock the salaries of federal officials who refuse to comply with its orders, although this only rarely has to be even threatened.

Q. *Can the Board take disciplinary actions?*

A. Yes. For example, for violations of the Hatch Act or prohibited personnel practices alleged by the Office of Special Counsel.

MSPB Regional Offices

LOCATION	ADDRESS	JURISDICTION
Atlanta Regional Office	401 W. Peachtree Street, NW 10th Floor Atlanta, GA 30308 (404) 730-2751 FAX (404) 730-2767	Alabama, Florida, Georgia, Mississippi, North Carolina, South Carolina
Boston Regional Office	10 Causeway Street Room 1078 Boston, MA 02222-1042 (617) 565-6650 FAX (617) 565-5903	Connecticut, Maine, Massachusetts, New Hampshire, Rhode Island, Vermont
Chicago Regional Office	230 South Dearborn Street 31st Floor Chicago, IL 60604-1669 (312) 353-2923 FAX (312) 886-4231	Illinois (all locations north of Springfield), Indiana, Michigan, Minnesota, Ohio, Wisconsin
Dallas Regional Office	1100 Commerce Street Room 6F20 Dallas, TX 75242-1001 (214) 767-0555 FAX (214) 767-0102	Arkansas, Louisiana, Oklahoma, Texas

LOCATION	ADDRESS	JURISDICTION
Denver Regional Office	730 Simms Street Suite 301 P.O. Box 25025 Denver, CO 80225-0025 (303) 231-5200 FAX (303) 231-5205	Arizona, Colorado, Kansas, Montana, Nebraska, Nevada, New Mexico, North Dakota, South Dakota, Utah, Wyoming
New York Regional Office	26 Federal Plaza Room 3137 New York, NY 10278 (212) 264-9372 FAX (212) 264-1417	New York, Puerto Rico, Virgin Islands, and the following counties in New Jersey: Bergen, Essex, Hudson, Hunterdon, Morris, Passaic, Somerset, Sussex, Union, Warren
Philadelphia Regional Office	U.S. Customhouse, Room 501 Second & Chestnut Streets Philadelphia, PA 19106- 2904 (215) 597-9960 FAX (215) 597-3456	Delaware, Pennsylvania, Virginia (except cities and counties served by Washington Regional Office—see below), West Virginia, and the following counties in New Jersey: Atlantic, Burlington, Camden, Cape May, Cumberland, Gloucester, Mercer, Middlesex, Monmouth, Ocean, Salem
St. Louis Regional Office	911 Washington Avenue Room 410 St. Louis, MO 63101-1203 (314) 425-4295 FAX (314) 425-4294	Illinois (Springfield and all locations south), Iowa, Kentucky, Missouri, Tennessee
San Francisco Regional Office	525 Market Street Room 2800 San Francisco, CA 94105- 2789 (415) 744-3081 FAX (415) 744-3194	California

LOCATION	ADDRESS	JURISDICTION
Seattle Regional Office	915 Second Avenue Room 1840 Seattle, WA 98174-1001 (206) 553-0394 FAX (206) 553-6484	Alaska, Hawaii, Idaho, Oregon, Washington and Pacific overseas areas
Washington Regional Office	5203 Leesburg Pike Suite 1109 Falls Church, VA 22041-3473 (703) 756-6250 FAX (703) 756-7112	Washington, D.C., Maryland, all overseas areas not otherwise covered, and the following cities and counties in Virginia: Alexandria, Arlington, Fairfax City, Fairfax County, Falls Church, Loudon, Prince William

MSPB Appeals Processing

Appeal Is Filed   **Within 20 days of effective date of agency personnel action**

MSPB Regional Office

Appeal acknowledged
Appeal entered in case management system
Case file requested from agency
Appeal assigned to administrative judge   —— 1-3 days from receipt of appeal

(If appropriate, show cause order issued
re: jurisdiction or timeliness)

Agency response and case file received
Discovery begins
Prehearing conference scheduled   —— 10-25 days from receipt of appeal
Notice of hearing issued
If show cause order issued, response received

Prehearing motions filed and rulings issued
Attempts to achieve settlement
Discovery completed   —— 10-60 days from receipt of appeal
Prehearing conference(s) held
Witnesses identified
If no hearing, close of record set

Hearing held   —— 60-75 days from receipt of appeal
Record closed

Initial decision issued   —— Within 120 days from receipt of appeal

---

Filing of Petition for Review (PFR) by   **Within 35 Days of Date of Initial Decision**
Appellant or Agency (or OSC or OPM as
intervenor)

Board Headquarters

PFR acknowledged
PFR entered in case management system
Case file requested from regional office   —— 1-3 days from receipt of PFR

(If appropriate, show cause order issued re:
jurisdiction, timeliness, or deficiency of PFR)

Response to PFR filed or Cross-PFR filed
Case file received   —— Within 25 days of date PFR is served
(If show cause order issued, response filed)

If cross-PFR received   —— Additional 25 days from date of
                                                              service of Cross-PFR

If extension of time request received and granted   —— Additional time specified in order
                                                              granting extension of time

Final decision issued   —— (Board time standard for issuance of
                                                              final decisions is 110 days)

Filing of Appeal with U.S. Court of Appeals   **Within 30 days of the party's receipt of**
for the Federal Circuit (or, in discrimination   **Board final decision**
cases, with the appropriate U.S. District Court
or EEOC)

Chapter 11

Office of Personnel Management

The Office of Personnel Management is not generally considered an appeals agency. Most of the appeals functions performed by its predecessor, the Civil Service Commission, were transferred to the Merit Systems Protection Board in the 1978 Civil Service Reform Act that created both OPM and MSPB. However, OPM does still have power to review certain types of disputes, including:

Classification Appeals

Who May Bring Appeals — A general schedule employee may appeal the classification of his or her position at any time. When a reclassification results in a reduction in grade the appeal generally must be filed within 15 calendar days of receiving notice of the action or after the action itself, whichever is later. An internal agency appeals process also may be available.

Wage system and nonappropriated fund employees must first appeal through the agency classification appeals system. An appeal to OPM must be filed within 15 days of receiving an unfavorable determination from the agency.

What May Be Appealed — An employee may appeal the classification or reclassification of a federal position, or whether the position is rightly included or excluded from the general schedule. Not appealable are the accuracy of a position description, the grade of a position to which an employee is detailed or an agency's proposed (not final) classification decision.

Bringing an Appeal — Generally no special form is required to file an appeal with OPM. However, it must be in writing and must state why the employee believes the classification is wrong. The appeal must include a description of the duties and qualifications for the position, names and addresses of the parties involved and other pertinent information.

An employee may use a representative to help prepare and present a classification appeal, so long as the representative has no conflict of interest with official duties.

A classification appeal may be filed regardless of whether the employee also is bringing some other type of appeal relating to the same dispute. However, a classification appeal can't be brought through a grievance procedure.

The appeal should be filed with the OPM regional office having geographic jurisdiction over the employee's work site (see list of OPM regional offices in this chapter). A request for a reconsideration of a regional office decision should be sent to OPM's Classification Appeals Office, 1900 E St. N.W., Washington, D.C. 20415. That office is under no obligation to accept a request for reconsideration, however. It generally reconsiders a decision only when evidence suggests a reasonable doubt that the decision was technically accurate.

For More Information — Information on classification appeals to OPM is contained in Subpart F, part 511 of Title 5, Code of Federal Regulations. Chapter 511 of the Federal Personnel Manual contains information on general schedule appeals, FPM supplement 532-1 for wage system appeals and FPM supplement 532-2 for nonappropriated fund employee appeals.

Termination of Grade or Pay Retention Benefits

Who May Bring Appeals — Grade or pay retention benefits accrue to employees placed in a lower graded position because of a reduction in force. These benefits generally last for two years; however, they may be ended by the agency if the employee declines a "reasonable offer" of another position during that time.

Such employees may appeal that action to OPM, so long as they are not members of a bargaining unit that provides for such review through a negotiated grievance procedure.

What May Be Appealed — The termination of grade and pay retention benefits based on the employee's rejection of a "reasonable offer" of other federal employment.

For an offer to be considered reasonable, it must: be in writing; inform the employee that entitlement to grade or pay retention will be ended if the offer is declined; be of tenure equal to or greater than that of the position creating the grade or pay retention entitlement; be fulltime, unless the employee's former position was not fulltime, and be in the same commuting area as the employee's position immediately before the offer unless the employee is subject to a mobility agreement.

Bringing an Appeal — There is no standard form for appealing the termination of grade or pay retention benefits. An appeal must be in writing and should include the pertinent names, addresses and phone numbers and the reasons for the employee's belief that the offered position was not a "reasonable offer."

The appeal should be filed with the OPM regional office having geographic jurisdiction over the employee's work site (see list of OPM regional offices in this chapter). It must be filed no later than 20 days after receiving notice that grade or pay retention benefits have been ended.

OPM generally makes its decision on the basis of a written record only. A decision is considered final, but OPM's Classification Appeals Office at 1900 E St. N.W., Washington, D.C. 20415, may reconsider one at its discretion when new information casts doubt on its accuracy. To gain this review, the employee must show that the information was not readily available at the time of the original decision.

For More Information — Rules governing the termination of grade or pay retention are found in Subpart C, part 536 of Title 5, Code of Federal Regulations. Procedures for filing such appeals are described in Book 536, Federal Personnel Manual Supplement 990-2.

Reconsideration of Examination Ratings

Who May Bring Appeals — Applicants for certain federal positions are rated according to factors including a written performance test. People who take these tests are assigned ratings by the examination office; the ratings are important in hiring decisions.

What May Be Appealed — An examination decision or the rejection of an application, by either OPM offices or by agencies that have examining authority.

Bringing an Appeal — A request for reconsideration should be filed with the examining office. It should be in writing and should state why the original decision was improper—factors that were not considered and similar arguments in favor of a reevaluation.

Requests for reconsideration are reviewed by someone other than the rater who made the original decision. If dissatisfied by that review the applicant may request a second review, which also must be sent to the original office for forwarding to a higher level.

There is no set time limit other than a policy that applicants who object to their ratings should act promptly. The filing of a request for reconsideration doesn't affect any other rights an applicant may have under law.

For More Information — Section 300.104(b) of Title 5, Code of Federal Regulations, provides guidance on the appeal of an examination rating or the rejection of an application. See also Chapter 337 of the Federal Personnel Manual.

Retirement, Insurance and Other Claims

In addition to the issues above, OPM may be asked to consider or reconsider several other types of decisions. These include:

• *Allegations of violations of the Fair Labor Standards Act.* FLSA is the law governing overtime eligibility in the federal workplace. Complaints should be filed with the appropriate OPM regional office, which investigates and issues a compliance order if violations are found. The OPM director has the discretion to reopen any case decided by the regional office. An employee alleging a violation of the FLSA may sue in a federal district court, either before or after receiving the final OPM decision.

• *Reconsideration of retirement claims.* A decision on a claim by the OPM retirement office provides that the person may request reconsideration, which must be filed within 30 days after the initial decision. The initial decision gives the address to contact to seek reconsideration. From there the decision generally may be appealed to the Merit Systems Protection Board, and from there to the U.S. Court of Appeals for the Federal Circuit.

• *Denials of life insurance coverage.* An employee, annuitant or former spouse may request that OPM consider a denial of basic insurance coverage, whether the initial denial was made by the employing agency or by OPM (agencies make the decisions for active employees and for former spouses not receiving annuities; OPM decides for annuitants and former spouses who are receiving annuities). A notice of denial will provide the address for the OPM office where the request for reconsideration should be filed. If an initial decision is made at the highest level of review available in OPM, however, it will not be subject to reconsideration. But the employee may challenge the OPM decision by filing suit in a federal district court or the U.S. Court of Federal Claims.

• *Health insurance enrollment.* Decisions on enrollment in the Federal Employees Health Benefits program are made by the employing agency, in the case of active employees, or by OPM, for retirees. The decisions will carry notice of the right to request reconsideration by OPM and the appropriate address. If an initial decision is made at the highest level of review available in OPM, however, it will not be subject to reconsideration. Any further challenge must be brought in a federal district court.

• *Health insurance claims.* An FEHB enrollee whose claim is denied by his or her health carrier has one year to ask the plan to reconsider the denial. If the firm upholds its denial, the individual may request consideration from OPM within 90 days after receiving that notice. Requests should be sent to OPM's Office of Insurance Programs, Insurance Review Division, P.O. Box 436, Washington, D.C. 20044. An enrollee may sue OPM in a federal district court to force reconsideration but a suit seeking payment of the disputed claim must be filed against the insurance carrier.

Questions and Answers

Q. *What role does OPM play in personnel appeals?*

A. Only a limited one. It is not an appeals agency in the sense that EEOC and MSPB are appeals agencies. However, OPM does have power to review or reconsider certain decisions made by agencies or by lower levels of OPM itself.

Q. *What may OPM review or reconsider?*

A. Classification appeals, termination of grade or pay retention benefits, examination ratings, allegations of violations of the Fair Labor Standards Act (overtime), retirement claims, denials of life insurance coverage, health insurance enrollment and health insurance claims.

Q. *What is OPM's authority in classification appeals?*

A. A general schedule employee may appeal the classification or reclassification of his or her position to OPM at any time. Wage system and nonappropriated fund employees must first appeal through the agency classification appeals system, and then to OPM. The appeal is filed at an OPM regional office. Employees may request reconsideration by the Classification Appeals Office at OPM headquarters. That office is under no obligation to accept a request for reconsideration, however.

Q. *What is OPM's authority over termination of grade or pay retention benefits?*

A. Employees may contest an agency's decision to end grade or pay retention benefits that they received when downgraded during a reduction in force (an agency may end such benefits before the normal two-year period expires if the employee declines a "reasonable offer" of another position during that time). The appeal should be filed with an OPM regional office. The Classification Appeals Office at OPM headquarters may reconsider regional office decisions.

Q. *What is OPM's authority to reconsider examination ratings?*

A. Applicants for federal positions who were rated by testing may ask the examination office to reconsider the rating. If dissatisfied, the applicant may request a second review which will be made at a higher level. This procedure applies as well to examinations done by agencies other than OPM. If an applicant applies to two or more OPM examining offices and receives different ratings, the difference is resolved by the OPM regional office in that area. Disputed ratings between regions or between a region and an examining office are resolved by the Career Entry Group at OPM headquarters.

Q. *What is OPM's authority over allegations of violations of the Fair Labor Standards Act?*

A. Complaints alleging that overtime is being improperly denied or paid at the wrong rate should be filed with the appropriate OPM regional office. The OPM director may reconsider the regional office's decision.

Q. *What is OPM's authority to reconsider retirement claims?*

A. Decisions on retirement claims are made by the OPM retirement office. That office allows for reconsideration by a higher level within the office.

Q. *What is OPM's authority over denials of life insurance coverage?*

A. Denial of basic life insurance coverage may be made either by OPM (for retirees and former spouses receiving annuities) or by an employing agency (for active employees and former spouses not receiving annuities). An employee, annuitant or former spouse may request that OPM reconsider that decision, unless it was made at the highest level of review available in OPM.

Q. *What is OPM's authority over health insurance enrollment?*

A. Decisions on enrollment in the Federal Employees Health Benefits program are made by the employing agency (for active employees) or by OPM (for retirees). OPM may reconsider these decisions, unless they were made at the highest level of review available in OPM.

Q. *What is OPM's authority over health insurance claims?*

A. Denial of a health insurance claim must first be contested with the insurance carrier. After a final decision from the carrier, the enrollee may ask for review by the Office of Insurance Programs, Insurance Review Division at OPM headquarters.

Q. *Are there further channels of appeal available after the final OPM decision?*

A. In most cases, yes. See the text of this chapter for details.

Office of Personnel Management
Regional Offices

LOCATION	DIRECTOR	JURISDICTION
Atlanta Richard B. Russell Bldg. 75 Spring Street, SW Atlanta, GA 30306 Comm/404-331-3459	Ronald E. Brooks	Alabama, Florida, Georgia, Mississippi, North Carolina, South Carolina, Tennessee, Virginia
Chicago Federal Office Building 31st Floor 230 S. Dearborn Street Chicago, IL 60604 FTS/353-2901 Comm/312-363-2901	Steven R. Cohen	Illinois, Indiana, Iowa, Kansas, Kentucky, Michigan, Minnesota Missouri, Nebraska, Ohio, North Dakota, South Dakota, West Virginia, Wisconsin
Dallas 1100 Commerce Street Dallas, TX 75242 FTS/729-8227 Comm/214-767-8227	Edward Vela, Jr.	Arizona, Arkansas, Colorado, Louisiana, New Mexico, Montana, Oklahoma, Texas, Utah, Wyoming
Philadelphia William J. Green Jr. Fed. Bldg. 600 Arch Street Philadelphia, PA 19106 FTS/597-4543 Comm/215-597-4543	Frederick A. Kistler	Connecticut, Delaware, Maine, Maryland, Massachusetts, New Hampshire, New Jersey, New York, Pennsylvania, Puerto Rico, Rhode Island, Vermont, the Virgin Islands
San Francisco Federal Building (Box 36010) 211 Main St., 7th Floor San Francisco, CA 94105 Comm/415-744-7237 FTS/484-7237	Joseph Patti	Alaska, California, Hawaii, Idaho, Nevada, Oregon, Washington, the Pacific Ocean Area
The Washington Standard Metropolitan Statistical Area Office of Personnel Management Washington, D.C. 20415		District of Columbia; Montgomery, Prince Georges, Charles, Calvert and Frederick Counties, Maryland; Arlington, Fairfax and Falls Church, Virginia, overseas areas, except the Pacific

General Schedule Classification Appeals

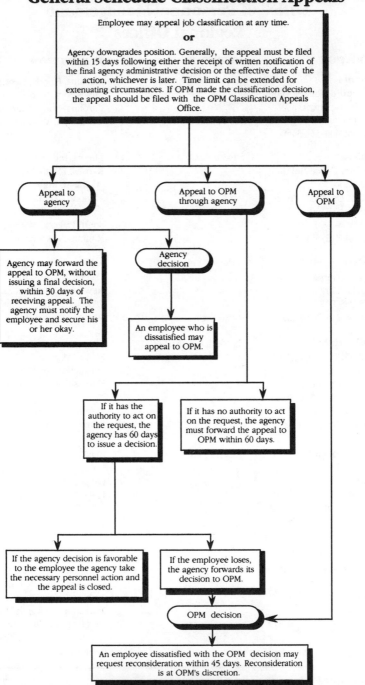

Employee may appeal job classification at any time.

or

Agency downgrades position. Generally, the appeal must be filed within 15 days following either the receipt of written notification of the final agency administrative decision or the effective date of the action, whichever is later. Time limit can be extended for extenuating circumstances. If OPM made the classification decision, the appeal should be filed with the OPM Classification Appeals Office.

Appeal to agency

Appeal to OPM through agency

Appeal to OPM

Agency may forward the appeal to OPM, without issuing a final decision, within 30 days of receiving appeal. The agency must notify the employee and secure his or her okay.

Agency decision

An employee who is dissatisfied may appeal to OPM.

If it has the authority to act on the request, the agency has 60 days to issue a decision.

If it has no authority to act on the request, the agency must forward the appeal to OPM within 60 days.

If the agency decision is favorable to the employee the agency take the necessary personnel action and the appeal is closed.

If the employee loses, the agency forwards its decision to OPM.

OPM decision

An employee dissatisfied with the OPM decision may request reconsideration within 45 days. Reconsideration is at OPM's discretion.

Chapter 12

Office of Special Counsel

The Office of Special Counsel, an independent government agency acting as a prosecutor before the Merit Systems Protection Board, is an organization from which employees in certain circumstances may obtain relief from personnel actions.

An employee may request the OSC to seek to postpone, or "stay," an adverse personnel action pending its own investigation. Such a stay order will be requested from the MSPB when the OSC has reasonable grounds to believe the action is the result of a prohibited personnel practice.

Under the 1989 Whistleblower Protection Act, employees who allege they were retaliated against for whistleblowing must first seek a stay through the OSC, but they may carry the request directly to MSPB themselves if it refuses.

The OSC has authority to issue subpoenas for documents or the attendance and testimony of witnesses and may require employees or other persons to give testimony under oath, sign written statements or respond formally to written questions.

Following an investigation of an alleged prohibited personnel practice, the OSC may recommend that an agency take corrective action. If no such action is taken, the OSC may ask the MSPB to order corrective action, and possibly to also discipline officials who violated civil service laws or rules. Officials who willfully refuse to comply with an MSPB order can be the subject of a further complaint.

OSC refers to the Justice Department any evidence of possible criminal violations that arise during its investigations.

The office also provides a channel for whistleblowers to disclose information without fear of retaliation from their agencies and enforces the Hatch Act.

Its effectiveness as a guardian of whistleblowers, however, has come under question. During the past few years some members of Congress have charged that the OSC is not doing enough to protect employees who report waste, fraud and abuse. As a result of adverse publicity, OSC's performance has been under review by Congress and the White House.

Who May File a Complaint

With few exceptions, current or former federal employees or federal job applicants in any agency of the executive branch, the Administrative Office of the U.S. Courts or the Government Printing Office may bring complaints to the OSC. Exceptions to this include employees of: a government corporation; the Central Intelligence Agency, Defense Intelligence Agency, National Security Agency or certain other intelligence agencies; the General Accounting Office; the U.S. Postal Service; the Postal Rate Commission, and the Federal Bureau of Investigation.

OSC will investigate alleged violations of the Hatch Act in any agency of the executive branch, the U.S. Postal Service, Postal Rate Commission and District of Columbia government.

What Actions May Be the Subject of a Complaint

OSC receives and investigates complaints of alleged prohibited personnel practices and other activities prohibited by civil service law or rule, especially retaliation for whistleblowing. An employee is considered a whistleblower who discloses information that he or she reasonably believes to show violations of law, rule or regulation, gross mismanagement, gross waste of funds, abuse of authority or danger to public health or safety.

OSC has authority to investigate allegations of age, race or sex discrimination, but normally defers such complaints to the channels existing in individual agencies and the Equal Employment Opportunity Commission. Labor relations matters do not fall under the jurisdiction of OSC unless prohibited personnel practices are involved.

Filing a Complaint

Any eligible employee may report an alleged prohibited activity to the OSC without being represented by an attorney. There is no time limit on filing a complaint. OSC provides complaint forms, but employees need not use them if they provide enough pertinent information. This should include:

• The name and address of the complainant and identification of the specific office involved.
• The job title, grade and employment status of the affected employee or employees.
• Information on the alleged violations of personnel laws or rules.
• A statement of facts providing evidence of violations and a

Prohibited Personnel Practices

Under the 1978 Civil Service Reform Act, federal agency heads, managers, supervisors and personnel officials are responsible for preventing certain personnel practices and for enforcing civil service laws, rules and regulations. This covers any employee who can take, direct others to take, recommend or approve any personnel action. When appealing a personnel action, an employee may raise an affirmative defense that the action was improperly based on a prohibited practice. If such a violation is found to have occurred, the action will be overturned, mitigated or sent back for reconsideration.

Prohibited personnel practices include:

• Discrimination on the basis of race, color, religion, sex, national origin, age, handicapping condition, marital status or affiliation.

• Soliciting or considering statements concerning a person under consideration for a personnel action unless the statement is based on personal knowledge and concerns the person's qualifications and character.

• Coercing the political activity of any person, or taking any action as a reprisal for a person's refusal to engage in political activities.

• Deceiving or willfully obstructing anyone from competing for employment.

• Influencing anyone to withdraw from competition for any position, whether to help or hurt anyone else's employment prospects.

• Giving unauthorized preferential treatment to any employee or applicant.

• Engaging in nepotism, defined as the hiring or promotion of relatives within the same agency component, or the advocating their hiring or promotion.

• Taking or failing to take, or threatening to take or fail to take, a personnel action because of an individual's legal disclosure of information regarding wrongdoing.

• Taking or failing to take, or threatening to take or fail to take, a personnel action because of an individual's exercising any appeal, complaint or grievance right; testifying or lawfully assisting any individual in the exercise of an appeal, complaint or grievance right; cooperating with or disclosing information to an agency inspector general or the Special Counsel; or refusing to obey an order that would require the individual to violate a law.

• Discriminating on the basis of personal conduct that does not adversely affect the performance of an employee or applicant or the performance of others, except that an employee or applicant's conviction for a crime may be taken into account in determining suitability or fitness.

• Taking or failing to take any other personnel action, or threatening to do so, if the act or omission would violate any law, rule or regulation of the merit system principles.

If a personnel action is allegedly based on a prohibited personnel practice (including reprisal for whistleblowing), the employee may file a complaint with the Office of Special Counsel, asking that the Special Counsel seek corrective action from the Merit Systems Protection Board. If the Special Counsel does not seek corrective action from the Board, there is no further administrative recourse, *except* in the case of complaints alleging that the personnel action was taken because of the employee's whistleblowing.

Under the Whistleblower Protection Act of 1989, an individual who alleges that a personnel action was threatened, proposed, taken, or not taken because of his or her whistleblowing may seek corrective action from the Board directly if the Special Counsel does not seek corrective action on his or her behalf.

description of the actions and events being reported.

Employees should include the specific action that shows wrongdoing, who was involved in the action, when it was taken or will be taken, and any pertinent documents. The employee also should indicate whether he or she grants permission to disclose his or her identity, should that become necessary to pursue the case.

For More Information

Although OSC will not give advisory opinions except in matters involving the Hatch Act, it will clarify its jurisdiction and advise an employee of information needed for OSC to take action on a problem. Contact the Office of Legislative and Public Affairs, The Office of Special Counsel, 1730 M Street, N.W., Washington, D.C. 20036, phone (202) or (FTS) 653-7984. A helpful pamphlet is "The Role of the Office of Special Counsel."

Complaints of prohibited personnel practices should be reported to Complaints Examining Unit, same address, phone (800) 872-9855 or (202) or (FTS) 653-7188.

Disclosures of information on violations of law, rule or regulation, gross mismanagement, gross waste of funds, abuse of authority or danger to public health or safety should be reported to Disclosure Unit, same address, phone (202) or (FTS) 653-9125.

Inquiries regarding the Hatch Act should be made to Hatch Act Unit, same address, phone (202) or (FTS) 653-7143.

Questions and Answers

Q. *What is the role of the Office of Special Counsel?*
A. To protect employees, former employees, and applicants for employment from prohibited personnel practices, especially reprisal for whistleblowing.

Q. *What are OSC's areas of responsibility?*
A. 1) receiving and investigating allegations of prohibited personnel practices and other activities prohibited by civil service law, rule or regulation and, if warranted, initiating corrective or disciplinary action, 2) providing a secure channel through which information evidencing a violation of any law, rule, or regulation, or gross mismanagement, a gross waste of funds, an abuse of authority, or a substantial and specific danger to public health or safety may be disclosed without fear of retaliation and without disclosure of identity except with the employee's consent, 3) enforcing the Hatch Act.

Q. *Can OSC investigators get evidence from federal employees?*

A. All federal employees are required to testify when asked and agencies must provide records to the OSC. The Special Counsel has authority to issue subpoenas for documents or the attendance and testimony of witnesses; persons may also be required to sign written statements or to respond formally to written questions.

Q. *Can the OSC handle discrimination cases?*

A. The OSC is authorized to investigate allegations of age, race, or sex discrimination. However, these are usually handled by the agencies and the Equal Employment Opportunity Commission. The OSC will normally defer discrimination complaints to one of them.

Q. *Can the OSC postpone or "stay" an adverse personnel action pending investigation?*

A. If the proposed action appears to have resulted from a prohibited personnel practice, the Special Counsel asks the Merit Systems Protection Board to delay the action until an investigation is completed.

Q. *In the legal sense, what is whistleblowing?*

A. Lawfully disclosing information to the Special Counsel, an inspector general, agency officials or others which you believe shows: 1) a violation of any law, rule, or regulation or 2) gross mismanagement, or waste of funds, an abuse of authority or a substantial and specific danger to public health or safety.

Q. *What is an "individual right of action?"*

An employee who believes he or she suffered retaliation for whistleblowing must first seek corrective action from the Special Counsel. If the Special Counsel ends its investigation of a complaint without seeking corrective action, the employee has 65 days from the date of the Special Counsel's written notice to file a whistleblower complaint called an "individual right of action" with MSPB. An employee also may file such a complaint with MSPB if 120 days pass after filing a complaint with the Special Counsel and there is no notification that it will seek corrective action.

Q. *If the Special Counsel ends the investigation of a whistleblower retaliation complaint, does this influence MSPB's decision?*

A. Under the Whistleblower Protection Act, MSPB may not take into account the Special Counsel's decision to terminate an investigation of a complaint. In fact, after 120 days with no notification of corrective action from the Special Counsel, the Special Counsel must obtain the complainant's permission to proceed. The Special Counsel must also gain permission to intervene in the complainant's appeal with the Board.

Q. *What is a prohibited personnel practice?*

A. A violation of various civil service laws and rules covering discrimination, merit-based hiring, nepotism, appeal rights, whistleblowing and other subjects (see list in this chapter). The restrictions apply to federal officials who can take, direct others to take, recommend or approve any personnel action. An actual personnel action (appointment, promotion, reassignment, suspension, and so on) may need to have occurred before a prohibited personnel practice can be found. Employees who believe they were victims of prohibited personnel practices may file a complaint with the Special Counsel. That office will investigate, and if the evidence warrants, the violation will be corrected or the official prosecuted before the Merit Systems Protection Board, or both.

Q. *Are there any agencies to which the prohibited personnel practices authority of OSC does not apply?*

A. It does *not* apply to employees in 1) a government corporation, 2) the Central Intelligence Agency, Defense Intelligence Agency, National Security Agency or certain other intelligence agencies excluded by the President, 3) the General Accounting Office, 4) the U.S. Postal Service or Postal Rate Commission, or 5) the Federal Bureau of Investigation.

Q. *Does an employee reporting an alleged prohibited personnel practice need the representation of an attorney?*

A. No. But in some cases it might be a good idea.

Q. *How does one submit a complaint to OSC?*

A. All information submitted to the OSC should be in writing; OSC provides complaint forms upon request. All complaints, disclosures and requests should be sent to: Office of Special Counsel, Complaints Examining Unit, 1730 M St. N.W., Washington, D.C. 20036.

Chapter 13

Grievances

Grievances are a means of resolving workplace disputes outside the appeals channels available through agencies such as the Merit Systems Protection Board. Although the word "grievances" most commonly is associated with unionized settings, a federal employee need not belong to a union bargaining unit in order to be covered by grievance procedures. Another category is the administrative grievance, a dispute-resolution channel available in most agencies. Each type of grievance has its own eligibility rules and its own scope of coverage, as described below.

Administrative Grievances

Agency administrative grievance systems are designed to provide a way to resolve disputes for which there is no other avenue of challenge. Their purpose is to provide a forum for internal review and resolution of employment-related matters, either formally or informally.

Agencies have a great deal of latitude in the design of such programs which are subject to general oversight by the Office of Personnel Management.

Rules generally require that the procedures give the employee a reasonable opportunity to present the matter and receive "fair consideration." This may or may not involve hearings, fact-finding and "other means of obtaining and assessing information pertaining to the dispute at hand."

Employees are guaranteed a reasonable processing time, freedom from restraint or reprisal, the right to be represented, and the right to official time to present the grievance, both for the employee and his or her representative, if one is used who also is an employee of the agency. (Entitlement to official time applies only if the individuals involved would otherwise have been on duty; rules do not provide official time to prepare a grievance.)

Each agency administrative grievance system also must provide for a fact-finding process; however, it is up to the agency to decide if one should be used in a given case. If a fact finder is used, that person may not be someone who has been involved in the grievance or who is subordinate to someone involved in the grievance. The fact finder may hold hearings or informal discussions or group meetings. He or she may have the authority to make a decision, recommend a decision or merely set out the facts.

Who May Bring Administrative Grievances

Administrative grievances most commonly are used by nonbargaining unit employees because bargaining unit employees generally are covered by a union contract that has a separate grievance system for them. However, union-represented employees also may use the administrative process where there is no negotiated grievance procedure, or where such a procedure excludes the matter at issue.

Employees may bring grievances either as individuals or as members of a group. In some cases, similar grievances by several employees are combined by management and one decision is rendered. An agency also may set its own standards for accepting and processing group grievances—requiring, for example, that all members of a group be part of the same organizational unit.

Employees specifically excluded from coverage of these systems include non citizens and aliens appointed to civil service jobs under various authorities, certain physicians, dentists and nurses ("Title 38" employees), members of the foreign service who are covered by the foreign service grievance system and other categories of employees as recommended for exclusion by the head of the agency and as approved by OPM.

Agencies excluded are the Central Intelligence Agency, Federal Bureau of Investigation, Defense Intelligence Agency, National Security Agency, Nuclear Regulatory Commission, Tennessee Valley Authority, Postal Rate Commission, U.S. Postal Service, Administrative Office of the United States Courts and the Panama Canal Commission.

What Types of Actions May Be Grieved

Subject to the restrictions listed below, administrative grievances are designed to address various matters of concern or dissatisfaction relating to federal employment. These include matters in which an employee alleges that coercion, reprisal or retaliation has been taken for filing a grievance.

Common examples of issues posed in administrative grievances include unwanted reassignments, challenges to performance ratings, challenges to the application of the agency's staffing policies, denial of training requests and disciplinary matters not appealable under other systems.

Important exceptions to grievance coverage are: the content of established agency regulations and policy; a matter on which the employee is entitled to file a grievance under a negotiated grievance procedure or an appeal to the Merit Systems Protection Board, Office of Personnel Management, Federal Labor Relations Authority or Equal Employment Opportunity Commission; nonselection for promotion or failure to receive a noncompetitive promotion; a preliminary warning notice of an action which, if taken, would be covered under the grievance system; the performance evaluation, job rating or other actions regarding a senior executive service appointee, under certain rules; the termination of an employee serving a trial period, including supervisory and other types of probation; the substance of performance standards and/or statements of work objectives; the granting, or failing to grant, of various awards; the granting or failure to grant of pay or bonuses under the Performance Management and Recognition System or the senior executive service evaluation system; the payment or failure to pay of a recruitment or relocation bonus, a retention allowance or a supervisory differential; the failure to request or grant an exception to dual compensation restrictions, and the termination of a time-limited excepted appointment and certain other limited appointments.

Also excluded from this grievance process are matters not subject to the control of agency management—for example, standard salary and benefit levels.

Filing an Administrative Grievance

Because of the discretion granted to agencies to design and carry out administrative grievance systems, the process for pursuing such a complaint varies greatly from one agency to the next. Employees should consult their own agencies' publications on their grievance systems to learn the form, content, time limits and other rules for filing a grievance where they work.

An employee must comply with the appropriate time limits, furnish sufficient detail to identify the matter being grieved, and specify the personal relief being requested.

Any time an employee submits a grievance in writing, a written decision must be issued that includes a report of the findings and reasons for the decision. This must be made by either an official at a higher organizational level than any employee involved in the grievance (unless one is the agency head), or by a designated official such as a fact finder who was given the power to make a final decision. Agencies may delegate authority to make final decisions.

The agency's decision is final. There is no further review available of administrative grievances.

For More Information

Agencies must publish and make available to employees copies of their administrative grievance systems. The publication may take the form of agency policy statements and regulations, or less formal forms such as pamphlets and brochures. Employees should be able to obtain these from their personnel offices.

General information on administrative grievances can be found in Chapter 771 of the Federal Personnel Manual and in 5 Code of Federal Regulations Part 771, "Agency Administrative Grievance System" (also published in the November 30, 1992, *Federal Register* beginning on page 56782).

Questions and Answers

Q. *What is an administrative grievance channel?*

A. A route for resolving grievances for which there is no other avenue of challenge.

Q. *Who has an administrative grievance system?*

A. Most executive agencies, military departments, and organizational units in the legislative and judicial branches that have positions in the competitive service are required to establish an agency administrative grievance system. Excluded are the CIA, FBI, Defense Intelligence Agency, National Security Agency, Nuclear Regulatory Commission, Tennessee Valley Authority, the Postal Rate Commission, U.S. Postal Service and Panama Canal Commission.

Q. *Are administrative grievance channels standardized among agencies?*

A. No. They vary considerably from agency to agency. Generally, they must give the employee a reasonable opportunity to present the matter and to receive fair consideration. They differ in the form, content and time limits required.

Q. *Where can I find out about the administrative grievance channel at my agency?*

A. Agencies must publicize them in policy statements, rules, pamphlets and brochures, and the like. These should be available in your personnel office.

Q. *Who is covered by an administrative grievance channel?*

A. Generally, all non-bargaining unit employees regardless of their appointment status (competitive or excepted service, temporary or career). There are some exceptions, however. And bargaining unit employees are covered in some places by agreement of both management and labor.

Q. *What subjects can be raised in administrative grievances?*

A. Matters of concern to the employee that are under the control of agency management—including unwanted reassignments, denial of training requests, challenges to performance ratings and disciplinary matters not appealable elsewhere. Also, subjects that are specifically excluded from a negotiated grievance procedure in a bargaining unit.

Q. *What subjects can't be raised in administrative grievances?*

A. The content of established agency regulations and policy; matters to which the employee was entitled to grieve through a negotiated procedure; the substance of performance standards or statements of work objectives; disputes over bonuses, and others.

Q. *What rights do employees have in administrative grievances?*

A. Reasonable processing time, assurance of freedom from restraint or reprisal, the right to be represented and the right to official time to present (but not to prepare) the grievance, the right to communicate with the servicing personnel office or its equivalent, establishment of a written grievance file whenever a written grievance is submitted and issuance of a written decision whenever a written grievance is filed.

Q. *What responsibilities do employees have in an administrative grievance?*

A. Meeting time limits, furnishing sufficient detail on which to base a decision and specifying the relief being requested (relief can only be personal and cannot involve a request for discipline or any other action affecting another employee). Failure to comply with any of these can result in the grievance being dismissed.

Q. *How is an administrative grievance filed?*

A. Follow the procedures set out by your agency.

Q. *Can group grievances be filed?*

A. Yes, subject to any limits that the agency sets out.

Q. *Can a matter be settled even after a grievance is filed?*

A. Yes. Government policy encourages this.

Agency Administrative Grievance Process

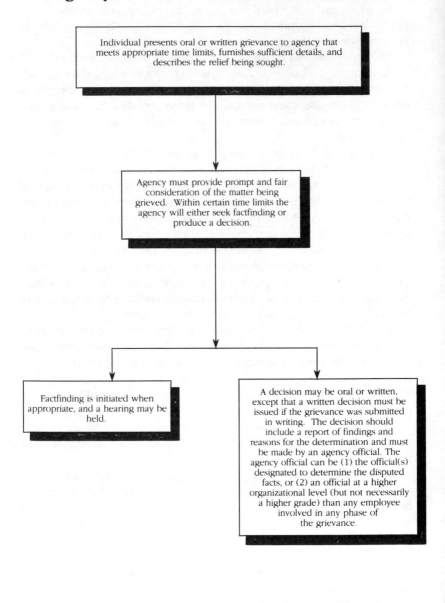

Individual presents oral or written grievance to agency that meets appropriate time limits, furnishes sufficient details, and describes the relief being sought.

Agency must provide prompt and fair consideration of the matter being grieved. Within certain time limits the agency will either seek factfinding or produce a decision.

Factfinding is initiated when appropriate, and a hearing may be held.

A decision may be oral or written, except that a written decision must be issued if the grievance was submitted in writing. The decision should include a report of findings and reasons for the determination and must be made by an agency official. The agency official can be (1) the official(s) designated to determine the disputed facts, or (2) an official at a higher organizational level (but not necessarily a higher grade) than any employee involved in any phase of the grievance.

Q. *Who hears an administrative grievance?*

A. Normally an official at a higher level than the one who made the decision being challenged and who was not involved in the original decision.

Q. *Can the hearing official's decision be appealed?*

A. No.

Grievances under Union-Negotiated Procedures

The 1978 Civil Service Reform Act put into law many of the union rights for federal employees that previously had existed only under executive orders, including the right to negotiate over grievance procedures. Under the law, labor and management are required to provide in any collective bargaining agreement procedures for the settlement of grievances, including questions of what can be taken to arbitration.

Since most contracts are negotiated locally, there is a great deal of variation regarding how grievance procedures will work and what will be covered—according to the latest statistics, there are now more than 2200 labor agreements in the executive branch. However, all of these contracts have been negotiated under the same basic law, the Reform Act.

That law requires that the grievance procedure be "fair and simple," provide for "expeditious processing" and include certain protections. Among these protections are the right of a union to bring a grievance on its own behalf or on the employee's behalf, the right of an employee to bring a grievance on his or her own behalf, and provisions that binding arbitration may be invoked for any grievance not satisfactorily settled between the agency and the employee or union.

Who May Bring Grievances under a Negotiated Procedure

Unlike most other forms of federal personnel appeals, a negotiated grievance is most commonly brought by a union representative— usually the local steward—rather than by the individual employee. There are several reasons for this.

A main reason is expertise. Union representatives have experience and resources that are beyond the easy reach of an individual.

The local union situation and the employee's status play important roles in negotiated grievance procedures. Those grievance rights are limited to employees covered by the contract. Thus, an employee must be a member (although not necessarily a dues-paying member) of a union local's bargaining unit to take advantage of the protections under that grievance procedure.

Employees covered by a negotiated grievance procedure have the right to bring such complaints on their own without the involvement— or support—of the union. In such cases the union does have the right to send a representative to any grievance proceeding.

Also, management may file a grievance against a union.

What Types of Actions May Be Grieved

The Civil Service Reform Act was in part designed to encourage union involvement in the federal government. Thus, its definition of what may be grieved under a negotiated contract is broad. It allows grievances on "any claimed violation, misinterpretation or misapplication of any law, rule or regulation affecting conditions of employment."

Specific exceptions under law are: prohibited political activities; retirement, life insurance and health insurance; suspension or removal for national security reasons; any examination, certification or appointment, and the classification of any position which does not result in the reduction in pay or grade of the employee.

Also, parties to a contract may exclude from coverage any matter they choose.

If a matter involves discrimination complaints, adverse actions, or actions based on unacceptable performance that are appealable under other channels (such as to the Merit Systems Protection Board or the Equal Employment Opportunity Commission), an employee may use the negotiated grievance procedure or the other appeals process, but not both.

Filing a Grievance under a Negotiated Procedure

The most common scenario, in which union help is invoked, begins with a meeting between the employee and a local union representative. The union rep interviews the employee and others and gathers other information that is pertinent to the matter. This may involve signing a complaint form and granting permission for the union official to see personnel records that otherwise would be closed.

The union at that point may decide not to pursue the matter any farther. The employee then would have the option of continuing on his or her own.

Should the union decide to pursue the case, however, a meeting with a management representative—often a second-level supervisor—will be requested. At this meeting either the union representative or the employee (usually the former) will state the case. The matter might be settled on the spot, or management might respond formally by a given date.

If management's position remains unacceptable to the employee side, binding arbitration can be invoked. This is another point where a union representative may decide to drop a case, since arbitration can be expensive and time-consuming. Also, unions often are concerned about possible fallout of an arbitration decision against them. Some unions have a policy that the national office must approve any decision to go to arbitration.

Should the case proceed to arbitration, the arbitrator will be chosen from a list provided by organizations such as the American Arbitration Association or Federal Mediation and Conciliation Service. The arbitrator will issue a decision that contains a finding of fact and law, and order a remedy if a violation is found. The remedy could include cancellation of the personnel decision that led to the grievance, with back pay and similar benefits, if appropriate to the case.

It is important to note that an employee can go through the grievance process as an individual, without union help. However, only a "party" to the contract—the union or the agency—can invoke arbitration. An arbitrator's decision can be appealed to the Federal Labor Relations Authority only by the union or management.

For More Information

Specific information on a local contract's grievance procedures is best obtained from the union local's office. The agency's local labor relations office also will have a copy.

General information on grievance procedures is contained in a publication from FLRA, "A Guide to the Federal Service Labor-Management Relations Statute," for sale by the Superintendent of Documents, U.S. Government Printing Office, Washington, D.C. 20402.

Questions and Answers

See Federal Labor Relations Authority chapter.

Discrimination and Adverse Action Disputes Covered by a Negotiated Grievance Procedure

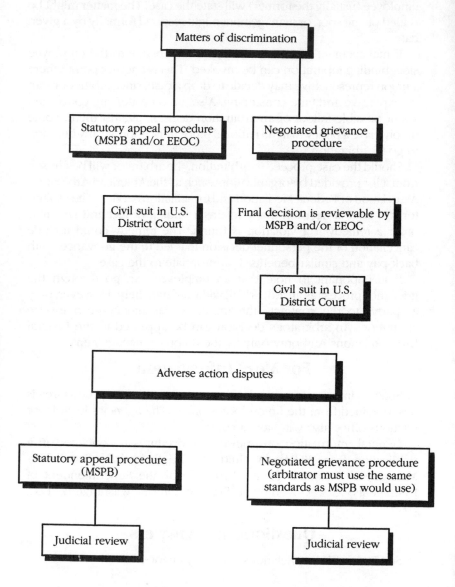

Chapter 14

Decisions

How to Use the Decision Index

The large index in this chapter is designed to provide an overview of important decisions in recent years on a variety of subjects that are commonly raised in federal personnel cases.

We have attempted to make the indexing system as consistent as possible. However, the reader should look under all headings that might be pertinent—for example, looking under both "Discipline" and "Leave" if in a situation where discipline was taken for alleged leave violations. We have provided cross-references to aid this process.

It is always a good idea to obtain a copy of the original decision, especially if the research is being done in preparation for a formal appeal. Administrative bodies and courts will only accept legal arguments taken directly from the earlier, presidential decisions. For a copy of a decision, contact the court or agency, providing the identifying number, date and case title that are given.

Federal courts have varying policies regarding charges for copies of opinions. Most assess a fee of a few dollars, but as this changes from time to time and from place to place, it is best to contact the clerk of that court first to ascertain its policy.

A court clerk's office may only maintain copies of decisions going back a certain period of time. For decisions no longer on file, the requester usually will have to research the case in one of the compilations that are available in law libraries, agency libraries and other places where legal research resources are kept.

Some of the court decisions in this index may not appear in such compilations because they were "unpublished" rulings. These decisions have the same force of law as "published" decisions but they are not considered precedential in nature because they break no new legal ground. We have included them, however, because they involve common types of disputes that would be of broad interest. To obtain copies of the full decisions, contact the courts that issued them. Also note that decisions can be overturned on appeal. Thus, a particular decision you might find could later have been reversed. This is a good reason to do research in legal compilations in addition using this index if you're more than just casually interested.

Compilations of the decisions of administrative agencies usually also are available in law libraries, agency libraries and other places where legal research resources are kept. The decisions also are generally available directly from the agencies that issued them.

(Chapter 5 contains a special table to help you further research court and administrative decisions.)

Administrative agencies generally assess no charge if only one copy is being requested and the decision is not unusually lengthy. The Equal Employment Opportunity Commission is an exception, charging a per-page fee for all opinions. Fee policies may change over time. Contact the agencies for information on the potential cost of a given decision.

Both the courts and the administrative bodies routinely provide copies of final decisions only. A specific request must be made to obtain legal briefs, supporting evidence or other background material on a case. Usually this will entail a charge per page copied. And such information may not be readily available, especially for older cases.

Should briefs and other papers not be available through the court or administrative body, they may still be available through the law firm that handled the case. Many rulings give the attorneys' names at the beginning on a title page or at the end in a list of those to whom the decision was sent. However, a law firm may have a policy of not providing such papers, or may charge not only for duplicating and

How to Get Copies of Decisions
Administrative Agencies

NAME	RESOURCE	ADDRESS
Merit Systems Protection Board	Decisions	Office of the Clerk, MSPB 1120 Vermont Avenue, N.W. Washington, D.C. 20419 (202) 653-7200
Federal Labor Relations Authority and the Federal Service Impasses Panel	Decisions	Office of Information Resources and Research Services 607 14th Street, N.W. Washington, D.C. 20424 (202) 482-6550 (FLRA) (202) 482-6670 (FSIP)
Comptroller General	Decisions	GAO Headquarters Room 1000 441 G Street, N.W. Washington, D.C. 20548 (202) 512-6000
Equal Employment Opportunity Commission	Decisions	EEOC's Information Handling Service Attention: Telemanagement 15 Inverness Way Englewood, CO 80150 (800) 525-7052 Commerce Clearing House 600 13th Street, N.W. Suite 700 South Washington, D.C. 20005, (202) 626-2200 Bureau of National Affairs 1231 25th Street, N.W. Washington, D.C. 20037 (202) 452-4200.

NAME	RESOURCE	ADDRESS
Labor Agreement Information Retrieval Service (LAIRS)	Indexing system of arbitration decisions operated by the Office of Personnel Management	LAIRS Section Office of Personnel Mgmt. Room 7429 1900 E St., N.W. Washington, D.C. 20415 (202) 606-2940

Federal Courts Most Commonly Appearing in the Index

(Address correspondence to "Clerk of Court")

NAME	ADDRESS
U.S. District Court for the District of Columbia	3rd Street and Constitution Avenue, N.W. Washington, D.C. 20001 (202) 273-0515
U.S. Court of Appeals for the District of Columbia Circuit	3rd Street and Constitution Avenue, N.W. Washington, D.C. 20001 (202) 273-0300
U.S. Court of Appeals for the Federal Circuit	717 Madison Place, N.W. Washington, D.C. 20439 (202) 633-6550
United States Court of Federal Claims (formerly called the United States Court of Claims)	717 Madison Place, N.W. Washington, D.C. 20439 (202) 219-9561
Supreme Court of the United States	1 First Street, N.E. Washington, D.C. 20543 (202) 479-3211

Federal Courts

United States Supreme Court

(Address correspondence to "Clerk of Court")

Supreme Court of the United States	One First Street, NW Washington, D.C. 20543

United States Courts of Appeals

District of Columbia Judicial Circuit
(District of Columbia)

3rd Street and Constitution Ave., NW
5th Floor
Washington, D.C. 20001

First Judicial Circuit (Districts of Maine,
Massachusetts, New Hampshire, Puerto
Rico, and Rhode Island)

1606 John W. McCormack
Post Office and Court House
Boston, Massachusetts 02109

Second Judicial Circuit (Districts of
Connecticut, New York, and Vermont)

40 Foley Square
Room 1702
New York, NY 10007

Third Judicial Circuit (Districts of
Delaware, New Jersey, Pennsylvania,
and Virgin Islands)

Room 21400, U.S. Courthouse
601 Market Street
Philadelphia, PA 19106

Fourth Judicial Circuit (Districts of
Maryland, North Carolina, South
Carolina, Virginia, and West Virginia)

1100 East Main Street
Richmond, VA 23219

Fifth Judicial Circuit (Districts of
Louisiana, Mississippi, and Texas)

600 Camp Street
New Orleans, LA 70130

Sixth Judicial Circuit (Districts of
Kentucky, Michigan, Ohio, and
Tennessee)

524 U.S. Post Office and
Courthouse Building
5th and Walnut Streets
Cincinnati, OH 45202

Seventh Judicial Circuit (Districts of
Illinois, Indiana, and Wisconsin)

219 South Dearborn Street
Room 2722
Chicago, IL 60604

Eighth Judicial Circuit (Districts of
Arkansas, Iowa, Minnesota, Missouri,
Nebraska, North Dakota, and South
Dakota)

1114 Market Street
Room 511
St. Louis, MO 63101-2077

Ninth Judicial Circuit (Districts of Alaska,
Arizona, California, Guam, Hawaii,
Idaho, Montana, Nevada, Northern
Mariana Islands, Oregon, and Washington)

121 Spear Street
San Francisco, CA 94105

| Tenth Judicial Circuit (Districts of Colorado, Kansas, New Mexico, Oklahoma, Utah, and Wyoming) | 1929 Stout Street Room C404 Denver, CO 80294 |

Tenth Judicial Circuit (Districts of
Colorado, Kansas, New Mexico,
Oklahoma, Utah, and Wyoming)

1929 Stout Street
Room C404
Denver, CO 80294

Eleventh Judicial Circuit (Districts of
Alabama, Florida, and Georgia)

56 Forsyth Street, NW
Atlanta, GA 30303

Federal Judicial Circuit

717 Madison Place, NW
Washington, D.C. 20439

United States District Courts

Alabama, Northern

140 U.S. Courthouse
1729 5th Avenue North
Birmingham, AL 35203

Alabama, Middle

P.O. Box 711
Montgomery, AL 36101

Alabama, Southern

Box 11, U.S. Courthouse
113 St. Joseph Street
Mobile, AL 36602

Alaska

222 West 7th Avenue, #4
Anchorage, AK 99513

Arizona

Room 1400
U.S. Courthouse and Federal Building
230 North 1st Avenue
Phoenix, AZ 85025

Arkansas, Eastern

P.O. Box 2381
Little Rock, AR 72203

Arkansas, Western

P.O. Box 1523
Fort Smith, AR 72902

California, Northern

P.O. Box 36060
450 Golden Gate Avenue
San Francisco, CA 94102

California, Eastern

2546 U.S. Courthouse
650 Capitol Mall
Sacramento, CA 95814

California, Central	312 North Spring Street Los Angeles, CA 90012
California, Southern	940 Front Street San Diego, CA 92189
Colorado	1929 Stout Street Room C-145, U.S. Courthouse Denver, CO 80294
Connecticut	141 Church Street New Haven, CT 06510
Delaware	844 King Street Lockbox 18 Wilmington, DE 19801
District of Columbia	U.S. Courthouse 3rd Street and Constitution Avenue, N.W. Washington, D.C. 20001
Florida, Northern	110 East Park Avenue Tallahassee, FL 32301
Florida, Middle	P.O. Box 53558 Jacksonville, FL 32201-3558
Florida, Southern	301 North Miami Avenue Miami, FL 33128-7788
Georgia, Northern	75 Spring Street, S.W. 2211 U.S. Courthouse Atlanta, GA 30335
Georgia, Middle	P.O. Box 128 Macon, GA 31202
Georgia, Southern	P.O. Box 8286 Savannah, GA 31412
Guam	6th Floor Pacific News Building 238 O'Hara Street Agana, Guam 96910

Hawaii	P.O. Box 50129 Honolulu, HI 96850
Idaho	550 West Fort Street Box 039 Boise, ID 83724
Illinois, Northern	219 South Dearborn Street Chicago, IL 60604
Illinois, Central	P.O. Box 2438 Springfield, IL 62705
Illinois, Southern	P.O. Box 249 750 Missouri Avenue East St. Louis, IL 62202
Indiana, Northern	102 Federal Building 204 South Main Street South Bend, IN 46601
Indiana, Southern	U.S. Courthouse 46 East Ohio Street Room 105 Indianapolis, IN 46204
Iowa, Northern	313 Federal Building and U.S. Courthouse 101 First Street, S.E. Cedar Rapids, IA 52401
Iowa, Southern	200 U.S. Courthouse East 1st and Walnut Streets Des Moines, IA 50309
Kansas	204 U.S. Courthouse 401 North Market Street Wichita, KS 67202
Kentucky, Eastern	P.O. Drawer 3074 Lexington, KY 40596-3074
Kentucky, Western	231 U.S. Courthouse 601 West Broadway Louisville, KY 40202

Louisiana, Eastern	U.S. Courthouse 500 Camp Street C-151 New Orleans, LA 70130
Louisiana, Middle	P.O. Box 2630 Baton Rouge, LA 70821-2630
Louisiana, Western	500 Fannin Street Room 106 Shreveport, LA 71101
Maine	U.S. Courthouse 156 Federal Street Room 102 Portland, ME 04101
Maryland	101 West Lombard Street Baltimore, MD 21201
Massachusetts	John W. McCormack Post Office and Courthouse Room 707 Boston, MA 02109
Michigan, Eastern	U.S. Courthouse 231 West Lafayette Boulevard Detroit, MI 48226
Michigan, Western	452 Federal Building Grand Rapids, MI 49503
Minnesota	708 Federal Building 316 North Robert Street St. Paul, MN 55101
Mississippi, Northern	P.O. Box 727 Oxford, MS 38655
Mississippi, Southern	245 East Capitol Street Suite 416 Jackson, MS 39201
Missouri, Eastern	1114 Market Street U.S. Court and Custom Building St. Louis, MO 63101

Missouri, Western	U.S. Courthouse 811 Grand Avenue Room 201 Kansas City, MO 64106
Montana	5405 Federal Building 316 North 26th Street Billings, MT 59101
Nebraska	P.O. Box 129 DTS Omaha, NE 68101
Nevada	300 Las Vegas Boulevard, South Las Vegas, NV 89101
New Hampshire	P.O. Box 1498 Concord, NH 03301
New Jersey	U.S. Post Office and Courthouse P.O. Box 419 Newark, NJ 07101
New Mexico	P.O. Box 689 Albuquerque, NM 87103
New York, Northern	P.O. Box 7367 Syracuse, NY 13261-7367
New York, Southern	U.S. Courthouse Foley Square New York, NY 10007
New York, Eastern	225 Cadman Plaza East Brooklyn, NY 11201
New York, Western	304 U.S. Courthouse 68 Court Street Buffalo, NY 14202
North Carolina, Eastern	P.O. Box 25670 Raleigh, NC 27611
North Carolina, Middle	P.O. Box V-1 Greensboro, NC 27402
North Carolina, Western	309 U.S. Courthouse 100 Otis Street Asheville, NC 28801-2611

North Dakota	P.O. Box 1193 Bismarck, ND 58502
Northern Mariana Islands	P.O. Box 687 Saipan, Northern Mariana Islands 96950
Ohio, Northern	102 U.S. Courthouse 201 Superior Avenue, NE Cleveland, OH 44114
Ohio, Southern	260 U.S. Courthouse 85 Marconi Boulevard Columbus, OH 43215
Oklahoma, Northern	411 U.S. Courthouse 333 West 4th Street Tulsa, OK 74103
Oklahoma, Eastern	P.O. Box 607 Muskogee, OK 74401
Oklahoma, Western	3210 U.S. Courthouse 200 NW 4th Street Oklahoma City, OK 73102
Oregon	503 Gus J. Solomon U.S. Courthouse 620 SW Main Street Portland, OR 97205
Pennsylvania, Eastern	Independence Mall West 601 Market Street 2609 U.S. Courthouse Philadelphia, PA 19106
Pennsylvania, Middle	P.O. Box 1148 Scranton, PA 18501
Pennsylvania, Western	P.O. Box 1805 Pittsburgh, PA 15230
Puerto Rico	Federal Building 150 Carlos Chardon Avenue Room 150 Hato Rey, PR 99018-1767

Rhode Island	119 Federal Building and U.S. Courthouse 1 Exchange Terrace Providence, RI 02903-1779
South Carolina	1845 Assembly Street Columbia, SC 29201
South Dakota	220 U.S. Courthouse and Federal Building 400 South Phillips Avenue Sioux Falls, SD 57102
Tennessee, Eastern	P.O. Box 2348 Knoxville, TN 37901
Tennessee, Middle	800 U.S. Courthouse 801 Broadway Nashville, TN 37203
Tennessee, Western	167 North Main Street 950 Federal Building Memphis, TN 38103
Texas, Northern	U.S. Courthouse 1100 Commerce Street Room 14A20 Dallas, 75242-1003
Texas, Southern	P.O. Box 61010 Houston, TX 77208
Texas, Eastern	106 Federal Building and U.S. Court- house 211 West Ferguson Street Tyler, TX 75702
Texas, Western	Hemisfair Plaza 655 East Durango Boulevard San Antonio, TX 78206
Utah	204 U.S. Courthouse 350 South Main Street Salt Lake City, UT 84101
Vermont	P.O. Box 945 Burlington, VT 05402

Virgin Islands	P.O. Box 720 Charlotte Amalie St. Thomas, VI 00801
Virginia, Eastern	P.O. Box 21449 200 South Washington Street Alexandria, VA 22320
Virginia, Western	P.O. Box 1234 Roanoke, VA 24006
Washington, Eastern	P.O. Box 1493 Spokane, WA 99210
Washington, Western	308 U.S. Courthouse 1010 Fifth Avenue Seattle, WA 98104
West Virginia, Northern	P.O. Box 1518 Elkins, WV 26241
West Virginia, Southern	P.O. Box 2546 Charleston, WV 25329
Wisconsin, Eastern	517 East Wisconsin Avenue 362 U.S. Courthouse Milwaukee, WI 53202
Wisconsin, Western	P.O. Box 432 Madison, WI 53701
Wyoming	P.O. Box 727 Cheyenne, WY 82001

Topic Guide to Decisions

Significant Decisions of Recent Years

Abbreviations used in the decisions: Equal Employment Opportunity Commission (EEOC); Comptroller General (CG); Federal Labor Relations Authority (FLRA); Federal Services Impasses Panel (FSIP); Merit Systems Protection Board (MSPB); Labor Agreement Information Retrieval Service (LAIRS).

APPEALS (see also SETTLEMENT AGREEMENTS)

The U.S. Court of Appeals for the Federal Circuit rejected an appeal from a woman who claimed she missed a deadline before the Merit Systems Protection Board because "her mail carrier had not delivered her mail in a timely fashion." The court said that she received a notice of the time limit at least three days before the deadline and thus could have filed her appeal on time. *(Barr v. MSPB, 91-3594, July 2, 1992)*

People appealing federal personnel decisions without using a lawyer can't be expected to know all the technicalities, but they must respond to clear instructions or risk having their cases dismissed, the U.S. Court of Appeals for the Federal Circuit said. *(Mendoza v. MSPB, 91-3202, June 10, 1992)*

While they were sympathetic to an employee's claim that he couldn't afford a lawyer in time to meet a deadline for pursuing a personnel appeal, judges of the U.S. Court of Appeals for the Federal Circuit said his case was properly dismissed for lack of timeliness. The court stressed that employees themselves, and not any legal help they may enlist, are "primarily responsible for the prosecution of their claims." *(Dominguez v. MSPB, 92-3002, May 14, 1992)*

The U.S. Court of Appeals for the Federal Circuit sent a warning to federal and postal employees against filing what it termed a "frivolous" appeal, by making the appealing employee responsible for repaying the government's cost to defend the case plus a $500 fine. *(McEnery v. MSPB, 91-3142, May 12, 1992)*

A union-represented employee wishing to challenge a personnel decision may pursue that challenge either through the grievance process or the unfair labor practice route but not both, the U.S. Court of Appeals for the District of Columbia said. Both types of challenges to the same action only can be considered, it said, only if "different factual and legal" situations arise between the filing of the first and of the second. *(American Federation of Government Employees v. FLRA, 91-1120, April 3, 1992)*

A federal appeals court refused to put a time limit on an employee seeking enforcement of a Merit Systems Protection Board order. The U.S. Court of Appeals for the Federal Circuit said that a hearing even five years later would not put an unreasonable burden on the agency to reconstruct what happened in a long-running dispute over the employee's job classification. *(Hoover v. Dept. of the Navy, 91-3227, March 3, 1992)*

The Merit Systems Protection Board gave an agency three options when interim relief is ordered to an employee in a personnel appeal: (1) Comply with the order and return the employee to his or her job with full pay and benefits, (2) place the employee in a nonduty status such as administrative leave if it decides that reinstatement would be disruptive to the work environment, or (3) place the employee in some other position—again after determining that a return to the former position would be disruptive. *(MSPB Doc. No. DC31518910527, February 19, 1992)*

The U.S. Court of Appeals for the 11th Circuit ruled that a federal employee who was embarrassed about details involving his drinking problem could not use a pseudonym when suing the U.S. Postal Service over his dismissal. It ruled that a plaintiff's name can only be withheld where the matters at hand are "highly sensitive and personal in nature," where there is a "real danger of physical harm" or for other reasons. *(Doe v. Frank, No. 91-5063, January 24, 1992)*

An agency that gave the Federal Labor Relations Authority the wrong address to send official communications can't be excused for missing an appeals deadline because a notice from FLRA went to the wrong destination, FLRA said. Thus, the agency lost out on its chance to contest an arbitrator's decision before the labor authority. *(43 FLRA No. 30, November 25, 1991)*

The foreign service board of appeals has no authority to review State Department decisions on the expiration or termination of limited, non-tenured appointments, said the U.S. District Court in the District of Columbia, *(Miller v. Baker, 90-409, October 22, 1990)*

The United States Claims Court said it has jurisdiction to hear claims from Army and Air Force Exchange Service employees but only those who are employed under contract to the agency. *(Moore v. U.S., 695-89C, October 12, 1990)*

The U.S. Court of Appeals for the District of Columbia ruled that excepted service employees cannot gain through negotiation appeals rights they don't have under civil service law. *(Dept. of the Treasury v.*

FLRA and NTEU, 88-1159, May 2, 1989)

A postal employee who didn't appeal his firing to the Merit Systems Protection Board until four years after the event occurred is entitled to an appeal and a hearing after showing good cause for missing the filing deadline. *(MSPB Decision No. CHO7528810490, April 12, 1989)*

The U.S. Court of Appeals for the Federal Circuit ruled that accepting a downgrade while fearing that the alternative is being fired is not an involuntary action and therefore can't be appealed to the Merit Systems Protection Board. *(Grossman v. USPS, 88-3051, Aug. 22, 1988)*

The U.S. Court of Appeals for the Federal Circuit ruled that a first line supervisor may be both the proposing and deciding official in a personnel action. *(Franco v. Dept. of HHS, 87-3567, June 2, 1988)*

The U.S. Court of Appeals for the Federal Circuit held that employees must prove that an error in a personnel action was "harmful" to them in order to have the action overturned. *(Bayne, et al, v. Dept. of Energy, 87-3545, May 4, 1988)*

The U.S. Court of Appeals for the District of Columbia ruled that a federal employee who refused to go through with an administrative hearing into her discrimination complaint did not forfeit her right to appeal to federal court. *(McRae v. Librarian of Congress, 87-5336, April 15, 1988)*

ANNUITIES — TAXES AND ACTIONS (see also RETIREMENT)

The North Carolina Supreme Court excused the state from refunding some $140 million in state income taxes paid by federal retirees and active duty military members before January 1, 1989. The court ruled that the state did not have to refund the money that was collected before the U.S. Supreme Court's ruling *(Davis v. Michigan)*, which quashed state laws that authorized taxing federal annuities but exempted state and local government pensions. *(Swanson v. N.C., NC SupCt, 64PA91, August 14, 1991)*

A U.S. Supreme Court decision significantly fueled hopes of federal, postal and military retirees in a score of states that they can recoup refunds for state taxes that were improperly withheld from their annuities. The court in a 6-3 ruling rejected a legal principle that many states had been using to deny refund requests since a 1989 decision found that those retirees had been unfairly taxed while retirees from other levels of government were not taxed. *(James Beam Distilling Co. v. Georgia, 89-680, June 20, 1991)*

Two rulings by the U.S. Supreme Court boosted chances that federal and military retirees in 23 states will get refunds of state taxes improperly taken from their federal annuities. (*American Trucking Association v. Smith, 88-325, and McKesson Corp. v. Division of Alcoholic Beverages and Tobacco, 88-192, June 4, 1990*)

ARBITRATION (see also GRIEVANCES)

The U.S. Court of Appeals for the Federal Circuit issued a decision that could make it harder for the Office of Personnel Management to step into arbitration cases, as it has the right to do when it believes a decision runs counter to federal employment laws or rules. The court said arbitrators considering disputes over federal employment actions must follow the same procedural rules used by the Merit Systems Protection Board, potentially setting time deadlines that would be hard for OPM to meet. (*Bloomer v. HHS, 91-3351, June 9, 1992*)

The U.S. Court of Appeals for the District of Columbia ordered arbitration to resolve a dispute between two postal unions regarding whose members should be assigned to deliver mail in a disputed zone. Such disputes are matters for the arbitration channel, not the federal courts, it said. (*USPS v. NRLCA and NALC, 90-5267, March 20, 1992*)

The U.S. Court of Appeals for the Federal Circuit said that while it has jurisdiction to review arbitrators' decisions, those cases must involve disputes over either unacceptable performance or an adverse action "for cause" against an employee. It declined to hear a dispute over a settlement agreement, saying it involved contract compliance that could only be appealed to the Federal Labor Relations Authority. (*Carney v. Dept. of Veterans Affairs, 90-3337, March 14, 1991*)

The U.S. Court of Appeals for the Federal Circuit held that an arbitrator's decision need not contain a detailed explanation of his reasoning unless a local union contract requires it. (*Wissman v. Social Security Administration, 87-3528, May 31, 1988*)

ATTORNEY'S FEES

An IRS special agent who was the subject of an investigation instigated by a House subcommittee looking for missing documents is stuck with a $15,000 bill for the services of a lawyer he hired to protect his rights during the probe. "Even though (the agent) was cleared of all suspicions of misconduct, his legal fees may not be deemed incurred in furtherance of the government's interest because the government's interest was not aligned with his personal interest," the U.S. Comptroller General said in denying his request for relief. (*CG Decision No. B-245648.2, July 24, 1992*)

The U.S. District Court for the District of Oregon ordered the U.S. Postal Service to pay $195,000 in attorneys fees incurred by a deaf-mute postal window clerk who successfully proved she was the victim of sexual harassment. The court rejected the postal service's contention that the amount was unreasonable. *(Nichols v. Frank, No. 89-635-FR, January 16, 1992)*

Three federal managers who were convicted on charges of breaking environmental laws can't be reimbursed for their legal fees, according to the U.S. Comptroller General, who said the defense "merely advanced the personal interest" of the trio. *(CG Decision B-242891, September 3, 1991)*

Federal employees appealing personnel actions against them generally are bound by the actions of their attorneys, even if they don't like the consequences. But the U.S. Court of Appeals for the Federal Circuit ruled that the principle doesn't apply in a case where the lawyer withdrew the appeal (without the consent of the employee) because he was overworked. *(Kipen v. MSPB, 91-3077, June 17, 1991)*

The government may be compelled to pay interim legal fees while the final amount is being determined when federal employees show that they were victims of discrimination, the U.S. Court of Appeals for the District of Columbia ruled. *(Trout v. Garrett, 88-5264, December 15, 1989)*

The U.S. Court of Appeals for the District of Columbia held that federal employees who are lawyers and who represent themselves successfully in challenges to personnel actions can be paid legal fees for their efforts. *(Jones v. Lujan, 88-5229, June 30, 1989)*

An employee who successfully defends himself against an adverse action by his agency is not entitled to compensatory time off in lieu of attorney fee payments. *(MSPB Doc.CH07528C0006, Sept. 6, 1988)*

BACK PAY

The U.S. Supreme Court refused to hear an appeal of a decision that federal employee who wins a claim that he was not promoted due to discrimination cannot collect interest on any back pay award that is granted. *(Brown v. Dept. of the Army, 90-1733, cert denied October 7, 1991)*

An employee who proved her accusations of discrimination before the Equal Employment Opportunity Commission won a monetary award but wound up owing money to the government because of her outside income after she left the government must apply to the Office of Personnel Management for relief, the U.S. Comptroller General said. *(CG Decision No. B-235638, December 4, 1990)*

Federal employees who win back pay cases claiming they were

denied promotions because of bias are eligible for interest on the award only if the promotion was of the mandatory type, said the U.S. Court of Appeals for the District of Columbia. *(Brown v. Secretary of the Army, 89-5371, and Mitchell v. Secretary of Commerce, 89-5375, November 9, 1990)*

When federal employees win challenges to personnel actions against them, the total outcome, not just part of it, determines whether they are entitled to back pay, said the U.S. Court of Appeals for the Federal Circuit. *(Fausto v. U.S., 90-5001, January 19, 1990)*

A postal employee cannot recover back pay for a suspension even though the legal action that led to the suspension was dropped, according to the U.S. Court of Appeals for the Federal Circuit. *(Callahan v. USPS, 89-3231, January 10, 1990)*

For the purposes of back pay claims a federal job may not be retroactively reclassified, the U.S. Comptroller General ruled. *(CG No. B-230404, April 5, 1988)*

The Federal Mediation and Conciliation Service upheld deductions amounting to more than $24,000 of a $25,000 back payment granted to an employee who won reinstatement after an improper firing from his federal job. *(No. 86K01932, Dec. 19, 1987)*

BARGAINING

When federal labor law requires that an agency bargain over a subject, the agency's duty to bargain extends even to requesting that outside parties—such as other levels of government—make changes that would allow the required bargaining to take place, the Federal Labor Relations Authority said. *(44 FLRA No. 103, May 22, 1992)*

The U.S. Court of Appeals for the District of Columbia backed a union's bid to bargain on a proposal that employees required to carry electronic pagers away from the job be compensated for their troubles. *(Dept. of the Navy v. FLRA, 91-1182, May 8, 1992)*

The Federal Labor Relations Authority ruled negotiable several union proposals regarding how an agency may use a new centralized computer system that contains information on agency personnel and programs, as well as classified data. *(44 FLRA No. 54, March 27, 1992)*

An agency has no duty to bargain on a union proposal during the term of a contract unless the proposal is a response to changes that management has made to the conditions of employment since the contract went into effect, the U.S. Court of Appeals for the Fourth Circuit ruled. Midterm bargaining is limited only to implementing such changes and accommodating employees adversely affected by them, the court said. (*Social Security Administration v. FLRA, 91-2065, February 25, 1992*)

A Federal Labor Relations Authority law judge, in ruling an agency improperly altered office space without bargaining with the local union, ordered management to knock down the walls of two offices that were built in the process. (*4-CA-10346, February 4, 1992*)

A federal union local was within its rights to put its fingers in the pie when the agency decided to establish an employee cafeteria, the Federal Labor Relations Authority decided. FLRA ruled various proposals about the design and services of the proposed facility to be negotiable as conditions of employment. (*43 FLRA No. 106, January 31, 1992*)

The U.S. Court of Appeals for the District of Columbia overturned a standard that the Federal Labor Relations Authority had been using to decide if certain federal union proposals are negotiable. FLRA mistakenly applied the standard only to proposals that also affected non-bargaining unit employees, the court said. (*Dept. of the Navy v. FLRA, 91-1123, January 14, 1992*)

The Federal Labor Relations Authority said it won't hesitate to order retroactive bargaining in cases where it believes such negotiations are needed to correct unfair labor practices. (*38 FLRA No. 83, December 14, 1991*)

Agency policies as they apply to employees while off-duty can still involve a "condition of employment" and require bargaining with a union, the U.S. Court of Appeals for the District of Columbia said. (*Dept. of the Air Force v. FLRA, 90-1561, December 10, 1991*)

A proposal to exempt from discipline federal employees who voluntarily admit to the use of illegal drugs, are rehabilitated and then remain drug-free was ruled negotiable by the Federal Labor Relations Authority. (*40 FLRA No. 68, May 10, 1991*)

The Federal Labor Relations Authority upheld the right to bargain over the percentages of health insurance premiums to be borne by employees and the agency in one of the few pockets of the executive branch where negotiation over benefits is allowed—the Army and Air Force Exchange Service. (*38 FLRA No. 32, November 21, 1990*)

A union proposal that would prohibit all but members of the bargaining unit from operating certain equipment was ruled negotiable by the Federal Labor Relations Authority. (*37 FLRA No. 113, October 30, 1990*)

The U.S. Court of Appeals for the District of Columbia gave the

Federal Labor Relations Authority wide latitude in deciding whether retroactive bargaining should be held on an issue. *(NTEU v. FLRA, 87-1165, August 14, 1990)*

The procedures an agency uses when investigating employees for misuse of government phones are subject to collective bargaining, ruled the Federal Labor Relations Authority. *(35 FLRA No. 135, May 31, 1990)*

A decision by the U.S. Supreme Court opened the door for bargaining over salaries for certain categories of federal workers whose pay is not governed by statute. While the decision leaves out the general schedule and vast bulk of the civil service, it is estimated that employees in some 40 sub-categories could use the decision as precedent for negotiating over their pay. *(Fort Stewart Schools v. FLRA, 89-65, May 29, 1990)*

The U.S. Court of Appeals for the 10th Circuit ruled that federal bargaining units may not contain both supervisory and nonsupervisory employees. *(Dept. of Energy v. FLRA, 86-2414, July 19, 1989)*

Keeping meals at a low cost for employees is a morale-builder and therefore can be justified as a negotiable item. *(89 FSIP 24, May 3, 1989)*

The U.S. Court of Appeals for the District of Columbia held that retroactive bargaining orders can be used regularly in cases where agencies refused to bargain over proposals that are later found to be negotiable. *(NTEU v. FLRA, 87-1165, Sept. 9. 1988)*

The U.S. Court of Appeals for the District of Columbia ruled non-negotiable a union proposal that an agency delay the start of a new program while the union studies its effects on bargaining unit members. *(U.S. Customs Service v. FLRA and NTEU, 87-1128, Aug. 23, 1988)*

The U.S. Court of Appeals for the District of Columbia said the Federal Labor Relations Authority has issued conflicting decisions on the duty to bargain over union proposals that affect nonbargaining unit employees and told FLRA to reconsider the issue and produce "intelligible" precedents. *(AFGE v. FLRA, 86-1447, 86-1642, Aug. 16, 1988)*

The U.S. Court of Appeals for the for the District of Columbia sharply limited bargaining rights for Veterans Administration professional medical personnel. *(Colorado Nurses Association v. FLRA, 87-1104, July 19, 1988)*

An agency must bargain with the resident union over imposing a dress code that would prohibit employees from wearing short pants. *(32 FLRA No. 34, May 31, 1988)*

Negotiations are allowed over an agency plan to share the profits for better productivity with the employees involved in the effort. *(32 FLRA No. 15, May 17, 1988)*

The Federal Labor Relations Authority said it has the power to review arbitrator awards affecting excepted service federal employees. *(32 FLRA No. 10, May 11, 1988)*

A labor contract clause requiring that employees be given 10 minutes on the agency clock before lunch time to clean up was ruled enforceable. *(31 FLRA No. 112, April 27, 1988)*

An Air Force policy that restricts eligibility for quality step increases to employees in grade steps 4 and above is negotiable. *(31 FLRA No. 107, April 22, 1988)*

The use of bicycles at work is an "internal security practice" and is not a subject for negotiation. *(31 FLRA No. 71, March 23, 1988)*

A federal agency may act on its own to require employees to wear uniform items if the action is taken in the name of internal security practices. *(31 FLRA No. 65, March 21, 1988)*

Overseas Defense Department teachers may negotiate over movement up the salary schedule rates, for longevity pay and the amount of annual and educational leave that they can receive. *(30 FLRA No. 69, Dec. 21, 1987)*

BONUSES AND INCENTIVES

Union proposals to dictate the method an agency would use for calculating the amount of monetary awards for excellent performance were ruled non-negotiable by the Federal Labor Relations Authority. *(45 FLRA No. 52, July 21, 1992)*

The U.S. Comptroller General said an agency plan to buy jackets with appropriate insignia as incentive awards for outstanding employee achievement is okay because such jackets (or presumably other kinds of apparel) can help agencies both recognize individual achievement and inspire it in others. *(CG Decision No. B-243025, May 2, 1991)*

An agency can't buy T-shirts with the Combined Federal Campaign logo as awards for employees who contribute generously to the charity drive, the U.S. Comptroller General ruled. There's no authority to do so under the Government Employees Incentive Awards Act, he said, adding that they would be considered "personal gifts." *(CG Decision No. B-240001, February 8, 1991)*

The U.S. Postal Service's Employee suggestion program does not create a "contract" between the agency and an employee, and those dissatisfied with their awards cannot appeal to the United States Claims Court, that court decided. *(Hayes v. U.S., 565-88C, April 17, 1990)*

The U.S. Court of Appeals for the Fourth Circuit ruled that negotiating over an employee bonus incentive program would interfere with management's right to determine its own budget. *(CA4 88-2131, September 14, 1989)*

The Federal Labor Relations Authority ruled that a union proposal for mandatory cash performance awards is not negotiable because it would have imposed mandatory requirements on the agency. *(37 FLRA No. 79)*

CONDITIONS OF EMPLOYMENT
(see also WORKING CONDITIONS)

The Federal Labor Relations Authority rejected a union's proposal that positions not be reclassified without the employee's consent, saying that law excludes classification of federal jobs from the "conditions of employment" over which unions may bargain. *(45 FLRA No. 119, September 14, 1992)*

The Federal Service Impasses Panel upheld a meal surcharge at a cafeteria in a remote worksite, saying the employees who work there on average are highly paid and that those with good appetites can get their money's worth. *(92 FSIP 71, May 19, 1992)*

A union proposal to allow employees to wear personal stereo headphones while at work would lead to everyone whistling a different tune, the Federal Service Impasses Panel said. FSIP agreed with management that employees should "focus their attention on their given tasks, instead of on entertainment, during the work day." *(91 FSIP 224, March 26, 1992)*

The Federal Labor Relations Authority said that eating and drinking arrangements can be part of the conditions of employment and that agencies cannot change them without negotiations. *(43 FLRA No. 124, February 14, 1992)*

The Federal Labor Relations Authority upheld bargaining on a union proposal that the agency provide either uniforms or a $400 annual uniform allowance for "dual status" technicians who sometimes must wear their military uniforms while performing their civilian duties. It said the proposal is negotiable as a condition of employment because it affects their civilian duties, and because the military uniform allowance they receive covers only uniforms to be worn while performing military duties. *(43 FLRA No. 101, January 31, 1992)*

The U.S Court of Appeals for the Ninth Circuit ruled that the Army must bargain with a union over paid holidays and disability insurance benefits for some civilian workers because those issues were conditions of employment. *(Dept. of the Army v. FLRA, 88-7004, 88-7158, September 18, 1990)*

The U.S. Court of Appeals for the District of Columbia held that the Veterans Administration has no duty to bargain over conditions of employment with its nurses and other health care professionals. *(New York State Nurses Association v. FLRA, USCA DC Cir., 88-1893, April 11, 1989 and Illinois Nurses Association v. FLRA, USCA DC Cir., No. 88-1891, April 12, 1989)*

An arbitrator ordered a supervisor to apologize to an employee for driving to her house at 11:45 pm and ordering her to report for an immediate fitness-for-duty examination when he didn't believe the subordinate's claim that she was too ill to work her shift. *(Case No. C4C-4B-C-36780, April 4, 1989, Michele Hoyman, arbitrator)*

An agency policy setting a specific hearing standard for a job was overturned on grounds that the standard was unrelated to safe and efficient performance of the job. *(EEOC Appeal No. 01881844, January 31, 1989)*

CONFLICT OF INTEREST

A federal employee who sends a resume to a person working for a firm under his agency's jurisdiction risks violating standards of official conduct if it appears he was seeking a job with the specific company rather than the industry in general. *(CG Decision No. B-229435.2, November 17, 1988)*

The U.S. Court of Appeals for the 4th Circuit ruled that improper civil service personnel actions may be prosecuted under the 1962 federal conflict-of-interest criminal statute. *(U.S. v. Lund, 87-5642, Aug. 1, 1988)*

An arbitration decision held that even the *appearance* of impropriety can be as harmful as a real conflict of interest when a federal employee decides to moonlight and an agency therefore is within its rights to forbid it. *(OHA, SSA and NTEU, LAIRS 18471)*

CONSTITUTIONAL RIGHTS

A federal employee who placed a sign on his truck reading "Hell With Bush" failed to convince a federal judge of the U.S. District Court for the Middle District of Georgia that Warner Robins Air Force Base, Ga., violated his right to free speech by prohibiting him from driving that truck on base as long as the sign remained. The judge ruled that the U.S. military has the right to curtail some kinds of speech on its bases when it believes order and discipline could be harmed. *(Ethredge v. Hail, No. 92-187-2-MAC(DF), June 5, 1992)*

Racially-charged comments about a supervisor are not protected free speech and can be the basis for firing a federal employee if they rise to the level of undermining government efficiency and discipline, said the U.S. Court of Appeals for the Federal Circuit. *(Henry v. Dept. of the Navy, 90-3018, May 10, 1990)*

A federal union has no statutory right to place an advertisement critical of management in a base publication, although it can gain that right through negotiation or established practice, the Federal Labor Relations Authority held. *(34 FLRA No. 172, February 28, 1990)*

The right of free speech did not protect a federal employee who sent to a member of the public an internal memo in which he accused his agency and a co-worker of race discrimination. *(MSPB Decision No. NYO7528710252, March 23, 1989)*

The U.S. Supreme Court ruled that national security considerations do not prevent federal employees from suing for violations of their constitutional rights. *(Webster v. Doe, 86-1294, June 15, 1988)*

An arbitrator ruled that an Air Force base may not prohibit union members from expressing to reporters their views about working conditions, saying that would infringe on First Amendment rights. *(FMCS No. 87-28443, June 3, 1988)*

CONTRACTING OUT

An agency isn't obligated to hold up its contracting-out efforts while a union challenges the move through the arbitration process, the Federal Labor Relations Authority ruled. FLRA said neither law nor rules require that management stay its decision while the grievance and arbitration process is pending, although such a requirement could be imposed if the two sides agreed to it in a contract. *(43 FLRA No. 79, January 10, 1992)*

Arbitrators have the power to reverse contracting-out decisions and order that the federal employees who lost their jobs be reinstated with back pay, the Federal Labor Relations Authority said in overturning its previous policy. *(43 FLRA No. 64, December 26, 1991)*

Agency decisions to contract out federal jobs to the private sector can be challenged through the grievance and arbitration process, the Federal Labor Relations Authority ruled in a case that could provide unions with a new tool to challenge such decisions. *(42 FLRA No. 31, September 27, 1991)*

Contract employees who performed work for the Nuclear Regulatory Commission were not performing "inherently governmental activities" and therefore cannot be barred by contracting-out regulations, the U.S. Comptroller General ruled. *(CG Decision No. B-242942, August 27, 1991)*

The U.S. Court of Appeals for the First Circuit opened the door for so-called *qui tam* suits brought by individuals in the name of the government seeking redress for fraud, giving federal employees a weapon to fight contracting out and earn money at the same time. *USCAFC, U.S. ex rel. Roland A. LeBlanc v. Raytheon Company, Inc., 9C-1246, September 4, 1990)*

An agency has to do more than simply downgrade positions to prove it is reorganizing a function to adhere to contracting-out procedures. It must prove that the reorganization involves "substance," ruled the Merit Systems Protection Board. *(Doc No. CH03519010356, June 22, 1990)*

The general counsel of the Federal Labor Relations Authority ruled that if the government fails to follow its own contracting-out procedures it is subject to challenges from unions. The counsel ruled that OMB Circular A-76 amounts to "applicable law" under federal labor statutes. *(Dept. of the Army v. NFFE Local 1263, No. 9-CA-90570, May 14, 1990)*

The U.S. Supreme Court ruled against employees wishing to challenge contracting decisions through grievance procedures but ordered a further legal look into the issue of whether A-76 is a "law" under language that gives management exclusive control over contracting only when all "applicable laws" are being followed. *(Dept. of the Treasury v. FLRA, 88-2123, April 17, 1990)*

The U.S Court of Appeals for the District of Columbia decided not to rehear a decision ruling that employees have no standing as disappointed bidders to challenge government decisions to contract out work to the private sector. *(NFFE v. Cheney, 88-5271, December 22, 1989)*

The U.S. Court of Appeals for the District of Columbia held that a federal union has no standing under the Administrative Procedures Act to challenge an agency decision to contract out federal jobs. *(NFFE v. Cheney, 88-5271, August 25, 1989)*

The U.S. Supreme Court agreed to resolve a dispute over whether federal unions can invoke arbitration over agency decisions to contract out civil service positions to the private sector. *(Dept. of the Treasury v. FLRA, 88-2123)*

DAY CARE

The U.S. Comptroller General said that if agencies want to help pay for the care of their employees' adult relatives or donate agency space for eldercare programs, Congress will have to authorize it. Appropriations may not be used for that purpose, the CG said. *(CG Decision No. B-247730, September 21, 1992)*

Bargaining was upheld on a union proposal that an agency's child care facility be open 24 hours a day and that the fees be comparable to those of similar centers run by another agency in the area. The Federal Labor Relations Authority held that such matters concern a condition of employment and that they were not restricted to the agency's discretion by law. *(43 FLRA No. 42, December 13, 1991)*

A union's proposal that half the spots available at a Navy facility's child care center be reserved for bargaining unit civilian employees was rejected by the Federal Service Impasses Panel. FSIP said the proposal would be unfair to both military personnel at the facility and to non-bargaining unit civilian workers. *(91 FSIP No. 70, December 6, 1991)*

The U.S. Comptroller General ruled that agencies may lease or construct child care facilities for federal employees if space is lacking in the government's inventory of buildings. *(CG Decision No. B-239708, January 31, 1991)*

The Secretary of the Air Force may set aside government funds to renovate or expand government buildings to provide child care facilities for the children of civilian employees — even to the extent of providing them at no charge to the parents. *(CG No. B-222989, June 9, 1988)*

DISABILITY BENEFITS
(see also REHABILITATION; RETIREMENT; DISABILITY)

The Office of Personnel Management failed to make clear what it means by requiring that an application for disability retirement be filed within a year after leaving federal service, the U.S. Court of Appeals for the Federal Circuit said. It ordered OPM to consider the application of a woman who mailed the forms before her cutoff date but which weren't received by OPM until after that date. *(Parker v. OPM, 92-3242, September 3, 1992)*

The key questions in assessing whether an agency met its obligation to accommodate a disabled employee are if the employee "could have performed the essential functions" of the position with the job changes sought and if the changes would impose an "undue hardship" on the employer, the U.S. Court of Appeals for the District of Columbia said. *(Langon v. Dept. of Health and Human Services, 90-5300, March 31, 1992)*

The disability retirement of an injured employee was voluntary because he had the option of taking a transfer to another job, the U.S. Court of Appeals for the Federal Circuit ruled. A resignation is only involuntary, it said, if "obtained through agency coercion, duress, deception or misinformation." *(Rodes v. Dept. of Transportation, 91-3571, March 12, 1992)*

The U.S. Court of Appeals for the Federal Circuit said a person with priority rights in a disability case has the claim to a position over someone else who may be brought in by certain types of new appointments, transfers or reemployments. But those priority rights "do not prevent an agency from filling a vacancy by detail or position change, such as by promotion of a current, qualified agency employee." *(Curtius v. MSPB, 91-3477, December 19, 1991)*

Civil service retirement law does not allow for an application for disability benefits after an employee has died, the U.S. Court of Appeals for the Federal Circuit said. *(Davis v. OPM, 91-3017, July 10, 1991)*

DISCIPLINE (see also DISMISSAL; SUSPENSION)

The U.S. Court of Appeals for the Federal Circuit overturned the firing on insubordination charges of a food delivery worker who refused to deliver food trays in carts he considered too dirty, saying that while his conduct was "out of line" it may have been understandable under the circumstances. It ordered a lesser penalty be imposed, pointing to evidence that the employee had good reason to be concerned about the cleanliness of the carts. *(Washington v. Dept. of Veterans Affairs, 91-3592, October 16, 1992)*

A union proposal to require that any discipline be imposed within 30 days of when a supervisor learned of an alleged infraction was ruled non-negotiable by the Federal Labor Relations Authority, which said the setting of any kind of limitation violates management's right to discipline employees. *(45 FLRA No. 100, August 31, 1992)*

Whether a disciplinary action against an employee is excessive depends, among other things, on whether similar action was taken against other employees who are "similarly situated," the U.S. Court of Appeals for the District of Columbia said. The court said the key test is whether comparable employees had been treated differently. *(Pension Benefit Guaranty Corp. v. FLRA, 91-1180, June 26, 1992)*

A reprimand of an employee on charges of misusing a computer electronic mail system was upheld by the Federal Labor Relations Authority, which said the employee had violated a "reasonable work rule" that he was aware of and that was consistent with the local labor-management contract. The rule prohibited sending messages outside the immediate division without approval of top management. *(45 FLRA No. 4, June 5, 1992)*

The U.S. Court of Appeals for the Federal Circuit was not amused by an attempt at ethnic humor made at a Navy facility, but it nonetheless ordered that the demotion imposed on a supervisor for his participation in it be reduced to a 14-day suspension. It said that was the penalty assessed to another supervisor involved in the incident — delivering a package with a racial overtone during business hours. *(Phillips v. Dept. of the Navy, 91-3311, March 26, 1992)*

The Federal Labor Relations Authority rejected bargaining on a union proposal that would have set up a table of disciplinary actions to guide the agency in disciplining employees. *(44 FLRA No. 38, March 17, 1992)*

An employee who forgot to type a two-character code in accessing a computer at work that then gave him unauthorized access to a check generating program should not have been disciplined for the mistake, the Merit Systems Protection Board said. *(MSPB Doc. No. PH07529110622, March 5, 1992)*

The U.S. Court of Appeals for the Federal Circuit set a new standard on suspending employees indefinitely for suspected off-duty misconduct. In sum, "it is incumbent upon the agency . . . to assure itself that the surrounding facts are sufficient to justify summary action," such as an immediate, indefinite suspension. *(Dunnington v. Dept. of Justice, 90-3427, February 27, 1992)*

The U.S. Court of Appeals for the Federal Circuit upheld the firing of an employee on charges including endangering his personal safety by not wearing a respirator while working in a contaminated area. Other charges against him included acting disrespectfully to a supervisor and failing to follow instructions. *(Daliberti v. Dept. of the Navy, 91-3318, December 26, 1991)*

The U.S. Court of Appeals for the Federal Circuit ruled that a former air traffic controller is entitled to know if he received unequal treatment when he was fired, along with 11,000 other controllers, for that same illegal strike. *(Templeton v. OPM, 91-3321, December 18, 1991)*

The firing of an FBI agent who refused to carry out certain assignments because of his personal and religious beliefs was upheld by the Seventh Circuit Court of Appeals, which said the agency is "entitled to insist that its agents follow orders." The agent, a Roman Catholic, refused to join investigations of several pacifist groups that were suspected of incidents of vandalism at military recruiting facilities. *(No. 91-1467, December 9, 1991)*

An agency may use instances of unacceptable performance up to a year old in disciplining an employee on such grounds, the U.S. Court of Appeals for the Federal Circuit said, rejecting an argument that only the employee's record during his current performance improvement plan should be considered. *(Addison v. Dept. of Health and Human Services, 91-3097, September 25, 1991)*

Federal employees appealing personnel actions and their agencies can settle their differences through oral contracts, the U.S. Court of Appeals for the Federal Circuit said, but it said such a contract wasn't reached in the case it was considering. *(Mahboob v. Dept. of the Navy, 90-3342, March 22, 1991)*

The Federal Labor Relations Authority upheld a ruling ordering a supervisor to write a letter of apology and take sensitivity training, among other things, for refusing to allow a diabetic employee to go home and take medication—ultimately he collapsed and had to be taken to a hospital. *(39 FLRA No. 114, March 21, 1991)*

Although an employee was sincere in his opposition to an agency policy that led to a dispute with his supervisors, that didn't relieve him of his duty to follow proper orders, the U.S. Court of Appeals for the Federal Circuit ruled in upholding a firing on insubordination charges. *(Gould v. National Archives and Records Administration, 90-3472, March 11, 1991)*

An employee may be held blameless for violating a settlement agreement with his agency if he "raises a non-frivolous factual issue," such as a medical emergency, the U.S. Court of Appeals for the Federal Circuit ruled. *(Stewart v. USPS, 90-3382, February 21, 1991)*

The U.S. Court of Appeals for the Federal Circuit upheld the unpaid 90-day suspension of a letter carrier on charges including "misrepresenting the amount of time necessary to complete his postal route." *(Box v. USPS, 90-3397, January 14, 1991)*

A charge of falsification of a government document requires not only that an answer was wrong, but also that the wrong answer was given with intent to deceive or mislead the agency, the U.S. Court of Appeals for the Federal Circuit ruled in dismissing travel fraud charges against a woman who it said could have honestly misinterpreted rules on who may qualify for travel expenses as a dependent. *(Cotlon v. Dept. of the Air Force, 90-3388, January 11, 1991)*

An arbitrator ordered the reinstatement of an employee who had been fired for burning a small American flag. The penalty for the incident, which the employee later apologized for, was too harsh, the arbitrator ruled, in ordering his reinstatement with back pay and restored benefits. *(LAIRS No. 20134, November 9, 1990)*

The U.S. Court of Appeals for the Federal Circuit upheld the demotion of a postmaster to a nonsupervisory job on charges of improperly handling bulk business mail that was either duplicative or misaddressed. *(Boley v. USPS, 90-3235, October 16, 1990)*

Despite the constitutional right to remain silent, a federal employee facing discipline may find that his refusal to answer questions can be held against him when an administrative judge is weighing charges, said the U.S. Court of Appeals for the Federal Circuit. *(McGuire v. Dept. of Treasury, 90-3120, September 13, 1990)*

The U.S. Court of Appeals for the Federal Circuit upheld the firing of a Social Security Administration supervisor who was charged with disclosing confidential information and accepting a free lunch from company officials applying for government contracts. *(Baker v. HHS, 89-3430, August 31, 1990)*

An employee's belief that an order he is given is senseless does not excuse him from the obligation to carry it out or face charges of insubordination, the U.S. Court of Appeals for the Federal Circuit said. *(Webster v. Army, 89-3369, August 9, 1990)*

A postal employee who was fired on charges including acting disrespectfully toward a supervisor deserves to have his firing reconsidered because prior discipline against him was partly overturned, the U.S. Court of Appeals for the Federal Circuit ruled. *(Lindo v. USPS, 90-3207, July 3, 1990)*

The Merit Systems Protection Board ruled that the Justice Department has cause to suspend an employee who was arrested after a magistrate found evidence he committed a crime for which he could be imprisoned. Thus, it has "reasonable cause" to suspend the employee since magistrates (and judges) are required to have sufficient evidence to issue such warrants, MSPB said. *(Doc. No. DA07528610554, May 25, 1990)*

An arbitrator overturned the firing of a Bureau of Prisons employee, taking time out to scold the agency for accepting unproved hearsay evidence against him and for releasing only those parts of the employee's background investigation that were damaging to him. (*FMCS Case No. 89-24576, May 23, 1990*)

A federal employee who used a government computer to help his wife's real estate business was given a suspension. He could have received a stiffer penalty, the Merit Systems Protection Board ruled. (*MSPB No. DC07529010125, April 18, 1990*)

A former Army civilian employee was sentenced in U.S. District Court in the District of Columbia to six months in prison for submitting a false claim to get $211,000 in benefits under the Federal Employees Compensation Act. (*9029, April 17, 1990*)

The Federal Labor Relations Authority ruled non-negotiable a union proposal that the Army consider only identical prior offenses when setting appropriate punishment for subsequent offenses. Management successfully argued that the proposal would prevent it from dealing with an employee's alleged habitual unacceptable behavior until the person committed an offense identical to an earlier one. MSPB found the proposal interfered with management's rights. (*34 FLRA No. 151, February 16, 1990*)

The U.S. Court of Appeals for the District of Columbia said the American Foreign Service Association should have gone first to the Foreign Service Labor Relations Board with a claim that the State Department violated its bargaining obligations, before going to federal court. (*AFSA v. Baker, 89-5130, February 16, 1990*)

The U.S. Court of Appeals for the District of Columbia upheld bargaining over pay in an area where a "grandfather" clause allowed continued wage bargaining in functions that had such rights before a 1972 law set up the prevailing rate wage system. (*USIA v. FLRA and NFFE, 88-1898, February 13, 1990*)

The Merit Systems Protection Board ordered the Army to reinstate an employee at the Tooele Army Depot, Utah, who was removed after striking his supervisor. Instead, MSPB imposed a 30-day suspension. (*MSPB Docket No. DE07528910010, January 1, 1990*)

An arbitrator upheld a seven-day suspension of a U.S. Customs employee who secretly recorded a meeting of employees called by an agency official, despite employees' contention that he did not know that unauthorized recording was punishable by penalties ranging from 30 days' suspension to removal. (*Arbitrator Stanley M. Block, October 30, 1989*)

The U.S. Court of Appeals for the Federal Circuit held that the First Amendment does not shield from discipline federal employees who solicit funds for a union publication from organizations that have official contacts with an agency. *(England v. Dept. of the Treasury, 89-3165, October 19, 1989)*

The U.S. Court of Appeals for the Federal Circuit held that an agency must prove, not just allege, instances of inadequate performance when taking a personnel action against an employee on performance grounds. *(Saint Thomas v. Dept. of the Navy, 89-3260, August 9, 1989)*

A federal employee may be fired for refusing to answer questions during an investigation if his agency has warned him that he is subject to discharge for not answering and that his reply can't be used against him in a criminal case. *(MSPB Decision No. DC07528810350, August 9, 1989)*

There can be mitigating and other extenuating circumstances that justify a penalty less than firing when a government employee assaults a co-worker. *(MSPB Decision No. BNO7528710144, July 26, 1989)*

The dismissal of a postal worker who allegedly stole a kitchen knife valued at $3.59 at a store was overturned as too harsh a punishment. *(MSPB Decision No. DA07528810277, July 10, 1989)*

The U.S. Court of Appeals for the Fourth Circuit ruled that federal agencies should not fire employees whose poor performance is caused by alcohol without first giving them an opportunity to complete an inpatient treatment program. *(Rogers v. Lehman, CA4, Nos. 88-2028, -2842, -2848, March 3, 1989)*

The U.S. Court of Appeals for the Federal Circuit said the harm done to a federal agency's image by an employee's misconduct can be a factor in taking adverse action against him. *(Case v. Dept. of Army, 88-3003, Sept. 8, 1988)*

The U.S. Court of Appeals for the Federal Circuit ruled that excessive absenteeism or tardiness so interferes with an agency's mission that they can be grounds for firing even an employee with an otherwise good work record. *(Law v. USPS, 88-001, July 26, 1988)*

The United States Claims Court ruled that while a federal employee cannot be fired for refusing to testify against himself, he can be removed for "failure to answer questions specifically and directly related to performance of official duties." *(Carr v. U.S., 323-84C, June 16, 1988)*

The Federal Labor Relations Authority upheld an arbitrator's finding that a federal prison employee was properly disciplined for jokingly placing a mouse or mole he had squashed in the kitchen in a roll for an inmate to eat. *(38 FLRA No. 112)*

DISCRIMINATION (see also HANDICAP)

Federal union-proposed contract language guaranteeing that "no discrimination will be tolerated on the basis of sexual preference and/or orientation" was upheld by the U.S. Court of Appeals for the District of Columbia. *(HUD v. FLRA, 91-1166, May 19, 1992)*

The U.S. District Court for the District of Columbia ruled that the Education Department did not discriminate against an employee who has cerebral palsy when it declined to promote him. Rather, it was his behavior on the job, including taking long breaks, losing interest in his work and failing to consistently perform well in his job that held him back from advancement, the court ruled. *(Decision No. 88-3581, May 13, 1992)*

A federal judge of the U.S. District Court for the Southern District of Ohio found in favor of a female lawyer who claimed that an all-male selection panel improperly rejected her for a teaching vacancy because of gender bias. The judge ruled that she had been singled out because of her gender for questions the male candidates were not asked. *(No. C-3-87-225, March 30, 1992)*

An Equal Employment Opportunity recommended decision in favor of employees drew fire from the Department of Housing and Urban Development, which criticized the administrative law judge, for wearing "traditional Hispanic garb" while hearing a discrimination case brought by Hispanic employees against the agency. *(EEOC Doc. Nos. 360-91-8127X & 360-91-81278X, March 18, 1992)*

An agency was wrong to assume that an employee knew the time limit for filing a discrimination claim, and it was irresponsible when it didn't specifically inform him of the paperwork deadline, the U.S. Court of Appeals for the District of Columbia ruled. *(Bayer v. Dept. of the Treasury, 90-5393, February 21, 1992)*

A federal appeals court reinstated the case of a Drug Enforcement Administration trainee because he provided the court with sufficient evidence of agency discrimination against him on the basis of his religion. *(Rosen v. Thornburgh, No. 90-6133, USCA. 2nd Circuit, March 13, 1991)*

After nearly 18 years in and out of administrative channels and the federal courts, six black employees of the Jacksonville, Fla., Naval Rework Facility lost in a bid to prove they were discriminated against by that agency in 1973. They were seeking back pay and other remedies for themselves and other black workers there. *(Johnson v. Garret, U.S. District Court for the Middle District of Florida, No. 73-702,*

March 6, 1991)

Proof of a discriminatory motive is key to deciding a claim of sex discrimination in a federal workplace bias case, the U.S. Court of Appeals for the District of Columbia said. *(Ramey v. Bowsher, 87-5305, October 5, 1990)*

The U.S. Court of Appeals for the Fourth Circuit ruled that litigants in "frivolous" federal employment discrimination suits are subject to financial penalties, even though they were able to show they had a *prima facie* case. *(Blue v. Dept. of Army, 88-1364, September 18, 1990)*

The U.S. District Court for the District of Columbia ruled that an Army Department employee's failure to contact an equal employment opportunity counselor bars him from proceeding under Title VII of the Civil Rights Act of 1964. *(Richards v. MSPB, DC DC, No. 89-1041-GHR, June 28, 1990)*

When an employee brings an appeal to the Merit Systems Protection Board claiming discrimination as well as other prohibited personnel practices, the board must decide both halves of the case at the same time, said the U.S. Court of Appeals for the Federal Circuit. *(Cruz v. Dept. of the Navy, 89-3359, June 25, 1990)*

Yelling at an employee of a group protected from workplace bias does not amount to discrimination when everyone else in the office gets the same treatment, a federal judge in the Eastern District of New York ruled. *(Sousa v. Hunter, 85-CV3703, June 6, 1990)*

Federal employees can be reimbursed for their legal costs in a settlement with an agency of an age discrimination complaint when the case also involves claims of another form or bias, such as sex discrimination, the U.S. Comptroller General ruled. *(CG Decision No. B-235902, May 22, 1990)*

The U.S. Court of Appeals for the Seventh Circuit held that administrative remedies, once initiated, must be exhausted before a suit may be filed in the federal courts alleging age discrimination in federal employment. *(McGinty v. Army, CA-7, No. 88-2534, April 25, 1990)*

The U.S. Supreme Court ruled that cases brought under Title VII of the 1964 Civil Rights Act—which prohibits various forms of discrimination—can be brought in state courts as well as in federal courts. *(89-431, April 17, 1990)*

The United States Claims Court said it has no jurisdiction over a race discrimination complaint from a former federal employee, even if the complaint is brought as a claim for lost wages and benefits. *(Bailey v.*

U.S., 576-89C, April 17, 1990)

A federal judge ruled guilty of racial bias one of the key federal agencies responsible for assuring that such discrimination does not occur in the federal workplace—the Merit Systems Protection Board—in a case where a board attorney claimed improperly low performances ratings. *(Tyson v. Levinson, 88-1068, February 7, 1990)*

The Merit Systems Protection Board has no jurisdiction over a claim by a preference-eligible employee of the Tennessee Valley Authority that he suffered age and race discrimination in a layoff, said the U.S. Court of Appeals for the Federal Circuit. *(Noble v. TVA, 88-3436, December 19, 1989)*

The U.S. Supreme Court refused to review a consent decree at Warner Robins Air Logistics Center, GA, that sets aside a certain number of promotions at the base for blacks as a remedy for past race discrimination. *(Poss v. Howard, 89-387, December 11, 1989)*

A federal judge approved more than $20,000 in damages and a retroactive promotion to a woman who had complained she was a victim of discrimination and retaliation. *(Whitley v. SBA, C-C-89-0028-M, December 6, 1989)*

The U.S. Court of Appeals for the Fifth Circuit held that it is not sex discrimination when an agency searches for outside candidates to fill jobs for which current employees are eligible. *(Risher v. Aldridge, 88-1504, December 5, 1989)*

Winning a claim against a federal official on charges of violating constitutional rights requires a higher standard of proof than is needed in a discrimination complaint, the U.S. Court of Appeals for the District of Columbia ruled. *(Whitcare v. Davey, 88-5339, November 17, 1989)*

The U.S. Court of Appeals for the District of Columbia ruled that a federal employee who was the victim of job discrimination should be placed in a position as close as possible to the one he was denied, even if that means "bumping" someone who had nothing to do with the discrimination. *(Lander v. Lujan, 89-5014, October 27, 1989)*

An employee was ordered demoted and a former supervisor barred from reemployment with the government for five years on charges of creating an "offensive, hostile and intimidating" workplace for a Jewish employee. *(MSPB Doc. No. HQ12068510015, March 16, 1988)*

The Federal Labor Relations Authority ruled negotiable a union proposal that management state a policy of not tolerating discrimination on the basis of sexual preference. *(39 FLRA No. 29)*

DISMISSAL (see also DISCIPLINE)

An agency has the right to weigh an employee's "dependability and utility" in deciding whether to continue his or her employment, the U.S. Court of Appeals for the Federal Circuit said. *(Kimble v. USPS, 91-3279, September 19, 1991)*

Certain managerial actions against administrative law judges can be appealed as if they were removals from office, but only if those actions interfere with the law judge's impartiality, said the U.S. Court of Appeals for the Federal Circuit. *(Sannier v. MSPB, 90-3463, April 23, 1991)*

The Merit Systems Protection Board reversed an administrative law judge's ruling that the U.S. Postal Service was wrong to fire an employee who had 23 absences for sick leave or leave-without-pay, a work pattern that USPS found unacceptable. *(MSPB Decision No. DE07529010113, March 20, 1991)*

The U.S. Court of Appeals for the Ninth Circuit ruled that a woman who lied during an agency's internal investigation into sexual harassment charges she brought was properly fired for making those false statements. *(CA9, No. 88-5884, June 6, 1990)*

The Merit Systems Protection Board ordered the Rock Island Arsenal flight detachment to rehire a civilian pilot whom it fired after he complained about how the unit was run. The case received additional publicity when one of his fellow pilots, who had testified for him, received a dead bird from an unknown person and had his garbage removed for investigation from his home by an Army provost marshal. *(CH07529010130 McRea v. Army, March 29, 1990)*

The U.S. Court of Appeals for the Federal Circuit ruled that a federal employee who was grossly negligent on the job can be fired for misconduct without warning. *(Fairall v. VA, 87-3311, April 13, 1988)*

DRUG TESTING

The Federal Service Impasses Panel upheld a proposal that employees who test positive for drug use have the right to union representation at a meeting with an agency doctor called to discuss the test results. *(92 FSIP No. 36, August 26, 1992)*

A federal judge in the Eastern California district upheld random drug testing of various medical employees but also restricted post-accident testing in the Air Force. Such "reasonable suspicion" testing must be limited to only "those employees for whom there is evidence they may have caused the accident or safety mishap in question." *(AFGE v. Wislon, S-89-1274, August 17, 1992)*

A federal judge in the Northern California district ordered that some two dozen Navy civilian job categories no longer be subjected to random drug testing, concluding that the government hasn't proved a connection with health and safety that would outweigh the employees' privacy interests. *(AFGE v. Cheney, 88-3823-DLJ, August 14, 1992)*

Union proposals designed to guarantee that any drug testing of employees be done "in strict compliance" with the Constitution and applicable laws and rules were ruled non-negotiable by the U.S. Court of Appeals for the District of Columbia. The court said the proposals would interfere with management rights to control the agency's internal practices. *(Dept. of the Interior v. FLRA, 91-1218, July 17, 1992)*

The Federal Labor Relations Authority rejected a union proposal that employees who pass drug tests be paid $25 to compensate them for "any negative impact such as humiliation and embarrassment" from being picked for testing. *(45 FLRA No. 24, June 19, 1992)*

Department of Health and Human Services drivers who don't carry passengers or have access to classified information should be excluded from the agency's random drug testing program, ruled Judge Harold Greene of the U.S. District Court in the District of Columbia. Greene ruled that the government's interest in testing those workers is no different than its interest in keeping any impaired drivers off the road and doesn't justify singling out HHS drivers for drug testing. *(AFGE v. Sullivan, 88-3594, March 24, 1992)*

A decision by the Federal Service Impasses Panel allowed employees to decide whether to tell the local union that they were picked for random drug testing. The union had asked that it be given the names within two weeks of any tests — although with the results omitted — so that it could ensure that the tests were indeed random and that no individuals were being singled out for frequent testing. *(91 FSIP No. 155, February 6, 1992)*

"Dual status" technicians, who must hold Reserve military positions to keep their civil service jobs, can be required to take drug tests under both military and civilian programs, the Federal Service Impasses Panel said. *(91 FSIP No. 248, January 29, 1992)*

The Federal Aviation Administration must give an air controllers union the names of all employees targeted for random drug testing, the Federal Labor Relations Authority ruled. *(FLRA No. 1-CA-10020, December 31, 1991)*

The U.S. Supreme Court refused to hear a challenge to drug testing of applicants for Justice Department attorney positions, a case that could have broader implications for applicants for other types of federal positions. Without comment, the justices declined to review a case in which a lower court said the government's interest in maintaining public confidence and trust in the people in those positions merited pre-employment drug screening. *(Willner v. Barr, 91-448, cert denied December 16, 1991)*

In order for a federal employee to qualify for protection against discipline on charges of drug use under the "safe harbor" program, that employee must voluntarily come forward and admit such use before the agency identifies him through other means as a possible user, the U.S. Court of Appeals for the Federal Circuit said. *(91-3317, October 11, 1991)*

A settlement reached in a lawsuit on drug testing of Health and Human Services employees provides that the agency will only order "reasonable suspicion" testing when the agency can show evidence that the employee had used drugs or was under their influence while on duty. Further, only those in safety or security positions designated for random testing will be subjected to reasonable suspicion testing for possible drug use away from the job. *(NTEU v. Sullivan, U.S. District Court for the District of Columbia No 90-0205-HHS, September 10, 1991)*

A federal judge in the Northern California district court ruled invalid parts of the Department of Veterans Affairs' employee drug testing program, restricting the number of positions to be subject to random and reasonable-suspicion testing, and overturning its post-accident testing program. *(C-88-20361-WAI, July 31, 1991)*

The Merit Systems Protection Board upheld the dismissal of a Federal Aviation Administration equipment technician who declined to take a mandatory drug test. He claimed the test was unconstitutional. *(MSPB Decision No. SE07528910074, July 25, 1991)*

An agreement was reached in a challenge by the National Treasury Employees Union to "random suspicion" drug testing in the Energy Department. In a settlement in federal district court in the District of Columbia, the two sides agreed that such testing will be allowed only when there is reason to believe an employee has used drugs at work or is working under the influence, or when the employee is working in a safety-sensitive position that is subject to random testing. *(NTEU v. Watkins, 89-1006-MB, May 24, 1991)*

People applying for federal jobs may be tested for illegal drugs in situations where incumbents of those positions might not be tested, the U.S. Court of Appeals for the District of Columbia ruled. *(Willner v. Thornburgh, 90-5156, March 29, 1991)*

A union proposal that an agency drug testing program comply with the Constitution, laws and rules is negotiable, the Federal Labor Relations Authority ruled. *(39 FLRA No. 107, March 15, 1991)*

A federal judge in the District of Columbia issued a permanent injunction against many aspects of the Food and Nutrition Service's program of drug testing employees. He said that FNS, a branch of the Agriculture Department, can impose such tests only when it can provide evidence of a reason to suspect drug use and when the position is a safety or security-related job subject to random drug testing. *(NTEU v. USDA, 88-2515, February 20, 1991)*

The Federal Labor Relations Authority ruled non-negotiable a union proposal to limit the number of times per year that employees may be compelled to take drug tests. FLRA said that would "directly interfere" with management's right to control security practices. *(38 FLRA No. 97, December 31, 1990)*

The U.S. Court of Appeals for the District of Columbia issued a split verdict on drug testing of federal employees, ordering restrictions against testing where an agency claims reason to suspect drug use, but opening the door for random testing of those holding high-level security clearances. *(Hartness v. Bush, 90-5050, November 16, 1990)*

A federal judge ruled too broad the Defense Mapping Agency rules for drug testing employees for "reasonable suspicion" of use, saying the symptoms DMA cited could be caused as easily by common illnesses, dissatisfaction with the workplace and even drinking too much coffee. *(NFFE v. Cheney, 89-1727, July 17, 1990)*

Random drug testing that covers 28,000 civilian Air Force employees can move forward, as a federal judge in the Eastern District of California considers a challenge to the policy. *(AFGE v. Wilson, C-89-1274, July 9, 1990)*

A federal judge in the District of Columbia ruled unconstitutional a Justice Department policy of testing lawyer applicants for its Antitrust Division for illegal drug use. *(Willner v. Thornburgh, U.S. District Court for the District of Columbia, No. 90-0535, May 15, 1990)*

The Federal Labor Relations Authority ruled that federal unions cannot be protected against suits that may arise from the government's drug testing program. *(35 FLRA No. 113, May 8, 1990)*

A federal district court in California rejected most of the Navy's controversial random drug testing program that sought to test 80,000 of its federal employees in 45 job categories. *(C88-3823-DLJ, C89-4112 and C89-4443, March 16, 1990)*

A federal district court judge in Washington D.C. ruled that federal employees holding top-secret level security clearances clearly can be tested randomly for illegal drugs, but the propriety of testing for those holding lesser clearances depends on individual circumstances. *(Hartness v. Bush, 89-0044-LFO, January 26, 1990)*

A federal judge issued a mixed ruling on drug testing at the Agriculture Department, barring random testing for certain inspectors and computer specialists but upholding it after accidents and in cases where there is reasonable cause to suspect drug use. *(National Treasury Employees Union et al, v. Yeutter, 88-2515, January 18, 1990)*

A temporary delay in the Navy's planned drug testing of civilian employees was ordered by the federal district court for Northern California. *(AFGE Local 1533 v. Cheney, C88-3823 (DLJ), December 29, 1989)*

The Fifth Circuit federal appeals court ruled against a broad challenge to random drug testing of federal employees, saying the order establishing the program is valid on its face. *(NTEU v. Bush, 88-3770, December 29, 1989)*

The U.S. Court of Appeals for the District of Columbia ruled that the Transportation Department's drug testing program was valid. *(AFGE v. Skinner, 87-5417, September 8, 1989)*

The U.S. Court of Appeals for the District of Columbia ruled that the Army may drug test without probable cause civilians who fly or service aircraft, who work in law enforcement, and who are drug counselors. *(NFFE v. Cheney, 88-5080, and AFGE v. Cheney, 88-5081, August 29, 1989)*

The U.S. Court of Appeals for the District of Columbia lifted a ban on random drug testing of Army civilian employees. *(NFFE & AFGE v. Carlucci, 88-5080, 88-5081, March 29, 1988)*

The U.S. District Court for the District of Maryland issued a permanent injunction barring the Army from subjecting two civilian employees to drug testing without reasonable suspicion of illegal drug use. *(Thompson v. Weinberger, R-87-393, IER Cases 7, March 3, 1988)*

The U.S. Supreme Court refused to hear a case on whether the Department of Transportation had authority to test more than 32,000 of its civil service workers since 1987 for illegal drug use, letting stand a lower court's decision that the agency acted within its legal powers.

(AFGE v. Skinner, 89-1272)

A federal judge banned random drug testing of General Services Administration employees, saying that the agency's claim that the tests are necessary were unproved. *(U.S. District Court for the District of Columbia, 89-0950-LFO)*

A federal judge in Washington D.C. gave the green light to the Department of Health and Human Services to drug test approximately 8500 employees in 45 job categories but the judge also agreed to partial injunctions for some aspects of the plan, ruling them unreasonable and/or overbroad. *(AFGE v. Sullivan, CA-88-3594 and NTEU v. Sullivan, CA-90-0205)*

The U.S. Supreme Court heard arguments in November on a case that could decide whether random drug testing of federal employees and job applicants will continue to be allowed. A decision is expected this year.

FURLOUGHS

The Federal Service Impasses Panel rejected a union proposal that employees facing a budget-related furlough be able to schedule their days so that they could receive unemployment compensation for the off time. *(91 FSIP 75, March 19, 1992)*

GRIEVANCES (see also ARBITRATION)

The U.S. Claims Court provided guidance on what types of cases federal employees may bring before it, in light of earlier rulings saying that grievance and arbitration procedures normally should be used instead of litigation. The court threw out the claims of all but a small portion of a group of Bureau of Prisons guards seeking overtime and premium pay, saying that most of the claimants had rights to use the grievance process. *(Albright v. U.S., 268-84C, September 11, 1992)*

Federal agencies and unions must continue to make the grievance process available to federal employees who for reasons of promotion, separation or death (for claims brought by their survivors) are no longer members of a bargaining unit, the U.S. Court of Appeals for the Federal Circuit ruled. *(Aamodt v. U.S., 91-5101 and Abundis v. U.S., 91-5102, September 10, 1992)*

A decision by the U.S. Court of Appeals for the Federal Circuit provided guidance to federal unions and agencies regarding which types of disputes can be carried to court and which are limited to the grievance and arbitration route. It said that the agency and union "must explicitly and unambiguously express in the words of the contract their intent to exclude the matter from the grievance and arbitration process" for court jurisdiction to apply. *(Muniz v. U.S., 91-1238, August 17, 1992)*

The Comptroller General said it will no longer issue decisions on matters subject to labor-management grievance and arbitration procedures, unless a contract specifically excludes a certain issue from its coverage. *(CG Decision No. B-222926.3, April 13, 1992)*

The U.S. Court of Appeals for the District of Columbia said agencies should loosen up on the information pertaining to employee grievances that they provide to unions, and that this can include recommendations of lower-level agency officials to their superiors regarding possible disciplinary actions. *(Case Nos. 91-1044, 91-1070 and 91-1087, January 7, 1992)*

A postal employee dissatisfied with the payment he received in a suggestion program should have contested the amount first inside agency channels, the U.S. Court of Appeals for the Federal Circuit said. It said the program allows suggesters to seek reevaluations of payments by the agency, and that they agree to use only this channel when they submit a suggestion. *(Hayes v. U.S., 90-5110, February 13, 1991)*

The grievance procedure is the rightful place for employment disputes in unionized federal work places to be aired, not the United States Claims Court, that court said. *(Andreen v. U.S., 548-88C, February 6, 1991)*

HANDICAP (see also DISCRIMINATION)

A federal judge in California permanently blocked a move by the U.S. Mint in San Francisco to fire several handicapped workers there for not meeting increased production quotas. The court found the policy violated the Rehabilitation Act and issued a permanent injunction that bars the removal of the handicapped workers for performance deficiencies. *(Case No. C-85-9196, U.S. District Court for Northern California, January 28, 1992)*

The U.S. Comptroller General allowed a federal agency to pick up the cost of transporting a handicapped employee from work to home when she has attacks from her cerebral palsy that occur, on average, three times a year. This is a "reasonable accommodation" of her handicap under the Rehabilitation Act, the CG said, noting that such expenditures should be made only in rare cases. *(B-243300, September 17, 1991)*

Once an agency "accommodates" a handicapped employee in assigning him to lighter duty, the employee cannot use that handicap as an excuse for substandard work or frequent absences—especially if he had performed adequately in that new assignment for a while, the Merit Systems Protection Board ruled. *(MSPB Decision No. DE07529010232, May 21, 1991)*

The Merit Systems Protection Board reduced a penalty against an alcoholic postal worker, but in the process established a principle that an addict's on-duty use of the substance that addicts him does not automatically give him a defense against disciplinary actions. *(MSPB Decision No. NYO7528810312, April 1, 1991)*

The U.S. District Court for the Northern District of California found that failure to provide reasonable accommodations for a qualified handicapped employee of the Labor Department violated the agency's obligations under the Rehabilitation Act of 1973, even though there was no proof of intentional discrimination. *(No. C-84-7012-VW (JSB), August 1, 1990)*

Federal employees claiming they were victims of handicap discrimination may bring such claims before the Merit Systems Protection Board even if they previously had appealed their cases to an arbitrator, the U.S. Court of Appeals for the Federal Circuit decided. *(Jones v. Dept. of the Navy, 89-3337, March 14, 1990)*

A federal agency's duty to reasonably accommodate a handicapped employee does not extend to offering a part-time worker a full-time job. *(MSPB Doc. DE07528710075, Aug. 15, 1988)*

The Rehabilitation Act does not require federal agencies to accommodate handicapped workers if problems posed by the handicap entail major changes in job duties and impose administrative or financial burdens on the agency. *(MSPB No. PH07528510760, Feb. 10, 1988)*

Merely claiming that a problem with alcohol was the cause for missing work is not enough to invoke protections of handicap laws, the Equal Employment Opportunity Commission ruled. It upheld the firing of a postal employee who claimed he was absent from work and couldn't call in because of his drinking. *(EEOC Decision No. 03900088)*

HEALTH AND SAFETY

A federal judge ruled that one of the largest federal and postal employee health plans must pay for expensive breast cancer therapy in the case of an enrollee's wife whose cancer was spreading. *(Nesseim v. MHBP, No. 92-1010, U.S. District Court for the District of South Dakota, April 3, 1992)*

A Navy facility that required motorcyclists to wear orange safety vests while riding on base is not required to supply such vests, the Federal Service Impasses Panel said. It told the employees who ride the machines to pay for the vests themselves. *(91 FSIP No. 125, January 29, 1992)*

An agency may buy safety shoes for a supply clerk who complained that he needed them to protect his feet while moving heavy objects. *(CG No. B-229085, Nov. 30, 1987)*

HIRING

The district court in the District of Columbia ordered the Office of Personnel Management to begin the rule making process that it said should have occurred when the Administrative Careers With America hiring program began. The program is the government's newest system for screening entry-level job applicants. *(NTEU v. Newman, 90-1165 (JHG), July 22, 1991)*

The U.S. Supreme Court extended broad protections for supervisors who badmouth subordinates applying for other federal jobs. It ruled that federal employees have no constitutional protection against critical statements about their job worth—even to the extent that such statements cause the loss of job opportunities. *(Siegert v. Gilley, 90-96, May 23, 1991)*

The Office of Personnel Management was wrong to say it lacked jurisdiction to hear an appeal of a denial of a job candidate on grounds that he lacked qualifications, said the U.S. Court of Appeals for Federal Circuit. *(Clayton v. Dept. of Justice, 89-3440, April 11, 1990)*

The U.S. Court of Appeals for the 1st Circuit ruled that persons with veterans preference cannot be passed over for federal job appointments merely because other candidates have superior qualifications. *(Keyes v. Secretary of Navy, 87-1707, Aug. 10, 1988)*

INVESTIGATIONS

A federal agency involved in a dispute with a union is not necessarily responsible for how an inspector general office conducts its own investigation into the matter, the Federal Labor Relations Authority said. *(45 FLRA No. 83, August 12, 1992)*

An agency may act without union consultation to use dogs to sniff for drugs and other contraband in its buildings and grounds. *(31 FLRA No. 2, Feb. 4, 1988)*

JOB RIGHTS

While it's well settled that federal employees don't have employment contracts for their jobs, the United States Claims Court gave one employee the chance to argue that she did have one — but eventually dismissed her case, saying that even if a contract existed, she didn't prove it had been violated. *(Hamlet v. U.S. 281-86C, October 2, 1992)*

The U.S. Supreme Court said there is no limit on the amount of time an employee can be away from his job for military reservist duty and then return and invoke his rights to reemployment. *(King v. St. Vincent's Hospital, 90-889, December 16, 1991)*

A civilian base security guard will be allowed to sue a four-star admiral who allegedly called him a liar after the guard had issued a traffic warning ticket to the military man's daughter. A divided Fourth Circuit Court of Appeals found that the admiral was not acting within the scope of official duties when he chided the guard, who had been summoned to the admiral's on-base residence where the admiral was tending his garden while in civilian attire. *(Johnson v. Carter, CA 4, No. 90-3077, July 8, 1991)*

A federal job is not protected by the Fifth Amendment right against takings of property for public use without proper compensation, the United States Claims Court said in rejecting an appeal from an employee fired on charges of unsatisfactory performance. *(Mobin v. U.S., 90-138C, January 23, 1991)*

LABOR-MANAGEMENT RELATIONS
(see also UNION ACTIVITIES)

A fax transmission is not the equivalent of a good old-fashioned hand-delivered letter for purposes of formal communications between management and a union, the Federal Labor Relations Authority said. It ruled that a fax transmission to a union local regarding an agency decision did not properly "serve" the union with notice of that decision—and the decision was therefore overturned. *(41 FLRA No. 79, July 31, 1991)*

The United States Claims Court said it has no authority to hear claims of federal employees seeking overtime pay for a period when they were covered by a union contract that made such pay subject to bargaining. *(Aamodt v. U.S., 623-89C, April 5, 1991)*

A federal appeals court ruled that the American Postal Workers Union owed the government back taxes on "associate" member dues. These are fees paid by individuals who join the union's health plan but who do not enjoy the full benefits of membership. *(APWU v. U.S. Court of Appeals for the District of Columbia, February 22, 1991)*

A federal union official doesn't have the right to use agency computers for union business unless a contract or past practice provides for it, ruled an arbitrator under the Federal Labor Relations

Authority whose decision was not challenged. *(5-CA-00587, February 8, 1991)*

A supervisor who said he no longer trusted an employee because he had filed an unfair labor practice charge interfered with that employee's right to assist his union, the Federal Labor Relations Authority ruled. *(39 FLRA No. 28, February 7, 1991)*

The Federal Labor Relations Authority set aside a settlement agreement that would have forced the U.S. Small Business Administration to pay an American Federation of Government Employees local nearly $7 million for administrative support. The FLRA ruled that the SBA official who executed the document was without authority and may have had a conflict of interest. *(FLRA No. 0-AR-1686, November 27, 1990)*

The Federal Service Impasses Panel found that a local union and management at Scott Air Force Base, Ill., were getting along so poorly that they were bringing "frivolous" cases before it. The remedy: the panel ordered the warring parties to attend a program to learn how to better cooperate with each other. *(FSIP Nos. 89, 110, 144, 160, 163 and 227, January 1, 1990)*

Both the union and management must request an arbitrator to reopen or modify an award that the Federal Labor Relations Authority has set aside or it will stand, the FLRA has ruled. In other words, the two sides must agree to the petition. *(39 FLRA No. 56)*

LEAVE (see also SICK LEAVE)

A retiree had no grounds to appeal the withholding of money from his final paycheck and annuity that the agency imposed to recoup an overpayment of annual leave, the U.S. Court of Appeals for the Federal Circuit ruled. It said that recoupment of overdrawn leave is not a reduction in pay, and thus not appealable to the Merit Systems Protection Board. *(Miller v. USPS, 91-3384, February 6, 1992)*

The Federal Labor Relations Authority ruled that unions may bargain over how federal agencies schedule work so that members who belong to Guard and Reserve units won't have to take annual leave when their military duty extends beyond 15 days. *(43 FLRA No. 91, January 24, 1992)*

A part-time federal employee's duty status, and not the number of hours he or she may work, determines eligibility for leave benefits, the U.S. Court of Appeals for the Federal Circuit ruled. *(Cutright v. U.S., 91-5031, January 14, 1992)*

The Federal Labor Relations Authority ruled an agency improperly denied bargaining unit employees administrative leave for the two days following the 1989 earthquake in the San Francisco area. The agency allowed the leave only for workers whose residences were damaged by the quake or who were confused about whether they should report to work. *(41 FLRA No. 5, June 6, 1991)*

Federal employees who buy nonrefundable airline tickets or hotel package deals and plan to use them while on leave are out the money if the government cancels their leave because of pressing official business, according to the U.S. Comptroller General. *(CG Decision No. B-241249, February 15, 1991)*

Federal employees requesting leave for military reserve duty must go through the same kind of procedures as when asking for other kinds of leave and are subject to an AWOL charge if time away is taken without permission, said the U.S. Court of Appeals for the Federal Circuit. *(Ellermets v. Dept. of the Army, 90-3058, October 16, 1990)*

A federal employee need not work a traditional 40-hour week in order to be considered a full-time permanent employee and enjoy sick and annual leave benefits, the United States Claims Court said. *(Cutright v. U.S., 172-88C, October 3, 1990)*

The Federal Labor Relations Authority ruled that an Army facility was wrong to charge a woman with a week of annual leave for time spent caring for her young son who had chicken pox. The Army had contended that the condition did not qualify as a "contagious disease" under the sick leave policy, saying chicken pox does not require isolation or quarantine. *(34 FLRA No. 49, January 12, 1990)*

Excessive leave use by government employees is a valid reason to deny them promotions, the U.S. District Court for the Eastern District of Michigan ruled. *(DC EMich. No 89-0113, January 8, 1990)*

Donated annual leave remaining after the death of a leave recipient must be restored to the donors. *(CG Decision No. B-234849, September 21, 1989)*

When the government closes offices by actions such as a presidential directive closing offices a day or a half day on Christmas or New Year's Eve, those employees who already are on annual leave are not entitled to be credited for this leave or paid additional salary for the time involved. *(CG Decision No. B-234596, August 23, 1989)*

A union proposal for parental leave for new fathers is negotiable. The proposal would allow use of annual and sick leave and leave without pay to the maximum permitted by law and regulation. *(33 FLRA No. 86, October 31, 1988)*

The U.S. Court of Appeals for the Federal Circuit upheld the Treasury Department's refusal to okay paid administrative leave to an employee recovering from traffic accident injuries. The court agreed with the agency's refusal to pay benefits because the employee, who had used up his sick leave, allegedly "was violating traffic regulations" at the time of the accident. *(Hambsch v. U.S., 87-1517, Sept. 14, 1988)*

The U.S. Court of Appeals for the 1st Circuit ruled that the Navy has no duty to bargain on a union proposal requiring it to put workers on paid administrative leave rather than lay them off during brief periods such as the Christmas holidays. *(Dept. of the Navy v. FLRA, 87-2024, Aug. 16, 1988)*

A union proposal that employees returning from maternity leave may request part-time employment or job-sharing on a temporary or permanent basis is negotiable. *(31 FLRA No. 22, Feb. 22, 1988)*

A federal employee who does not schedule annual leave in advance and in writing and who forfeits the leave due to the exigencies of public business may not have that leave restored. *(CG No. B-229228, Jan. 21, 1988)*

LIABILITY

The U.S. Comptroller General relieved several State Department cashiers of liability for the loss of some $350,000 in travelers checks because his office found a "general lack of concern and sense of laxity which pervaded" the department's operation and management of its headquarters cashiers operation. *(B-235147.2, August 14, 1991)*

A State Department employee who was temporarily placed in charge of government funds while the regular cashier was elsewhere was held liable for an "unexplained" loss of $1000 by the U.S. Comptroller General. *(CG Decision No. B-238898, April 1, 1991)*

The U.S. Comptroller General ruled proper a Customs Service settlement in a case where one of its employees had her car broken into while it was parked in an agency parking lot. *(CG Decision No. B-241443, March 14, 1991)*

Federal employees using government-leased vehicles generally are responsible for paying their own parking tickets, the U.S. Comptroller General's office has ruled. *(CG Decision No. B-239511, December 31, 1990)*

The U.S. Supreme Court said that the government cannot be bound by bad advice it gives to employees about their benefits. *(OPM v. Richmond, 88-1943, June 11, 1990)*

Agencies may allow dependents of their employees to accompany them as passengers in government-owned or leased vehicles, but if there is an accident, the government may be held liable for damages. *(CG Decision No. B-231814, January 19, 1989)*

The U.S. Court of Appeals for the District of Columbia ruled that federal employees may not seek personal damages against officials of their agencies who claim they violated their constitutional rights in the course of a disputed personnel action. *(Spagnola v. Mathis, 84-5530 and Hubbard v. EPA, 85-5145, Sept. 30, 1988)*

The U.S. Court of Appeals for the District of Columbia upheld the firing of a federal union official on charges of making unfounded accusations against local agency managers, declaring that the accusations were not protected free speech because they didn't affect a matter of "broader public interest." *(Barnes v. Small, 86-5536, March 8, 1988)*

A federal appeals court ruled that four IRS officials must stand trial for allegedly causing the illegal arrest of an IRS employee, having him publicly searched, and humiliating him in front of his co-workers. He was arrested for allegedly failing to pay $60 in unpaid court fees dating back eight years. *(USCA 4th Circuit, No. 91-1122)*

The U.S. Supreme Court refused to hear a case in which three federal managers were found guilty of breaking environmental laws has raised new concern about their personal liability for official actions. The trio was sentenced to three years of probation and 1000 hours of community service. *(Dee v. U.S., 90-877)*

LUMP-SUM SUIT

The U.S. Court of Appeals for the Federal Circuit rejected the claim of federal and postal retirees that their lump-sum annuity payments were improperly taxed. Also upheld was an extra 10 percent tax assessed against those taking the lump-sum under age 55. *(Shimota v. U.S., 91-5017, September 12, 1991)*

The U.S. Supreme Court refused to hear a challenge to the taxation of the retirement lump-sum payments, in effect upholding the decisions of two lower courts that the government was within its rights to tax the jumbo payments taken by many federal and postal retirees despite their claim that the money already has been taxed. *(Shimota v. U.S., 91-1241)*

The U.S. Claims Court upheld the IRS in a long-running dispute with federal retirees who maintain that their lump-sum annuities are being double taxed *(Shimota v. U.S.)*

OFF-DUTY CONDUCT

A federal judge in the District of Columbia district court held unconstitutional the ban against federal and postal employees accepting money for free-lance article writing, speeches and other forms of appearances. He issued an injunction against the ban but didn't put the injunction into effect pending an appeal by the government — an appeal that later was filed, keeping the ban alive until an appeals court decision. *(90-2922, March 19, 1992)*

A federal employee who has been authorized to conduct private business on the side has First Amendment rights to advertise that business, the Federal Labor Relations Authority ruled. *(39 FLRA No. 39, February 12, 1991)*

Federal agencies have a legitimate interest in controlling off-the-job professional activities of employees that may reflect badly on the agency, the U.S. Court of Appeals for the District of Columbia ruled. *(Williams v. IRS, 90-5078, November 20, 1990)*

OVERTIME

An employee who said he was told he could receive a certain amount of overtime pay when he earlier had read regulations that said he couldn't, "knew or should have known" that the payment he received was excessive and must return it, the Comptroller General ruled. *(CG Decision No. B-246967, June 2, 1992)*

The Federal Labor Relations Authority said that a union proposal requiring that the agency provide advance notice to employees of overtime assignments was negotiable, but it ruled several other proposed limits on overtime policy as interfering with management's rights. *(44 FLRA No. 113, May 28, 1992)*

An agency didn't have to pay several of its employees overtime or grant compensatory time off for traveling during a Sunday to arrive in time to set up a training course on Monday, the U.S. Comptroller General ruled. The agency was not obligated to compensate them for their Sunday involvement because no work was performed during the travel and the agency had control over scheduling of the training event, the CG ruled. *(CG No. B-245417, February 10, 1992)*

The U.S. Court of Appeals for the District of Columbia ruled non-negotiable a union proposal that employees be given overtime pay for delays in leaving the worksite because of security measures. *(Dept. of the Air Force v. FLRA, 90-1530, December 27, 1991)*

National Labor Relations Board employees can't collect overtime pay or receive time off for travel to and from union representation elections, the U.S. Comptroller General ruled. Why? Because the NLRB "retains a degree of control" over the events, the CG reasoned. *(CG No.*

B-229363.2, December 23, 1991)

The United States Claims Court was told to reconsider a decision that denied a form of overtime pay available to U.S. Customs Service inspectors who helped with the 1980 Mariel boatlift of refugees from Cuba. The U.S. Court of Appeals for the Federal Circuit told the lower court to hold a trial in which the Customs inspectors may argue that the situation created an implied authority for that pay. *(National Treasury Employees Union, et al. v. U.S., 90-5122, December 11, 1991)*

The U.S. Court of Appeals for the Federal Circuit upheld the method of calculating overtime pay for federal firefighters, endorsing a lower judge who said that while the system is a "crazy quilt" it is probably the best that can be done under the circumstances. *(Abreu v. U.S., 91-5054, October 24, 1991)*

Several federal law enforcement officers called to work unusual hours in a "short term emergency situation"—in this case a prison riot—were not entitled to regularly scheduled overtime pay in addition to the other forms of premium pay they earned through the assignment, the U.S. Comptroller General held. *(CG Decision No. B-242411, October 22, 1991)*

An agency can be compelled to make someone available to fetch food for employees working long overtime assignments given on such short notice that they couldn't arrange for their own meals, the Federal Labor Relations Authority said. *(41 FLRA No. 57, July 12, 1991)*

A group of nearly 600 current and former border patrol agents with the Immigration and Naturalization Service received a second chance to be reimbursed on claims that they were not paid their customary salary, including overtime, while they were on leave. The U.S. Court of Appeals for the Federal Circuit said the statute of limitations on such claims was six years, not the two years that the U.S. Claims Court cited in dismissing their claims. *(Acton v. U.S., 90-5153, May 20, 1991)*

Federal employees who are eligible for overtime pay are entitled to it only if they actually work those designated hours even if the hours were "regularly scheduled" by the agency or "irregular," the U.S. Comptroller General ruled in a case involving Army Corps of Engineers river bank repairers. *(CG Decision No. B-224854.2, May 16, 1991)*

The U.S. Court of Appeals for the Federal Circuit turned down an appeal from a group of federal firefighters and law enforcement personnel for compensation for delays in receiving overtime pay, saying the case was filed after the end of a two-year statute of limitations that applies in such matters. *(Doyle v. U.S. 90-5148, April 30, 1991)*

A postal employee who won a challenge to a demotion is not eligible for out-of-schedule overtime pay for the change in her working hours that the demotion caused, the U.S. Court of Appeals for the Federal Circuit ruled. *(White v. USPS, 90-3423, April 17, 1991)*

A policy of denying overtime pay for brief work-related activities before and after a shift was upheld by the United States Claims Court, which said the activities have only a "minimal" effect on employees. *(Riggs v. U.S., 131-89C, October 23, 1990)*

Because agencies now have general power to decide which of their employees are entitled to overtime pay, the presumption is that the issue is broadly subject to bargaining, the United States Claims Court said. *(Ackerman, et al. v. U.S., 674-89C, October 2, 1990)*

The grievance and arbitration procedure, not the federal courts, is normally the proper home for complaints about overtime pay brought by union-represented federal employees, the United States Claims Court ruled. *(Bevill v. U.S., 403-89C, September 13, 1990)*

Federal employee claims for overtime pay are subject to a two-year statute of limitations, not a six-year limit, said the United States Claims Court. *(Acton v. U.S., 269-89C, August 1, 1990)*

The U.S. Comptroller General ruled that the government may grant overtime or compensatory time off to employees who must travel outside of their normal duty hours to attend courses for which the government has no scheduling control. *(CG No. B-230405, June 29, 1990)*

The United States Claims Court said that Customs Service agents who worked overtime processing immigrants during the Mariel boat lift from Cuba in 1980 were properly paid at the standard time-and-a-half overtime rate. *(NTEU v. U.S. , 292-86C, May 24, 1990)*

The U.S. Court of Appeals for the Federal Circuit rejected a lawsuit claiming overtime pay by several hundred IRS agents, on grounds that the matter must be resolved in a grievance under the labor-management contract—even though the contract did not include overtime as a subject to be resolved in that way. *(Carter, et al. v. Gibbs, 88-1576, March 30, 1990)*

The United States Claims Court has told the government that it must show good reason why more than 500 employees in technical, engineering and related jobs have been made ineligible for overtime pay. *(Abundis, et al. v. U.S., 22-88C, November 9, 1989)*

The United States Claims Court ruled that federal employees who are required to eat meals while at work should not be paid overtime for that time unless they also are performing "substantial labor." *(Nerserth, et al, v. U.S., 102-88C, July 24, 1989)*

An employee cannot be paid a claim for overtime if work during that time was not officially ordered or approved. *(CG Decision No. B-231024, April 12, 1989)*

Employees working at a military installation who are detained when the base conducts a "no notice" exercise cannot receive overtime pay for their trouble. *(30 FLRA No. 68, Dec. 18, 1987)*

Certain employees of Toole Army Depot, Utah, were made eligible for overtime or leave lost for an extra day's work incurred when their workweek was shifted on just one day's notice in order to accommodate a visit from the Secretary of the Army, under a decision by a Federal Mediation and Conciliation Service arbitrator. *(FMCS No. 92-05052)*

PAY, GENERAL (see also SPECIAL RATE PAY)

An arbitrator ruled that National Guard regulation that prohibits the payment of severance pay to "civilian technicians" who lose their military status is improper. He ordered the Guard to give the individual his severance pay. *(Arkansas National Guard and NFFE Local 1671, Federal Mediation and Conciliation Service No. 91-25958, October 5, 1992)*

The U.S. Supreme Court ruled that individuals who win back pay awards based on findings of illegal discrimination on the job must pay taxes on the money. *(U.S. v. Burke, et al, 91-41, May 26, 1992)*

The Federal Labor Relations Authority ordered back pay for to a group of Customs inspectors who lost out on eligibility for extra pay when their shifts were changed without bargaining with their union. *(44 FLRA No. 92, May 4, 1992)*

The U.S. Marshals Service failed to pay a female branch chief the same salary it was paying to several men performing "substantially equal work" and thus violated the Equal Pay Act, the U.S. Claims Court ruled. *(Ellison v. U.S., 663-88C, March 13, 1992)*

An appellate court ordered "front pay" to a retired federal employee who successfully claimed he was forced out because of his age and didn't want to accept the alternative of going back to his former position. The decision by the U.S. Court of Appeals for the 11th Circuit may break new ground regarding the remedies available to employees who win such bias claims, which traditionally have been restricted to reinstatement with back pay for salary lost due to the discrimination. *(Lewis v. Federal Prison Industries, 88-3570, February 18, 1992)*

The Federal Service Impasses Panel upheld wage and benefit proposals made in bargaining on behalf of nonappropriated fund employees at two Navy and Army bases. The decisions follow a ruling in 1991 by the Federal Labor Relations Authority saying that pay and fringe benefits not established by statute, such as those applying to these employees, are subject to collective bargaining. *(91 FSIP 182, February 10, 1992 and 91 FSIP 200, February 11, 1992)*

A law that allows special raises for federal supervisors who find themselves earning less than their blue collar subordinates does not require such increases but rather leaves the discretion in the agency's hands, the U.S. Court of Appeals for the Federal Circuit ruled. *(Huston v. U.S., 91-5074, February 10, 1992)*

An employee who ended up with a pay cut because he relied on bad information from his agency about the salary he would earn in a new position should be restored to his former level of pay, the Merit Systems Protection Board ruled. The board ruled that a "reasonable person would have been misled" by the misinformation from his employer, the Defense Logistics Agency. *(Paszek v. Defense Logistics Agency, MSPB Doc. No. CH07529010138, October 7, 1991)*

An agency is obligated to bargain over changes in environmental differential pay, which goes to employees exposed to certain dangers and hazards, unless the local union specifically waives its right to negotiate on the subject, the Federal Labor Relations Authority said. *(42 FLRA No. 22, September 23, 1991)*

A pilot program of productivity gainsharing, in which individual employees share with the agency in the money saved through better performance, became a "condition of employment" to affected employees and its future thus subject to bargaining, the Federal Labor Relations Authority held. *(41 FLRA No. 84, July 31, 1991)*

An Army installation was ordered to reimburse employees there who lost money because it changed the time between the end of a pay period and the delivery of the pay check from the normal 7-9 days to 12. Management should have negotiated the matter with the local union, ruled the Federal Labor Relations Authority. *(41 FLRA No. 76, July 30, 1991)*

The United States Claims Court issued a mixed ruling on the issue of pay entitlement of federal law enforcement officers during time off from the job. In general, it upheld claims for special pay such as Sunday premium pay in situations where they took annual leave instead of working, but not in situations where they were originally scheduled to work and then were told their services were not needed, and where no leave time was charged. *(Armitage v. U.S. 139-89C, June 20, 1991)*

The U.S. Comptroller General ruled that a former IRS employee doesn't have to pay back the government $1,094 she received in overpayments for temporary appointments because the government was at fault and she could not reasonably be expected to "know and understand the complexities of federal personnel regulations governing the establishment of pay rates and step advancements." *(CG Decision No. B-238580, May 10, 1991)*

The IRS acted within its discretion in reclassifying certain mail processing jobs from the wage grade to the general schedule pay system, the U.S. Court of Appeals for the Federal Circuit said, denying a claim for compensation for lost pay and restoration to the wage grade system from a group of affected employees. *(Bosco v. U.S., 90-5132, May 1, 1991)*

The U.S. Comptroller General approved a request to retroactively compensate the workers for having worked with toxic substances up to a six-year statute of limitations on such claims. *(CG Decision No. B-238323, February 21, 1991)*

The United States Claims Court said it has authority to review disputes over severance pay for fired federal employees under the Severance Pay Act. *(Hedman v. U.S., 356-86C, August 27, 1990)*

Special pay practices such as Sunday premium pay are only negotiable when the practices are standard in the private sector in a federal facility's local area, ruled the Federal Labor Relations Authority. *(26 FLRA No. 37, July 12, 1990)*

The U.S. Court of Appeals for the Sixth Circuit ruled that federal law does not give letter carriers the right to keep higher pay rates after transferring from urban to rural routes. *(CA6, No. 89-1897, June 10, 1990)*

The United States Claims Court refused to hear a case seeking premium pay in a unionized workplace, saying that such challenges must be brought through grievance procedures. *(Adams v. U.S., 749-88C, May 31, 1990)*

The Federal Service Impasses Panel ruled that a federal agency may require its employees to receive their pay through direct deposit into bank accounts, but added conditions that gave the employees favorable treatment from the banks and the opportunity to receive paychecks in hardship cases. *(89 FSIP 206, December 29, 1989)*

The United States Claims Court said employees who normally

receive premium pay for working undesirable shifts can enjoy an entitlement to that higher pay if they are assigned instead to other shifts. *(Gahagan, et al. v. U.S., 265-88C, December 20, 1989)*

The Comptroller General ruled that for federal employees to get hazardous duty pay for future work around asbestos and other dangerous substances they must show by clear and convincing evidence that an agency decision to deny the extra pay was arbitrary and capricious, or the General Accounting Office (which is headed by the Comptroller General) will not consider the matter. *(CG Decision No. B-235461, December 19, 1989)*

A union local's proposal that among other things would have made non-smoking federal employees eligible for hazardous duty pay for being exposed involuntarily to second-hand smoke was rejected. *(89 FSIP 139, August 16, 1989)*

A federal employee is responsible for paying "reasonable" attention to whether the proper deductions are being taken from his pay check and must refund the money his agency failed to properly deduct from his salary. *(CG No. B-226465, March 23, 1988)*

The U.S. Comptroller General held valid an Office of Personnel Management regulation that bases severance pay on the last permanent appointment rather than any temporary appointment held at the time the individual leaves government. *(CG Decision No. B-223184, March 23, 1988)*

The Federal Services Impasses Panel killed a move by two Navy activities to delay permanently the pay days of their civilian employees by four days. *(87 FSIP 11, 22 and 161, March 22, 1988)*

An employee is out of luck when his or her check bounces because the government failed to deposit a pay check in his or her bank account. *(CG Decision No. B-228632, March 10, 1988)*

PAY RAISES

The United States Claims Court turned down a group of Voice of America broadcast foremen who claimed their pay was improperly capped for several years in the 1980s, causing some of them to earn less than subordinates whose pay was exempt from the caps because their own salaries were set in negotiations. *(Averi v. U.S., 619-87C, May 17, 1991)*

The U.S. Court of Appeals for the Federal Circuit rejected a federal employee's claim that her raises have been calculated incorrectly since she became eligible for retaining her former salary when downgraded in a RIF. *(Chaney v. Veterans Administration, 90-3020, June 25, 1990)*

The U.S. Court of Appeals for the District of Columbia ruled legal the conversion of certain foreign service positions to the general schedule, even though the incumbents lost eligibility for cost-of-living and within-grade raises. *(Olds v. U.S. Information Agency, 88-5373, February 27, 1990)*

PERFORMANCE APPRAISALS

The U.S. Court of Appeals for the Federal Circuit reversed the dismissal of an employee for poor performance because the standards used to rate him were "backwards" and too vague. The standards were backwards, the court said, because they defined what the employee should not do, not what he should. *(Cordioli v. Dept. of the Navy, 91-3531, August 21, 1992)*

An arbitrator has the authority to raise the performance ratings of federal employees if he decides the agency violated policy when making the ratings, the Federal Labor Relations Authority said, but such an increase should not be automatic. Instead, the arbitrator must decide what the employee's rating would have been had management evaluated him properly. *(45 FLRA No. 54, July 22, 1992)*

A union's bid to receive the names and locations of bargaining unit employees who received outstanding or commendable personnel evaluations was rejected by the U.S. Court of Appeals for the District of Columbia, which said the disclosure would violate the Privacy Act. *(FLRA v. Dept. of Commerce, 91-1175, April 24, 1992)*

The U.S. Court of Appeals for the District of Columbia ruled negotiable a union's proposal that personnel evaluations be provided to employees within 45 days of their development or receipt by a supervisor. The proposal said that if the time limit were exceeded, the evaluation could not be used and material damaging to an employee's rating would have to be destroyed. *(Dept. of the Treasury v. FLRA and NTEU, 91-1139, April 14, 1992)*

A federal appeals court overturned the performance-related demotion of an employee, saying the agency failed to show that the rating standards it used had been approved by the Office of Personnel Management. The U.S. Court of Appeals for the Federal Circuit said that the government's failure to present that evidence is not only a "serious" flaw in such a case, "it is fatal." *(NATCA and Shuffler v. Dept. of Transportation, 91-3524, March 19, 1992)*

Bargaining was required on a union proposal that an agency may not use any information in rating an employee's performance that wasn't made available to the employee being rated, the Federal Labor

Relations Authority said. *(44 FLRA No. 5, February 21, 1992)*

A group of male supervisors of the U.S. Forest Service reached a settlement in a legal battle against the agency for requiring that job performance be measured against their record in hiring minorities and women. *(Gates v. Madigan, Civ. A. No. S-91-0033-DFL-PAN, U.S. District Court for the Eastern District of California, September 26, 1991)*

The United States Claims Court said it lacks jurisdiction to review disputes over federal employee performance ratings, even if those cases are presented as claims for money improperly denied. *(Free v. U.S., 585-86C, June 27, 1989)*

The U.S. Court of Appeals for the Fourth Circuit ruled that the Air Force is not required to negotiate a union proposal to grant mandatory bonuses to civilian employees receiving high performance ratings. *(CA4 88-2171, June 3, 1989)*

The U.S. Court of Appeals for the District of Columbia ruled that union proposals that go to the heart of agency discretion on evaluating employee performance are not negotiable. *(Patent Office Professional Association v. FLRA, 87-1824, May 5, 1989)*

Performance standards that are "impossibly absolute in nature" are invalid. The standards required the employee to perform exactly as described, with no mistakes. *(MSPB Doc. No. SL04328710306, April 3, 1989)*

Arbitrators have the power to correct improper employee performance ratings if they decide that management hasn't followed the established performance standards or if the standards were applied improperly. *(30 FLRA No. 127, Jan. 28, 1988)*

PHYSICAL REQUIREMENTS

The Federal Labor Relations Authority ordered bargaining on a management decision to remove diabetic air traffic controllers from line positions but stopped short of ordering that those affected be restored to their former duties. *(42 FLRA No. 5, September 11, 1991)*

The Federal Labor Relations Authority weighed in with its own opinion on disciplining an employee for an incident supposedly caused by his being overweight, saying an arbitrator was wrong to offer to overturn a suspension if the employee slimmed down. *(36 FLRA, No. 39, July 13, 1990)*

Agencies may not purchase running shoes for federal employees who are required to pass fitness tests and to meet certain physical requirements. *(CG Decision No. B-234091, July 7, 1989)*

PRIVACY

A federal judge in Texas ruled that the IRS may no longer ask its employees about any connection to illegal drugs or whether they have experienced any "problems" related to drug use. The ruling came in a case in which the National Treasury Employees Union challenged certain questions on Standard Form 85P, a security questionnaire. *(U.S. District Court for Western Texas (Austin Division) Case No. A-89-CA-924, August 31, 1992)*

A federal union may not take a role in random, unannounced inspections of vehicles or people entering agency facilities, the Federal Labor Relations Authority said, ruling that a number of union proposals would violate management's right to set its internal security practices. *(45 FLRA No. 95, August 20, 1992)*

The U.S. Court of Appeals for the Third Circuit ruled that release of names and addresses to a federal union was allowed as a routine use of that information. *(Federal Labor Relations Authority and American Federation of Government Employees v. Dept. of the Navy, No. 90-3690, May 26, 1992)*

The U.S. District Court for the District of Columbia ordered the U.S. Postal Service to furnish home addresses of employees to a union seeking to represent them. This constitutes a "routine use" of the information and therefore is not, as the postal service maintains, a violation of the Privacy Act. *(NLRB v. USPS, No. 92-0195, May 5, 1992)*

The U.S. District Court for the Eastern District of Pennsylvania ruled that the U.S. Postal Service was within its rights in training a video camera on an individual employee although the camera had been used in performing general surveillance in the work area. *(91-678, March 13, 1992)*

IRS employees may use pseudonyms when dealing with the public, the Federal Service Impasses Panel said in a case where a union contended that the employees otherwise are at risk of harassment or assault from disgruntled taxpayers. *(91 FSIP No. 229, March 10, 1992)*

The U.S. Court of Appeals for the Second Circuit ruled against the routine disclosure of names and home addresses of bargaining unit members to unions for their recruiting efforts. The court said employees have a "measurable privacy interest" at stake and that there is no "relevant public purpose" in giving out the information. *(FLRA v. Dept. of Veterans Affairs, 91-4049, March 5, 1992)*

Federal employees can't use the Privacy Act as a backdoor to challenge the way their positions are classified, said the U.S. Court of

Appeals for the District of Columbia. It said the proper route for employees to challenge their job's classification is through an appeal to the Office of Personnel Management. *(Kleiman v. Dept. of Energy, 90-5284, February 25, 1992)*

The U.S. Court of Appeals for the Third Circuit, citing a U.S. Supreme Court decision, said that federal employees have a privacy interest under the Freedom of Information Act that protects them against release of their names and home addresses to unions and other organizations that may wish to solicit them for membership. *(FLRA v. Dept of the Navy, 90-3690, September 13, 1991)*

The U.S. Court of Appeals for the First Circuit ruled that the Navy's Portsmouth (N.H.) shipyard was correct to refuse to release to a federal union the names and addresses of bargaining unit members there. The Privacy Act prohibits such a release, the court said. *(FLRA v. Dept. of the Navy, 90-1948, August 13, 1991)*

The U.S. Court of Appeals for the Federal Circuit upheld the firing of a supervisor on charges of participating in unauthorized background check of a fellow employee. *(Morgan v. Dept. of the Army, 91-3091, May 22, 1991)*

The U.S. District Court for the District of Columbia refused the government's request for a summary judgment to dismiss the complaint of a fired Department of Education employee who said that a search of her office and desk violated her right to privacy. *(McGregor v. Greer 88-2544 SSH, September 27, 1990)*

The U.S. Court of Appeals for the District of Columbia ruled that a federal union has the right to get the names and addresses of its bargaining unit employees if it lacks adequate means to communicate with them otherwise. *(FLRA v. Dept. of Health and Human Services and consolidated cases, 87-1147, August 9, 1990)*

The U.S. Court of Appeals for the District of Columbia ruled that the Justice Department violated the privacy rights of a federal employee when it contacted an outside agency to check up on his leave use rather than ask him first. *(Waters v. Thornburgh, 88-5178, October 31, 1989)*

The U.S. Court of Appeals for the District of Columbia ruled that the names and addresses of federal retirees cannot be released to the National Association of Retired Federal Employees. *(NARFE v. Horner, 86-5446, July 7, 1989)*

The right of a federal union to receive detailed information on the job title, grade, sex and race of every employee in the facility was upheld by the FLRA. *(32 FLRA No. 19, May 17, 1988)*

The U.S. Court of Appeals for the 3rd Circuit held that federal unions have a right to the home addresses of bargaining unit employees to mail them labor literature. *(Dept. of the Navy v. FLRA, 87-3005, March 3, 1988)*

The Sixth Circuit Court of Appeals turned down a federal union seeking the home addresses of bargaining unit employees for recruiting and other purposes. *(FLRA v. Dept. of the Navy, No. 91-3450)*

The U.S. Supreme Court refused to review the decision by the U.S. circuit court for the District of Columbia which denied federal employee unions the home addresses of employees in their exclusive recognition units. *89-444, 89-853)*

The U.S. Supreme Court let stand a 1989 appeals court ruling that the government does not have to provide the National Association of Retired Federal Employees with the names and addresses of retired federal and postal employees.

PROBATIONARY EMPLOYEES

A probationary federal employee fired for being unable to physically perform his job has no appeal rights beyond the very restricted rights granted to people in such positions, the U.S. Court of Appeals for the Federal Circuit said. This applies even if the condition that hampered his work existed prior to his being hired, it added. *(Knox v. MSPB, 92-3218, August 18, 1992)*

The Foreign Service Grievance Board has the power to prevent the removal of probationary foreign service employees, the U.S. Court of Appeals for the District of Columbia said, even though the Secretary of State has great leeway to fire them by denying them tenured status. *(Miller v. Baker, 90-5398, July 10, 1992)*

Although a former federal employee was surprised to learn that she was in probationary status, that does not change the fact that she was a probationer, the U.S. Court of Appeals for the Federal Circuit said. She was not provided with incorrect information regarding her status, the judges noted, but rather made a wrong assumption based on a lack of information. *(Poores v. Dept. of the Treasury, 91-3273, June 25, 1992)*

For a probationary federal employee to successfully appeal his firing by claiming political bias he must show discrimination "based on affiliation with [a] party or candidate," the U.S. Court of Appeals for the Federal Circuit said. *(Bante v. MSPB, 91-3275, June 9, 1992)*

Postal workers who are dismissed during their probationary period have no right to challenge the firings unless they have disabilities covered under the Rehabilitation Act of 1973, the U.S. Court of Appeals for the District of Columbia Circuit ruled. The four workers were fired within 90 days of joining USPS. *(American Postal Workers Union v. USPS, CA DC, 90-5022, August 9, 1991)*

PROMOTION

A union proposal that provided for an automatic promotion if an employee spent a year in grade with satisfactory performance was ruled non-negotiable by the Federal Labor Relations Authority. *(45 FLRA No. 37, July 1, 1992)*

Agency documents having to do with decisions on which employees might be promoted are exempt from disclosure under the Freedom of Information Act because they involve management's "deliberative process," the U.S. Court of Appeals for the District of Columbia ruled. *(AFGE v. Dept. of Commerce, 86-5390, July 13, 1990)*

The Federal Labor Relations Authority upheld the right of federal unions to receive copies of interview questions used by agency promotion panels. *(36 FLRA No. 13, June 21, 1990)*

The Federal Labor Relations Authority ruled that a federal union does not have the right to have an observer on an agency's promotion panel. *(34 FLRA No. 121, February 1, 1990)*

The Federal Labor Relations Authority ordered the Army to turn over to a union a promotion file on a position outside of the bargaining unit. The union said it needed the file to determine if it had good reason to file a grievance on behalf of a bargaining unit employee who was not chosen for the opening. *(FLRA 4-CA-70874, January 22, 1990)*

The U.S. Court of Appeals for the District of Columbia ruled non-negotiable a union proposal that current employees be given first crack at promotions before outside applicants could be considered. *(Dept. of Treasury v. FLRA, 87-1234, Sept. 23, 1988)*

The U.S. Court of Appeals for the Federal Circuit held that federal employees have a "heavy burden" of proving that they should be retroactively promoted even after winning a personnel appeal. *(Naekel v. Dept. of Transportation, 87-3274, June 28, 1988)*

The U.S. Court of Appeals for the District of Columbia ruled that a within grade raise is "a variety of promotion" and a federal employee thus has no property right to one. *(Jacqueline A. Thomas Griffith v. FLRA, 86-5720, March 25, 1988)*

An employee promoted to a supervisory or managerial position who does not satisfactorily complete the probationary period must be returned to a job at no lower grade and pay than the one from which the person was promoted. However, that person may be fired during the probationary period for causes unrelated to supervisory or managerial performance. *(MSPB No. SF04328610610, Jan. 5, 1988)*

An arbitrator may order a promotion that was denied by agency management "only if the arbitrator finds a direct connection between an improper agency action and the failure of a specific employee to be selected for promotion." *(30 FLRA No. 70, Dec. 22, 1987)*

QUI TAM

A ruling by the 11th Circuit federal appeals court expanded the right of federal employees to sue contractors on false claims charges on behalf of the government. Such so-called *qui tam* suits can result in the employee becoming eligible for up to 30 percent of any money recovered if the contention eventually is upheld. *(Williams v. NEC Corp, 89-3973, May 29, 1991)*

REDUCTIONS IN FORCE

A general reduction-in-force notice that announces the abolishment of all positions within an employee's competitive area by a specific date can help form the basis for separation pay eligibility, the U.S. Comptroller General ruled. *CG Decision No. B-246832, June 22, 1992)*

The Merit Systems Protection Board erred by not fully considering a former Army employee's claim that his reemployment rights were violated after a layoff, the U.S. Court of Appeals for the Federal Circuit said. The court told MSPB to take a full look at his contention that he had priority rights over another person who was hired to fill a vacancy in his former function. *(Baxter v. Dept. of the Army, 91-3019, May 6, 1991)*

Retirement-eligible employees who lose their jobs through reductions-in-force and are forced to retire cannot also collect severance pay, the U.S. Court of Appeals for the Sixth Circuit ruled. *(Muller v. Lujan, No. 90-1583, March 18, 1991)*

Excepted service federal employees can be given the same bump-and-retreat rights in layoffs that apply to competitive service workers, but only if no distinction is drawn between those in a bargaining unit and those not, the U.S. Court of Appeals for the District of Columbia ruled. *(MSPB v. FLRA, 88-1268, September 14, 1990)*

Rules that provide job protection during reductions-in-force can be extended to excepted service employees. *(31 FLRA No. 26, Feb. 23, 1988)*

REHABILITATION (see also DISABILITY BENEFITS)

A "last chance" agreement where an employee enters rehabilitation rather than being fired on charges of substance abuse can apply to alleged abuse of substances other than the one for which the employee was treated, the U.S. Court of Appeals for the Federal Circuit ruled. *(89-3442, January 23, 1991)*

Federal employees with drinking problems cannot be fired unless they first get a specific warning from their agencies that continued misbehavior will lead to their removal, the Merit Systems Protection Board ruled. *(DE07528810362, April 4, 1990)*

REIMBURSEMENT (see also TRANSFERS AND RELOCATIONS; TRANSPORTATION; TRAVEL, OFFICIAL GOVERNMENT)

The U.S. Comptroller General rejected an Interior Department request that it reimburse an employee it required to become a registered professional engineer. The employee took the necessary state-administered examination and then asked Interior to pay for it. The CG said it's well-established that "the costs of qualifying for a federal position are personal to the employee." *(CG No. B-248955, July 24, 1992)*

Federal employees have to pay for their own business cards, the U.S. Comptroller General reaffirmed. A senior Agriculture Department official reasoned that the cards were "the most practical, economical, commonly recognized and business-like way" to show the public the extent of the agency's contract personnel's authority. The CG said, however, that the official's assertions are "no more persuasive" than others that have been rejected in the past. *(CG Decision No. B-246616, July 17, 1992)*

The U.S. Comptroller General asked Congress to allow the Education Department to reimburse a newly hired employee who, relying on erroneous information from the agency, incurred $19,000 in normally not reimbursable relocation costs. *(CG Decision No. B-246004, March 23, 1992)*

Agencies can pay registration fees for their employees to attend Federal Executive Board training sessions, the U.S. Comptroller General decided. *(CG No. B-245330, December 17, 1991)*

Agencies cannot be arbitrary in computing meal costs for employees. *(CG Decision No. B-231776, July 13, 1989)*

REINSTATEMENT

An agency violated federal labor law when it didn't reinstate an employee until more than two months after an arbitrator ordered the action, said the Federal Labor Relations Authority. It added that because of the foot-dragging the employee didn't receive a back pay check due to him until more than six months after he won his case. *(44 FLRA No. 111, May 27, 1992)*

The Merit Systems Protection Board ruled that federal employees injured at work do not have restoration rights to permanent light-duty positions. *(MSPB Decision No. SF03538810389-1, May 21, 1991)*

A Federal Labor Relations Authority law judge ordered the reinstatement of two National Treasury Employees Union stewards at an IRS office in Boston, saying they were improperly removed from their union posts by NTEU after filing an unfair labor practice complaint against the local's president. *(1-CO-90015, March 26, 1990)*

REPRESENTATION

A union representative should be given the combination to the lock on a restricted office even though she doesn't work in that office and normally wouldn't have access to the combination, the Federal Labor Relations Authority said. *45 FLRA No. 121, September 18, 1992)*

The Federal Labor Relations Authority upheld a union proposal to require that union representatives be sent to certain temporary work sites, rejecting the agency's argument that the proposal interfered with its rights to assign employees. *(45 FLRA No. 108, September 3, 1992)*

The U.S. Court of Appeals for the District of Columbia upheld an order forcing the U.S. Postal Service to post a notice saying that employees covered under labor contracts have the right to consult a union representative before an interrogation that might lead to discipline. *(USPS v. NLRB, 91-1373, June 30, 1992)*

An agency violated federal labor law when it tried to force a union steward to disclose information from an employee he was representing, the Federal Labor Relations Authority ruled. FLRA said a union rep has the right to maintain confidentiality of such discussions since an employee must be free to make "full disclosures to his or her representative in order to obtain adequate advice and a proper defense." *(44 FLRA No. 83, April 29, 1992)*

Federal unions are entitled to information from management that is "necessary"—not merely "relevant"—to their duty to represent employees, the U.S. Court of Appeals for the District of Columbia said. It reversed a decision to provide the union with a copy of a disciplinary letter sent by upper management to a supervisor against whom a union member had filed a grievance. *(Dept. of the Air Force v. FLRA, 91-1042, February 28, 1992)*

A federal union may not charge a fee for its representational activities even if that fee would apply to union members and non-members alike, the Federal Labor Relations Authority said. FLRA said that charging any such fee would interfere with an employee's right to refrain from assisting a union. *(44 FLRA No. 8, February 26, 1992)*

The Federal Labor Relations Authority ruled negotiable a union proposal that a management representative conducting an interview with an employee notify him of any union representation rights he might have during the session. FLRA said the proposal didn't create new representation rights—but merely helped enforce existing ones— and didn't interfere with management's right to assign work to its representatives. *(43 FLRA No. 117, February 10, 1992)*

"Effective or not," a federal union did its duty to represent a bargaining unit employee in a personnel dispute when it interceded with management on her behalf, even though no formal grievance was filed, the Federal Labor Relations Authority said. *(43 FLRA No. 50, December 19, 1991)*

The U.S. Court of Appeals for the District of Columbia said that the government can be forced to reimburse federal unions on the basis of the market rate for legal services they provide in pursuing an appeal on behalf of an employee—not just the actual expenses they incurred. *(AFGE v. FLRA, 88-1375, September 3, 1991)*

Federal employees who successfully represent themselves in personnel disputes are not eligible for legal fees, the U.S. Court of Appeals for the District of Columbia ruled. *(Lawrence v. Bowsher, 84-5443, May 10, 1991)*

Federal unions may not charge representation fees for pursuing grievances for bargaining unit employees who are not dues-paying members, since that would improperly "discriminate against non-members on the basis of their membership status," the Federal Labor Relations Authority ruled. *(38 FLRA No. 57, November 30, 1990)*

Federal unions may negotiate to gain the use of franked "penalty" mail for representation purposes, such as negotiations and handling grievances and appeals, said the Federal Labor Relations Authority. *(35 FLRA No. 109, May 7, 1990)*

The U.S. Supreme Court held that federal employees cannot sue their unions in federal court over failure to represent them—their final appeal is with the Federal Labor Relations Authority. *(Karahalios v. NFFE Local 1263, 87-636, March 6, 1989)*

The U.S. Court of Appeals for the District of Columbia ruled that individual employees dissatisfied with their union's decision to stop pursuing an unfair labor practice charge cannot press an appeal themselves. *(Hanlon and Sanders v. FLRA, 87-1094, Oct. 18, 1988)*

The U.S. District Court for the Eastern District of California ruled that federal employees without counsel in discrimination suits should not be deprived of the opportunity to have their cases heard because they make the mistake of naming the agency instead of the agency head as defendant. *(Hollcroft v. Dept. of Treasury, S-87-838 MLS, June 9, 1988)*

The U.S. Court of Appeals for the Federal Circuit held that a federal employee is responsible for the quality of his representation in a personnel appeal and cannot use the excuse of "utter incompetence" of his union representative. *(John DiCeasare v. USPS, 87-3411, Feb. 10, 1988)*

The U.S. Supreme Court ruled that employees have a constitutional right to a jury trial when they sue unions for failing to represent them adequately in disputes with their employers. Although the case involved workers in the private sector, experts said the ruling would apply to postal employees, as well, but probably not federal employees. *(Chauffeurs, Teamsters and Helpers Local 391 v. Terry 88-1719)*

RESIGNATIONS

A federal employee faced with the "unpleasant alternative choices" of resigning or being fired and who quits is presumed to have acted voluntarily, the U.S. Court of Appeals for the Federal Circuit said. *(Ramos v. Dept. of the Army, 91-3491, February 14, 1992)*

Federal employees who resign on the advice of their agencies rather than be laid off can be eligible for severance pay, the U.S. Claims Court said, saying such a resignation in effect is an involuntary separation. *(Bell v. U.S., 687-88 C, May 8, 1991)*

When a federal employee resigns, the resignation is effective then and there, unless expressly noted otherwise on an agency's notification of personnel action, the Merit Systems Protection Board ruled. *(MSPB Decision No. DE07529010045, March 20, 1991)*

An employee who resigns and later contends he was forced into the decision must show improper acts by the agency and not just that he was faced with an "unpleasant" choice between resigning and being fired for cause, said the U.S. Court of Appeals for the Federal Circuit. *(Latham v. USPS, 90-3134, July 17, 1990)*

The United States Claims Court refused to rule involuntary a resignation by a contracting officer who had been notified that he would be transferred on an uncertain future date. *(Giknis v. U.S., 162-88C, March 20, 1990)*

RETIREMENT (see also ANNUITIES — TAXES AND ACTIONS; LUMP-SUM SUIT; RETIREMENT, DISABILITY; SPOUSE/SURVIVOR ANNUITY)

A retired federal employee who didn't apply for enhanced annuity benefits until seven years after his retirement deserves a chance to have his claim heard, the U.S. Court of Appeals for the Federal Circuit ruled. It said the retiree only then became aware that he might be eligible for the benefit, and no harm was done to the government by his delay. *(Nuss v. OPM, 91-3482, September 8, 1992)*

A prenuptial agreement signed by a federal employee who remarried late in life doesn't take precedence over a form he signed designating his federal retirement death benefits to his new wife, the Merit Systems Protection Board ruled. *(MSPB Doc. No. DE0831910 50511, May 21, 1992)*

A federal employee who announces his intent to retire and then changes his mind before the effective date must clearly inform his agency of his reversal, the U.S. Court of Appeals for the Federal Circuit said. It refused to rule involuntary the retirement of an employee who said he had wanted to withdraw the application before its effective date but who provided insufficient evidence that he made that clear to his agency. *(Davis v. Dept. of the Army, 91-3131, April 27, 1992)*

A federal employee who felt his agency rushed him into retirement didn't meet the test of having retired involuntarily, the U.S. Court of Appeals for the Federal Circuit said. The employee must prove he "involuntarily accepted agency conditions, the circumstances permitted no other alternative, and the circumstances were created by agency acts," the ruling said. *(Maher v. Dept. of the Army, 90-3254, April 16, 1992)*

A survivor's annuity can be part of a property settlement in a federal retiree divorce case, even if the initial order of divorce doesn't provide for one, the U.S. Court of Appeals for the Federal Circuit said. It was considering how survivor annuities fit into "bifurcated" (split) divorce cases in which a divorce decree is issued and the settlement of property is left for later. *(Newman v. Love and Penn, 91-3268, April 15, 1992)*

The government was correct in crediting a retiree's military service toward his civil service annuity rather than toward a Social Security benefit, the U.S. Court of Appeals for the Federal Circuit ruled. The retiree wanted the time added to his Social Security credit to qualify for an annuity under that system. But the court said the law required crediting toward his civil service annuity because otherwise his designated survivor's benefit would have been reduced. *(Fermin v. OPM, 91-3562, April 8, 1992)*

Time spent as a cadet-midshipman at the United States Merchant Marine Academy is not creditable for civil service retirement purposes, the U.S. Court of Appeals for the Federal Circuit ruled. *(Whalen v. OPM, 91-3438, March 17, 1992)*

To be eligible for a discontinued service annuity a federal employee must be given a notice of a specific date when he or she will be involuntarily separated in order to make the resignation involuntary, the U.S. Court of Appeals for the Federal Circuit said. *(Beasley v. OPM, 91-3286, September 26, 1991)*

The U.S. Court of Appeals for the Federal Circuit criticized the Office of Personnel Management for "mishandling" a federal retirement claim, saying that while the amount of money involved is small by government standards, it was important to the retiree and that he deserved better treatment. *(Gromo v. OPM, 91-3071, September 19, 1991)*

The U.S. Court of Appeals for the Federal Circuit said the time limit for appealing a denial of an application for regular retirement should be waived because the employee received a series of confusing letters from both OPM and MSPB regarding what type of evidence he needed to support his claim. *(Cuajunco v. OPM, 91-3212, September 5, 1991)*

A federal employee need not actually be involved in fighting fires to be considered a firefighter and eligible for early retirement benefits that apply to that occupation, the U.S. Court of Appeals for the Federal Circuit ruled. *(Felzien v. OPM, 90-3445, April 17, 1991)*

The government can't deduct a federal annuity from a military reservist's disability pay, the U.S. Comptroller General ruled. *(CG Decision No. B-237973, March 22, 1991)*

Although a federal retiree who is receiving an erroneously high annuity may come to depend on the extra money, he is still obliged to repay the government when it discovers its mistake, the U.S. Court of Appeals for the Federal Circuit ruled. *(Laurenzano v. OPM, 91-3004, March 14, 1991)*

A postal employee who worked under an unusual part-time arrangement of four hours on-duty and four hours of leave without pay each day deserves only partial retirement credit for the time served, said the U.S. Court of Appeals for the Federal Circuit. *(True v. OPM, 90-3310, February 25, 1991)*

A federal employee who received his annuity lump-sum payment eight months after retirement is eligible for neither interest on the payment nor a claim for damages, the U.S. Court of Appeals for the Federal Circuit held. *(Rathjen v. OPM, 90-3387, February 12, 1991)*

A formal appointment into a civil service position is needed to make time served creditable for federal retirement, and some who consider themselves federal employees may not actually have that status, a ruling from the U.S. Court of Appeals for the Federal Circuit said. *(Arenal v. OPM, 90-3372, January 14, 1991)*

A survivor's annuity does not come automatically to the beneficiary of a federal retiree's estate; it must be applied for while the survivor is still living, the U.S. Court of Appeals for the Federal Circuit ruled. *(Davis v. OPM, 90-3186, November 6, 1990)*

The U.S. Court of Appeals for the Federal Circuit ordered the Merit Systems Protection Board to look into whether the weekend days following an employee's last day of work should count as time served for computing retirement eligibility. *(Lim v. OPM, 90-3377, October 26, 1990)*

Federal and postal employees who were given the chance to transfer into the new FERS retirement system were told clearly that the choice was irrevocable and cannot back out of it now claiming they were misinformed, said the U.S. Court of Appeals for the Federal Circuit. *(Springer v. OPM, 90-3193, August 6, 1990)*

The West Virginia state Supreme Court ruled that when dividing marital property, contributions of one spouse to the civil service retirement system may be counted as a shared asset of the couple, but contributions to Social Security may not. *(Loudermilk v. Loudermilk, No 19367, July 12, 1990)*

Time spent working as a "private roll" employee of a federal agency does not count toward a civil service retirement benefit, the U.S. Court of Appeals for the Federal Circuit ruled. *(Bisson v. OPM, 89-3410, July 6, 1990)*

A federal employee cannot receive retirement credit for time he would have worked had he not been injured, the U.S. Court of Appeals for the Federal Circuit said *(Sabado v. OPM, 90-3106, June 12, 1990)*

Time spent working for a "proprietary" corporation owned by a government agency (such as the CIA) does not count toward a federal annuity if the employee is not appointed to the civil service and contributions to the retirement fund are not withheld from the company and the employee, the U.S. Court of Appeals for the Federal Circuit said. *(Bevans v. OPM, 89-3396, April 12, 1990)*

The U.S. Comptroller General ruled that a retired Navy regular officer who was employed by the U.S. Senate will not have his retired pay reduced additionally after a bonus he received from his Senate job increased his combined retired-Senate salary above the executive level V rate. Only basic pay is counted for purposes of the Dual Compensation Act, the CG said. *(B 238189, March 22, 1990)*

RETIREMENT, DISABILITY (see also DISABILITY BENEFITS; RETIREMENT)

A federal employee who had scads of medical and other evidence showing that he had a severe back injury that qualified him for disability retirement nevertheless had to take it all the way to the Merit Systems Protection Board before he got relief. An administrative law judge who upheld an Office of Personnel Management decision that he did not qualify finally was overturned by the full MSPB board. *(MSPB Decision No. CH831E8910309, May 20, 1991)*

The Merit Systems Protection Board ruled that disability retirements cannot be denied government employees when the "light duty" jobs offered them as an alternative are not of the same "tenure" as their present positions. *(MSPB Decision No. DE831E8910185, March 22, 1990)*

An agency has no duty to file for a disability retirement or seek a medical exam before moving to fire an employee on charges of being disruptive in the workplace. *(MSPB Doc. No. SL07528710120, April 6, 1989)*

SECURITY AND SECURITY CLEARANCES

IRS employees represented by the National Treasury Employees Union will not have to answer questions regarding their mental health during background checks unless they hold security clearances, under an agreement reached between the agency and the union. *(NTEU v. Dept. of Treasury, 89-924, U.S. District Court for Western Texas, January 3, 1992)*

An agency's right to search union property located on its site cannot be restricted in bargaining, ruled the Federal Labor Relations Authority. *(36 FLRA No. 8, June 19, 1990)*

The Federal Labor Relations Authority ruled that a union local may bargain for stricter measures to protect employees at agency headquarters against the hazards of assault and theft. *(35 FLRA No. 78, April 26, 1990)*

The U.S. Court of Appeals for the District of Columbia upheld a president's prerogative to suspend union rights of certain groups of federal employees by citing national security concerns. *(AFGE v. Reagan, 87-5335, March 24, 1989)*

The U.S. Court of Appeals for the Federal Circuit ruled that federal employees who lose their jobs because their security clearances have been withdrawn cannot bring a monetary claim before the United States Claims Court. *(Carr v. U.S., 88-1472, January 5, 1989)*

The U.S. Supreme Court ruled that the Merit Systems Protection Board has no business reviewing the reason why an agency refused to grant an employee a security clearance. *(Dept. of the Navy v. Eagan, 86-1552, Feb. 23, 1988)*

SETTLEMENT AGREEMENTS

An agreement settling a personnel dispute, which included a written admonishment being put in the employee's file, didn't specify what that letter was to say and thus the agency was free to write whatever it wished, the U.S. Court of Appeals for the Federal Circuit said. It rejected the employee's claim that the letter shouldn't have contained the agency's allegations that led to the dispute. *(Ramos v. Dept. of the Treasury, 91-3500, July 10, 1992)*

An oral contract settling a personnel dispute between a federal employee and an agency is just as enforceable as written settlement, said the U.S. Court of Appeals for the Federal Circuit, which said an oral agreement was reached in a case that went before an arbitrator. It said the employee was bound by that agreement—which was taped—even though it was never put in writing. *(Nixon v. Dept. of the Navy, 92-3167, June 11, 1992)*

An agency that has reached an agreement with the local union regarding the procedures to be used in exercising one of its rights— here, to reassign employees and set new performance standards— doesn't have to bargain again when it actually takes such actions, the U.S. Court of Appeals for the District of Columbia ruled. It said the Federal Labor Relations Authority set an improper precedent on the issue that would have required further bargaining in almost all such cases, even though the issue already had been resolved by contract. *(Dept. of the Navy v. FLRA, 91-1211, April 24, 1992)*

An attorney handling a federal employee's personnel appeal is presumed to have the authority to settle the case on the employee's behalf, the U.S. Court of Appeals for the Federal Circuit said. It added that such a settlement will be considered valid unless the employee shows proof that he did not authorize his lawyer to enter into a settlement agreement. *Amin v. MSPB, 91-3271, December 17, 1991)*

The U.S. Comptroller General quashed a settlement between the Defense Investigative Service and an employee the agency had wanted to dismiss for alleged misconduct. The agreement, negotiated between DIS and the employee's attorney, allowed him to opt out of a 12-month duty extension (the period was intended to make the relocation payment proper) and permitted him to use accumulated sick and annual leave until he resigned. *(CG Decision No. B-239592, August 23, 1991)*

A settlement agreement between a federal employee and his agency that is reached before the Merit Systems Protection Board does not create a contract that falls under the review of the United States Claims Court, that court ruled. Any disputes arising from that settlement—most commonly, whether the parties are living up to what they promised—fall under MSPB's jurisdiction, it said. *(Good v. U.S., 90-1063C, August 22, 1991)*

An agreement that settles a personnel dispute between a federal employee and his agency is a contract, and it is within a law judge's power to interpret that contract if another disagreement arises, said the U.S. Court of Appeals for the Federal Circuit. *(Hanson v. Dept. of the Army, 90-3327, October 4, 1990)*

An employee who agreed to resign if his agency would cancel his removal must abide by that agreement, even if he contends the agency reneged on its promise to grant him disability retirement instead. *(MSPB Doc. No. PH075287CO267, March 3, 1989)*

SEXUAL HARASSMENT

The U.S. Postal Service is to blame for creating a hostile work environment for a deaf and mute postal worker who succumbed to the sexual advances of her supervisor, the U.S. District Court for the District of Oregon ruled. *(89-635-FR, September 4, 1991)*

The U.S. District Court for Massachusetts said that a federal employee may pursue a personal damages suit against her supervisor for alleged sexual harassment, despite the government's move to take over as the defendant in the case. The court in a procedural ruling said that actions such as those alleged weren't within the scope of employment and that the complaint can proceed against him in his "private, individual capacity." *(Wood v. U.S., 89-0166-S, January 29, 1991)*

The U.S. Court of Appeals for the Ninth Circuit held that a female plaintiff states a prima facie case of hostile environment sexual harassment when she alleges conduct which a reasonable woman would consider sufficiently severe or pervasive to alter the conditions of employment and create an abusive working environment. *(Ellison v. Brady, CA 9, 89-15248, January 23, 1991)*

The Merit Systems Protection Board canceled the demotion of a postal superintendent on sexual harassment charges because he had no prior disciplinary record, the alleged offense was his first and "playful touching was part of the work environment" at the site. *(MSPB Decision, No. AT07528810522, March 13, 1990)*

SICK LEAVE (see also LEAVE)

A federal appeals court upheld the firing of a 10-year postal employee with an otherwise spotless attendance record, on charges of submitting a false claim for one day of sick leave. *(Beverly v. USPS, U.S. Court of Appeals for the Federal Circuit, No. 90-3002, July 3, 1990)*

The U.S. Comptroller General ruled that a federal agency properly approved sick leave for a federal employee who stayed at home while his child was suffering from conjunctivitis. A state (Alaska) health official stated that the child would have been unable to attend a day care center with that contagious eye condition, the CG noted. *(B-238784, June 15, 1990)*

Although an agency may be suspicious of an employee's motives in requesting extended sick leave, the request must be granted if he presents valid medical evidence for the leave, a Merit Systems Protections Board hearing officer ruled. *(MSPB Decision No. BN07529010087, April 6, 1990)*

An arbitrator upheld the firing of a federal warehouseman who was suspended for 30 days after being caught performing as a rock musician while on sick leave. *(LAIRS No. 19654, March 2, 1990)*

An employee who used annual leave instead of sick leave may be permitted to retroactively substitute sick leave for annual leave in order to avoid losing the annual leave, because he was given bad advice on the subject by his agency. *(CG Decision No. B-233945, February 24, 1989)*

SMOKING

The Federal Service Impasses Panel rejected a union bid to have tables set aside in an Air Force Academy visitor center for civil service workers to smoke, arguing that the smoke would be circulated through the central ventilating system and into non-smokers' lungs. *(91 FSIP No. 275 and 92 FSIP No. 80, August 11, 1992.)*

While generally agreeing with a plan to ban indoor smoking at a Navy facility, a labor panel said the agency went too far when it proposed that employees who wished to smoke outdoors build their own shelters. Instead, the Federal Service Impasses Panel said the employer should provide for outdoor smoking that is reasonably accessible to employee work stations and sheltered from the elements. *(91 FSIP 251, February 10, 1992)*

Unless a union "clearly and unmistakably" waives its right to bargain over smoking policy at a facility, negotiations must be held over the agency's plans to change that policy, the Federal Labor Relations Authority said. It ordered the agency to restore a smoking room it eliminated when it went to an outdoor smoking-only policy, and to begin negotiations on the subject. *(43 FLRA No. 96, January 28, 1992)*

An agency that has entered an agreement with a union regarding smoking policy at its facilities cannot unilaterally break that agreement, the U.S. Court of Appeals for the Fourth Circuit ruled. *(HHS v. FLRA, 90-1068, December 26, 1991)*

The Federal Service Impasses Panel upheld firm restrictions on smoking at a health-related federal agency, the Centers for Disease Control, which argued that allowing smoking on the premises "does not protect adequately the health of nonsmokers and fails to consider the agency's overall mission." *(91 FSIP No. 91, July 24, 1991)*

Agency authority to make work areas smoke-free was taken a step farther by a Federal Labor Relations Authority decision allowing a ban on the sale of smoking materials on its premises. *(40 FLRA No. 55, April 30, 1991)*

The Federal Service Impasses Panel upheld a proposed management policy of assigning smoking breaks to employees who abuse the general smoking policy at the work site. *(90 FSIP No. 222, March 15, 1991)*

The Federal Service Impasses Panel approved as a designated agency smoking zone an outdoor picnic area that is covered but otherwise not protected from the elements, and 75 yards from the building.*(90 FSIP 217, December 20, 1990)*

The Health and Human Services department must negotiate over its workplace smoking policy just like any other agency, despite the claim by HHS that it has a stronger reason than the others to make its work areas smoke-free, the U.S. Court of Appeals for the District of Columbia held. *(HHS v. FLRA, 88-1867, November 30, 1990)*

Restricting the hours that smoking will be permitted in a federal office is not sufficient protection to non-smokers from dangerous second-hand smoke, said the Federal Service Impasses Panel. *(90 FSIP*

The Federal Labor Relations Authority upheld an arbitrator's decision that an agency improperly revoked its designated smoking areas without consulting the union local. (35 FLRA No. 144, May 31, 1990)

Individual federal employees do not have the authority to designate their own work areas as smoking zones under the government's general policy against smoking in the work place, the U.S. Court of Appeals for the District of Columbia said. (IRS v. FLRA and NTEU, 88-1550, May 1, 1990)

The Federal Service Impasses Panel ruled in the case of two agencies that smoking accommodations among employees should be limited to outside areas that are "reasonably accessible" and protected from the elements. (89 FSIP 198, April 27, 1990 and 90 FSIP 58, April 27, 1990)

Smokers at Griffiss Air Force Base, NY, will be allowed to smoke in designated smoking areas inside activity buildings when the outside air temperature falls below 35 degrees or the weather is otherwise inclement, under an agreement imposed by the Federal Services Impasses Panel. (89 FSIP 214, January 24, 1990)

A tentative contract between the Social Security Administration and the American Federation of Government Employees that was rejected by a vote of AFGE members in the agency was ordered into effect. The Federal Service Impasses Panel ordered that the contract be carried out as it was negotiated, rejecting AFGE's request to change clauses concerning smoking policy and alternative work schedules (flexitime). (89 FSIP 132, December 22, 1989)

The U.S. Court of Appeals for the 10th Circuit upheld the right of federal unions to negotiate over anti-smoking policies. (Indian Health Service v. FLRA and NFFE, 88-1304, September 15, 1989)

Agencies may use appropriated funds to pay for smoking cessation programs for their employees, although they are not required to do so. (CG Decision No. B-231543, February 3, 1989)

Federal Labor Relations Authority held negotiable a union proposal that smokers and nonsmokers in the workplace be separated by installing floor-to-ceiling partitions and acquiring "smoke-eaters" to supplement the existing ventilation system. (32 FLRA No. 31, May 31, 1988)

The U.S. District Court for the District of Columbia ruled that a supervisor's failure to enforce his federal agency's mandatory policy limiting smoking in the workplace could subject him to an employee's

personal injury suit. *(Caroll v. TVA, 87-1957, March 7, 1988)*
SPECIAL RATE PAY

A federal judge in the District of Columbia ordered that the annual general schedule raises should have been the starting point for calculation of "special rate" raises in the early 1980s, when some special rate federal employees received lower amounts than their colleagues. But the decision didn't immediately pave the way for any payments in the long-running dispute, leaving the actual dollar settlements to be calculated through further negotiations. *(NTEU v. Newman, 83-0279 JGP, June 28, 1991)*

The U.S. Court of Appeals for the Federal Circuit ruled that special rate employees illegally were denied pay raises that went to their general schedule counterparts. It directed a lower court to see who should be compensated and how much. *(NTEU, POPA v. Horner, Nos. 87-1506, 87-1507 and 88-1075, March 7, 1989)*

A union proposal that employees start receiving higher (special rate) pay if they are detailed for more than 20 days to a job paying the bonus salary is negotiable. *(31 FLRA No. 53, March 11, 1988)*
SPOUSE/SURVIVOR ANNUITY (see also RETIREMENT)

The former spouse of a federal retiree who was given wrong information regarding the procedure for leaving a survivor annuity got sympathy but no help on her claim for the money from the U.S. Court of Appeals for the Federal Circuit. The court said that despite the "equities" of her case, the law prohibits paying an annuity to her and it is up to Congress to provide her with any relief. *(Koyen v. OPM, 91-3088, August 27, 1992)*

A federal appeals court sided with a retiree in a dispute over his choice for a survivor annuity, saying that while he "could have acted differently" his wishes should carry great weight. The U.S. Court of Appeals for the Federal Circuit ordered the Office of Personnel Management to allow him to designate his new wife as the beneficiary of the annuity even though the deadline to make such a choice—one year after a remarriage—long had passed. *(Berg v. OPM, 92-3160, June 12, 1992)*

The U.S. Court of Appeals for the Federal Circuit rejected a claim for a survivor annuity from the widow of a federal retiree who said her husband never was formally informed that he had to make that election in writing, claiming that "senior citizens do not read notices sent to them." The court said two letters he was sent constituted adequate notice, adding that it is the retiree's duty to take care of such matters.

(Austin v. OPM, 91-3567, June 12, 1992)

A divorce decree can make a retiree ineligible for a lump-sum retirement payment if it gives a former spouse rights to part of an annuity, the U.S. Court of Appeals for the Federal Circuit said. *(Donlan v. OPM, 90-3066, July 6, 1990)*

The U.S. Court of Appeals for the Federal Circuit overturned an Office of Personnel Management position on annuities for former spouses of federal and postal employees, saying Congress intended to make a larger group eligible for such annuities than OPM would allow in rules it published. *(Newman v. Tiegeler, 89-3365, February 28, 1990)*

The U.S. Court of Appeals for the Federal Circuit ruled that former spouses of federal employees may be eligible for a survivor's annuity in cases where their spouses qualified for either regular or disability retirement. *(Horner v. Hollander, 89-3208, February 5, 1990)*

The U.S. Court of Appeals for the Federal Circuit rejected a claim for a survivor annuity in a case where it was alleged that an employee was given incorrect advice that her retirement coverage would continue for a month after leaving federal employment. *(Allen v. OPM, 89-3144, November 1, 1989)*

The U.S. Court of Appeals for the Federal Circuit held that the government is obliged to send annual notices to retirees regarding the option to select or reject a survivor annuity for their spouses. *(Harris v. OPM, 89-3147, October 13, 1989)*

The U.S. Court of Appeals for the Federal Circuit held that a retired federal employee may choose a spousal annuity for his wife even though he missed the deadline for requesting that kind of annuity because his personnel office gave him "confusing" advice. *(Torre v. OPM, 88-3157, Aug. 2, 1988)*

SUSPENSION (see also DISCIPLINE)

The U.S. Court of Appeals for the Federal Circuit said that a 40-day suspension of an employee was too great a penalty, considering that only one of the four administrative charges against him was upheld. It ordered the penalty reduced to a reprimand. *(Snow v. Dept. of Agriculture, 91-3612, May 21, 1992)*

An employee who voluntarily stays home from work may not appeal an action taken against him for doing that, the U.S. Court of Appeals for the Federal Circuit said. It added, however, that some circumstances, such as an enforced leave of absence, are effectively the same as a suspension and can be appealed on those grounds. *(Perez v. MSPB, 91-3108, April 17, 1991)*

A forestry supervisor who allegedly altered a time and attendance record and a travel document to keep his agency from finding out that he had left his crew to go back to his duty station was suspended for 60 days and the penalty was upheld by the Merit Systems Protection Board. *(MSPB Decision No. DEO7529010286, January 21, 1991)*

The Federal Labor Relations Authority overturned a suspension of an employee who refused to run a work-related errand during off-duty hours, saying he had the right to refuse to perform government work on his own time without compensation. *(38 FLRA No. 102, January 4, 1991)*

An agency may keep an employee on unpaid suspension while it prepares to fire him on a misconduct charge even though the suspension may last several months, ruled the U.S. Court of Appeals for the Federal Circuit. *(Engdahl v. Dept. of the Navy, 89-3326, April 17, 1990)*

A federal protective officer who twisted another's injured foot in an apparently well-meaning, albeit rough way to welcome him back to work after a long medical recovery—and resulted in yet another injury costing the co-worker another 45 days off the job—lost a bid to have his 10-day suspension lifted. *(LAIRS No. 20246)*

TAXATION (see also ANNUITIES — TAXES AND ACTIONS)

Living quarters allowances paid to certain federal employees stationed overseas are exempt from FICA (Social Security) taxes, the U.S. Court of Appeals for the Federal Circuit ruled. *(Anderson v. U.S., 90-5002, March 21, 1991)*

Employees of nonappropriated fund agencies such as officers clubs who work overseas are still subject to U.S. income tax on their wages, said the U.S. Court of Appeals for the District of Columbia. *(Matthews v. Commissioner of Internal Revenue, 89-1423, July 3, 1990)*

The United States Claims Court ruled that housing allowances paid to federal employees stationed overseas are not subject to Social Security or Medicare taxes. *(Anderson, et al, v. U.S., 1-87T, March 24, 1989)*

The U.S. Supreme Court ruled that states cannot tax federal annuities if them exempt state and local government retirees from the same levies. *(Davis v. Michigan Dept. of the Treasury, 87-1020)*

The U.S. Supreme Court agreed to decide if federal and postal retirees in Virginia—and by implication, in several other states—will be eligible for tax refunds for the years the states taxed their annuities without also taxing state government workers' pensions. *(Harper v. Virginia Department of Taxation)*

TEMPORARY DUTY

A federal employee away on temporary duty who performs work at yet another site may receive per diem for both locations, the U.S. Comptroller General ruled. *(CG No. B-244666, February 14, 1992)*

Agency employees who are "drafted" into a temporary assignment should not get special pay if employees who volunteered do not also get such cash awards, said the Federal Service Impasses Panel. *(91 FSIP No. 55, March 1, 1991)*

Agencies may keep employees on temporary assignments much longer than generally has been allowed but they must take into account the length of the assignment and reduce per diem and should advise employees of all potential liabilities of such an arrangement. *(CG Decision No. B-234262, June 2, 1989)*

TRAINING

It's up to an agency to prove it gave the proper training to an employee in an up-or-out type career path if it decides the employee should be out, said the U.S. Court of Appeals for the Federal Circuit. *(Wright v. Dept. Transportation, 89-3284, March 30, 1990)*

Federal employees who fail to live up to on-the-job training agreements with their agencies can be required to pay back the cost of the training course. *(CG Decision No. B-233734, May 30, 1989)*

TRANSFERS AND RELOCATIONS

A proposal that employees designated as "surplus" be put on an agency-wide list of available employees has been ruled negotiable by the Federal Labor Relations Authority, which said it did not interfere with management's right to assign employees. *(45 FLRA No. 21, June 18, 1992)*

A transferred federal employee who moved into an apartment at his new location while continuing to search for a house didn't lose his eligibility for temporary quarters subsistence expenses, the Comptroller General ruled. The employee's agency had denied his claim for 30 days of that allowance, pointing out that he had signed a one-year lease on the apartment and had moved some of his household goods into it. *(CG Decision No. B-246479, June 9, 1992)*

A Federal Service Impasses Panel arbitrator accepted a union proposal that, all other thing being equal, the choice of which employee will get a noncompetitive reassignment will be based on seniority, saying the proposal didn't unduly interfere with management's discretion to make assignments. *(91 FSIP No. 196, June 1, 1992)*

The government has the right to recoup a relocation allowance it paid to an employee who later left his new position before the one year of service required to keep the money had expired, the U.S. Comptroller General said. It added that it was improper for the employee to try using unused sick and annual leave to keep his name on the employment rolls long enough to serve out the time. *(CG Decision No. B-238271.2, January 31, 1992)*

The U.S. Comptroller General issued a ruling clarifying the issue of reimbursement of meals expenses for federal employees and their families living in temporary quarters while preparing for a permanent transfer. The cost of meals, including groceries, is a reimbursable expense in such situations. *(CG Decision B-245015, November 4, 1991)*

The U.S. Comptroller General approved several costs incurred by an employee being transferred, including more than $500 he had to forfeit earnest money on a house he was buying. The CG ruled that because the official transfer was the "proximate cause" of these misfortunes, they may be paid by the government. Also approved were the costs of having to obtain a new driver's license for his wife and telephone calls related to real estate transactions. *(CG Decision No. B-241710, May 13, 1991)*

The U.S. Comptroller General upheld a general agency policy of not paying the costs to ship employee-owned vehicles overseas in a transfer, saying there was no obligation to examine each situation case-by-case. *(CG Decision No. B-227534.5, March 7, 1991)*

The U.S. Comptroller General issued a detailed ruling on what expenses are reimbursable for building ones own home at a new duty station after an official transfer. The upshot—many costs are reimbursable. *(B-233484, July 6, 1990)*

The U.S. Comptroller General asked Congress to make an exception and allow an individual entering the government in a "manpower shortage" position to be paid the full amount of his relocation expenses as erroneously specified in travel orders. *(B-237667, April 27, 1990)*

Agencies may reimburse employees for paying their friends to help them pack household goods in connection with an official transfer as long as they are moving themselves and the claimed amounts are "reasonable." *(CG Decision No. B-232600, August 3, 1989)*

A federal employee who transfers to a new duty station in another state but fails to complete a service agreement must repay the relocation expenses for which the agency paid. *(CG Decision No. B-230338, June 2, 1989)*

When the spouse of an employee who is being transferred drives the family's second car to the new location, reimbursement of per diem costs is proper because this was an authorized mode of transportation. *(CG Decision No. B-232370, May 10, 1989)*

Federal employees on house-hunting trips preparing for official transfers may be reimbursed for their own per diem costs but not for the costs of boarding pets while they are away. *(CG No. B-227189, March 25, 1988)*

Employees may ship their boats at government expense when transferring to new duty stations if the agency agrees. *(CG No. B-228803, Feb. 5, 1988)*

A federal worker retiring overseas who had a new car shipped directly from there to New York City can't be reimbursed for delivery from the Big Apple to a stateside residence because he didn't use that car at his overseas station. *(CG No. B-226426, Jan. 19, 1988)*

TRANSPORTATION

Federal employees serving overseas may take up to two years after retirement to resettle back to their previous location and be reimbursed for travel and transportation expenses—but there are limits, said the U.S. Comptroller General. *(CG Decision No. B-248013, September 8, 1992)*

A union local's bid to have its members join the public transit subsidy program was rejected by the Federal Service Impasses Panel, which noted that the subject already has arisen at the national level between the agency and the union. *(92 FSIP No. 56, May 14, 1992)*

The Federal Labor Relations Authority sided with a union that wanted to bargain over the agency's participation in the program in which agencies can subsidize employees for taking public transit to and from work. *(44 FLRA No. 34, March 17, 1992)*

An agency missed the bus when it refused to negotiate over a proposal that it "ensure the employee's transportation home" at night after overtime assignments of workers dependent on public transportation, the Federal Labor Relations Authority held. FLRA said there is authority to pay cab fare when the overtime-delayed travel home "is during infrequently scheduled public transportation or darkness." *(43 FLRA No. 65, December 26, 1991)*

Federal agencies may use appropriated funds to, in effect, pay their employees to use public transportation. Specifically, they may participate in state and local programs designed to encourage such use, the U.S. Comptroller General ruled. *(CG Decisions No. B-243677 & B-243674, May 13, 1991)*

TRAVEL, OFFICIAL GOVERNMENT

A union proposal that certain employees be issued travel advances in lieu of using government-sponsored credit cards on travel was ruled non-negotiable by the Federal Labor Relations Authority. FLRA further denied bargaining on a union proposal that all charges on such cards be billed directly to the government, and not to the employees. *(43 FLRA No. 37, November 29, 1991)*

The U.S. Comptroller General rejected an Energy Department proposal to allow its employees on official travel to begin and end official travel where they wish if the government saves money in the process. While the arrangements initially would be a boon to employees, in the long run it would undermine the government's ability to negotiate cheaper fares for the bulk of its employees, the CG said after consulting with the General Services Administration. *(B-243622, August 29, 1991)*

End of fiscal year temporary duty travel expenses must be charged to the appropriation current for the year in which a particular travel expense in incurred when that travel spans two fiscal periods, as is often the case near the end of a fiscal year, said a U.S. Comptroller General ruling. *(CG Decision No. B-238110, May 7, 1991)*

Federal agencies paying travel and per diem for employees they are honoring at ceremonies may not only pay for their spouses to accompany them but also may extend their stays, as well, the U.S. Comptroller General ruled. *(CG Decision No. B-241987, April 25, 1991)*

Although attending the funeral of a fellow federal employee is normally not considered reimbursable official travel, it may be allowed when it is considered important to the mission of the agency, said the U.S. Comptroller General. *(CG Decision No. B-239887, January 25, 1991)*

The U.S. Comptroller General ruled that federal law allows federal employees to be driven by government vehicle between their homes and airports and other "common carrier terminals" in conjunction with official travel. *(CG Decision No. B-210555.44, January 22, 1991)*

The U.S. Comptroller General reaffirmed a policy that allows agencies to grant compensatory time off or overtime for employees who must travel outside of normal duty hours. *(CG Decision No. B-*

236327.2, November 13, 1990)

Airline "frequent flyer" bonuses earned by traveling federal employees are agency property and can't be turned over to the employee for personal use even if the agency can't take advantage of the benefits itself, the Comptroller General ruled. *(CG Decision No. B-220542.12, August 2, 1990)*

The U.S. Comptroller General ruled that since a United States airline's service had been "unreliable," an agency could reimburse an employee assigned to Honduras for flying his two children home on a Honduran airliner to the states for spring recess. Normally government employees are required to fly with U.S. carriers. *(B-198930.3, June 25, 1990)*

The U.S Court of Appeals for the Federal Circuit said an agency was wrong to fire an employee on charges of making a misleading statement on a travel reimbursement claim. *(Case No. 89-3201, March 30, 1990)*

A federal employee used airline frequent flyer points based on his government-paid official travel to obtain free tickets for his own use. He owes Uncle Sam for the fair market value of those tickets, the U.S. Comptroller General ruled. *(B-233388, March 23, 1990)*

The U.S. Comptroller General ruled that federal employees who are summoned to appear at discrimination hearings are entitled to be reimbursed for their travel expenses. They are "in an official duty status," he decided. *(B-235845, March 12, 1990)*

A federal employee who left government quarters for commercial lodging while on temporary duty because she found the government digs substandard need not be reimbursed for switching, the U.S. Comptroller General decided. He noted that he will not substitute his judgment for that of the federal agency, which claimed that shortcomings in its quarters had been corrected on the day she left. *(No. B-233841, January 26, 1990)*

Federal employees who stay in temporary quarters at government expense after moving to another duty station also may claim per diem if they have to travel away from those temporary quarters to perform other duty, the U.S. Comptroller General ruled. *(CG Decision No. B-232503, November 9, 1989)*

The U.S. Comptroller General ruled that agencies may elect to pay for the travel and transportation of employee spouses to join husbands and wives who are being honored by their agencies. Agency heads may consider the expenses "necessary," the CG said. *(CG Decision No.*

B-233607, October 26, 1989)

If an agency gives an employee the right to make an oral response to a proposed notice of removal that requires travel, it must reimburse him if he undertakes that travel. *(CG Decision No. B-233387, September 7, 1989)*

The Drug Enforcement Administration may approve official travel abroad by its employees on foreign-flag carriers in certain circumstances to avoid terrorist attacks. *(CG Decision No. B-235495, August 23, 1989)*

An agency is justified in withholding reimbursement for all costs incurred during travel when it is proven that part of the request for reimbursement was falsified. *(CG Decision No. B-232858, April 21, 1989)*

Federal travel regulations can be revised to allow employees overseas to transport home at government expense a privately owned vehicle even if no vehicle was transported overseas initially. *(CG Decision No. B-230448, February 17, 1989)*

Time spent waiting for an airplane while on official travel doesn't count as overtime because an employee is not performing regular work during that time. *(CG Decision No. B-226191.2, January 4, 1989)*

The government, not federal travelers, owns those certificates overbooked hotels give guests whose reservations are not honored. *(CG Decision No. B-228696, March 10, 1988)*

The Comptroller General denied a claim for an extra day's per diem by a federal employee who said that while he could have reached his official travel destination the same day, he was too tired to finish the trip. *(CG No. B-229103, Feb. 29, 1988)*

Employees taking advantage of "frequent flyer" upgrades to business or first class seats on airlines while on official travel must reimburse the government for the value of the VIP treatment. *(CG No. B-220542)*

UNIFORMS

Federal employees have the right to wear union pins at work, even if they are dressed in uniform, said the Federal Labor Relations Authority in a case where management claimed that wearing pins would detract from the appearance and morale of employees. *(38 FLRA No. 63, November 30, 1990)*

The Customs Service can require its uniformed employees to add a new bicentennial patch to their uniforms but must negotiate with the National Treasury Employees Union over who is to pay for them, the

Federal Labor Relations Authority ruled. Cost of the patches is $2.50 each. *(35 FLRA No. 1, March 2, 1990)*

The U.S. Court of Appeals for the 9th Circuit ruled that federal agencies may prohibit the wearing of union pins on work uniforms. *(Nos. 87-7138 and 87-7146, Sept. 1, 1988)*

UNION ACTIVITIES (see also ARBITRATION; BARGAINING; GRIEVANCES)

Individual federal employees are not "parties" to union representation elections and have no right to challenge the results of those elections before the Federal Labor Relations Authority, FLRA said. This is the case even if the employees were eligible to vote in the election and even did so, FLRA said. *(45 FLRA No. 28, June 23, 1992)*

A contract between an agency and a union may limit who can scrvc as a union shop steward, the U.S. Court of Appeals for the District of Columbia said. *(IRS v. FLRA, 91-1247, May 5, 1992)*

A federal employee is protected from discipline when asserting union rights guaranteed by a contract, the Federal Labor Relations Authority said. It ruled that pressing a contractual right is just an extension of the employee's right to join or assist a union. *(43 FLRA No. 86, January 17, 1992)*

It is an unfair labor practice for an agency to deny a local union the right to distribute union information at a work site where there is a practice of allowing employees to deliver other kinds of materials to each others' desks, the Federal Labor Relations Authority held. *(43 FLRA No. 33, November 27, 1991)*

The Federal Labor Relations Authority ordered the reinstatement of an agency attorney fired after he engaged in "protected" union activity. *(FLRA No. 3-CA-90456, February 28, 1991)*

The Federal Labor Relations Authority strengthened the hands of union stewards by declaring that discussions between them and federal employees facing discipline are "protected activities" and an agency may not try to coerce the unionist to disclose what was said. *(38 FLRA No. 103, January 8, 1991)*

Agencies may seek elections that might lead to the disbanding of an existing bargaining unit when there is a "reasonable doubt" that a majority of the employees still supports union representation, ruled the Federal Labor Relations Authority. *(36 FLRA, No. 59, July 31, 1990)*

A federal employee who works full-time on union duty still can be disciplined despite his official time status, the Federal Labor Relations Authority ruled. *(35 FLRA No. 126, May 16, 1990)*

An arbitrator ruled that the Air Force acted properly in giving a 14-day suspension to an employee who spent 30 minutes on personal matters after receiving permission to be absent from his duties only for union business. *(89-05245-8943, May 2, 1990)*

Agency management may not imply to union officials that their performance rating would be higher if they spent less time on union duties, the Federal Labor Relations Authority held in saying such statements can improperly "coerce or intimidate" the employees out of union activities. *(35 FLRA No. 94, April 30, 1990)*

The Federal Labor Relations Authority issued two rulings against federal unions on a point that is a perennial sore spot for them, their duty to represent bargaining unit members who do not pay dues. In two decisions involving an American Federation of Government Employees local, FLRA stressed that unions may not suggest that an employee will receive preferential treatment by actually joining the organization. *(35 FLRA No. 64, April 16, 1990, and 35 FLRA No. 79, April 27, 1990)*

When a federal agency improperly denies a bargaining unit member the right to have a union representative present during an investigatory interview, the agency must repeat the session with a union official present and reconsider the disciplinary action, the Federal Labor Relations Authority held. *(35 FLRA No. 56, April 6, 1990)*

The Federal Labor Relations Authority ordered the retroactive promotion with back pay of an employee who it found had been bypassed for advancement because of his union activities. *(35 FLRA No 15, March 14, 1990)*

The Federal Labor Relations Authority ruled negotiable a union proposal that an employee with whom a supervisor is discussing the issuance of an opportunity-to-improve performance letter be entitled to union representation at the meeting. *(34 FLRA No 154, February 23, 1990)*

The Federal Labor Relations Authority ordered Hill Air Force Base to stop trying to intimidate a union steward who received two reprimands for upstaging management. *(FLRA-7-CA-80186, February 14, 1990)*

An appeals court said that just because an arbitration case moves slowly, that doesn't mean the union has abandoned it and doesn't give grounds for dismissing the complaint. *(Gunn and AFGE v. VA, 89-3114, January 3, 1990)*

An arbitrator ordered the consolidation of more than 1600 unfair labor practice complaints regarding use of official time for American Federation of Government Employees union representatives at the Social Security Administration. *(No. DF-89-R-000, October 31, 1989, Francis X. Quinn, Arbitrator)*

The U.S. Court of Appeals for the Federal Circuit ruled that it has "very limited" jurisdiction over challenges to arbitrator's decisions involving postal employees. *(Burke v. USPS, 89-3225, October 31, 1989)*

The U.S. Court of Appeals for the District of Columbia ruled that federal unionists who resort to racial stereotyping in their publications are not protected from discipline by labor-management law. *(AFGE v. FLRA, 87-1199, June 27, 1989)*

A federal union's responsibility does not extend to the conduct of one of its local officials who allegedly told an employee that he would have to join the union in order to get an apartment in a building owned by the official. *(FLRA ALJ Decision No. 9-CO-70014, November 3, 1988)*

A union local that agreed in a contract not to post derogatory or personal attacks on agency officials must live up to that promise. *(FMCS Decision No. 88-18299, October 18, 1988)*

The U.S. Court of Appeals for the District of Columbia ruled that a federal union local facing a representation challenge from a rival union should expect no help from the host agency. *(AFGE v. FLRA, 87-1083, March 4, 1988)*

A federal district judge ruled that the IRS improperly taxed the American Postal Workers Union for income received from its nonpostal employee associate members who joined the union to take advantage of APWU's health insurance plan. *(APWU v. U.S. District Court for the District of Columbia No. 88-1091)*

A federal union official won't have to apologize to an Air Force colonel for disobeying him by initially refusing to leave the colonel's office when the military man abruptly ended a meeting that had grown unpleasant. An arbitrator found that his refusal was excusable because he did leave after a short time (about 10 minutes)—a period that the arbitrator found a reasonable cooling off period. *(Maxwell v. American Federation of Government Employees Local 997, FMCS No. 91-07809)*

The Federal Labor Relations Authority ruled that federal agencies cannot discontinue subscriptions to publications devoted entirely to federal employee news without giving unions the chance to bargain over the cancellations. *(37 FLRA No. 73)*

UNION DUES

Agency management "should have as little involvement as possible" with the issue of bargaining unit employees having union dues withheld from their paychecks, the Federal Service Impasses Panel said. *(91 FSIP No. 293, May 5, 1992)*

The U.S. Court of Appeals for the Federal Circuit rejected a refund request by the National Association of Postal Supervisors for nearly $700,000 in taxes and interest on "associate member" dues from its health insurance plan in the early 1980s. *(NAPS v. U.S., 90-5160, September 11, 1991)*

The United States Claims Court ruled taxable associate member dues paid by outside subscribers to their health plans when profit is the main motive for charging those fees. *(NAPS v. U.S., 99-89-T, August 14, 1990)*

The Federal Labor Relations Authority ordered the U.S. Mint to pay a union back dues for the temporary employees the agency refused to recognize as bargaining unit members. *(35 FLRA 120, May 14, 1990)*

The Labor Department failed to withhold union dues over several pay periods for five of its employees and therefore must pay the union out of appropriated funds, the U.S. Comptroller General ruled. *(CG Decision No,. B-235386, November 16, 1989)*

WHISTLEBLOWING

To be covered by whistleblower protections a federal employee must reasonably believe that the information he is disclosing is evidence of a violation of law or rule or serious mismanagement, the U.S. Court of Appeals for the Federal Circuit said. *(Haley v. Dept. of the Treasury, 92-3077, October 13, 1992)*

The broadened protections of federal employees provided by the 1989 Whistleblower Protection Act don't apply to personnel actions taken before the date of the law's enactment on July 9 of that year, the U.S. Court of Appeals for the Federal Circuit ruled. *(Knollenberg v. MSPB, 91-3226, January 14, 1992)*

In one of the first rulings under the 1989 Whistleblower Act, the Merit Systems Protection Board ordered a 30-day suspension against a personnel director on a charge of threatening to fire a subordinate on performance grounds, an action that MSPB decided really was an attempt to retaliate against the subordinate for whistleblowing. MSPB ruled that the standard of proof in such disciplinary cases should be the same as in corrective actions, a policy that may make it easier to win claims of retaliation. *(MSPB Doc No. HQ12159010005, August 16, 1991)*

The Whistleblowers Protection Act does not cover employees of the U.S. Postal Service, the Merit Systems Protection Board ruled. *(MSPB No. NY07528910594, June 5, 1991)*

Filing an equal employment opportunity complaint does not constitute whistleblowing and does not guarantee an employee the same protections as those who disclose fraud and waste, the Merit Systems Protection Board ruled. *(MSPB Decision No. NY 075290S0119, January 7, 1991)*

WORK ASSIGNMENT

Management's right to assign work includes the right to "determine the particular duties to be assigned, when work assignments will occur and to whom or what positions the duties will be assigned," the Federal Labor Relations Authority said in rejecting bargaining on a number of union proposals that it said would interfere with those rights. *(44 FLRA No. 70, April 16, 1992)*

Management at MacDill Air Force Base, Fla., ordered civilian firefighters to paint their fire station. They refused, pointing out that the contract between Local 153 of the National Federation of Federal Employees and the base forbids assigning them work outside of their job descriptions. The union prevailed before the Federal Labor Relations Authority. *(38 FLRA No. 11, November 9, 1990)*

An arbitrator upheld the Department of Veterans Affairs in its decision to discipline a 64-year-old security guard who had refused to work overtime. A labor agreement gave management the prerogative to force overtime, he ruled. The guard's punishment: a letter of admonishment. *(LAIRS No. 20013)*

WORK SCHEDULES

A planned arrangement in which employees would be polled regarding their preferred work schedule, and additional alternative schedules made available if enough expressed interest, was endorsed by the Federal Service Impasses Panel. *(92 FSIP No. 15, August 17, 1992)*

Complaints from clients and a backlog of work were compelling enough reasons for the Federal Service Impasses Panel to agree to the cancellation of a compressed work schedule at a Health and Human Services payroll office. *(92 FSIP No. 124, June 29, 1992)*

Compressed work schedules may not be appropriate in federal offices with few employees or "thinly staffed" work areas, said the Federal Service Impasses Panel. It said that although such schedules, such as working four ten-hour days instead of five eight-hour days, are good for family life, commuting times and morale, the needs of the employer can outweigh those considerations. *(91 FSIP No. 190, June 23, 1992)*

An alternate work schedule that an agency initiated on its own cannot be ended without bargaining with a union local that came into existence after the program began, the Federal Labor Relations Authority ruled. *(44 FLRA No. 50, March 26, 1992)*

An agency's interests in accomplishing its mission can outweigh its employees' desire to have flexible work schedules, the Federal Service Impasses Panel said in two cases where it rejected union arguments in favor of four-day workweeks. *(91 FSIP No. 129, September 12, 1991 and 91 FSIP No. 174, September 18, 1991)*

The Federal Labor Relations Authority found that an agency was not required to bargain over a work schedule change that saw a half-hour added to the daily lunch break and the work day extended by the same amount of time. *(41 FLRA No. 6, June 6, 1991)*

The Federal Service Impasses Panel ordered the elimination of a 4-day workweek at a hospital, ruling that management proved that the policy made its operations suffer as its patient case load increased. *(91 FSIP 148, May 30, 1991)*

A federal agency is obligated to bargain on a union proposal that "whenever possible," employees' two days off per week be consecutive and preferably on Saturday and Sunday, the Federal Labor Relations Authority ruled. *(40 FLRA No. 60, May 3, 1991)*

WORKING CONDITIONS (see also CONDITIONS OF EMPLOYMENT)

Bargaining was upheld on a union proposal that an employee lounge not be altered until arrangements had been completed for comparable space after a renovation. The Federal Labor Relations Authority said that because the proposal merely would retain the status quo, it doesn't interfere with management's general right to control the physical workplace. *(45 FLRA No. 90, August 17, 1992)*

A union's hopes that the existence of a shower in a current facility would set a precedent for having one in a new location were sent down the drain by the Federal Service Impasses Panel. The union proposed in bargaining that the parties "acknowledge the existence of a shower stall" at the current site as a prelude to bargaining over such facilities at a future site. *(92 FSIP No. 40, June 23, 1992)*

A Federal Service Impasses Panel arbitrator who visited the Housing and Urban Development San Francisco regional office found the place congested and confused, and as a result ordered management to alter the office space by adding new partitions and raising the height of those already existing, despite HUD's claim that it couldn't afford to make those changes. *(91 FSIP No. 95, May 27, 1992)*

So long as there is no compelling management need to assign seating to federal employees, those employees can be free to choose their own work sites in a given office, the Federal Labor Relations Authority ruled. *(41 FLRA No. 99, August 23, 1991)*

An agency was upheld on a ban against eating or drinking near sensitive electronic equipment by the Federal Labor Relations Authority, which said management's right to determine its internal security "includes the right to take actions which are part of its plan to safeguard its physical property." *(41 FLRA No. 85, July 31, 1991)*

The U.S. Comptroller General said that the Federal Trade Commission could use appropriated funds to pay for the installation of cable television at employees' homes—but for a reason unlikely to be matched in any other agency. FTC monitors TV advertising and officials felt they needed to install their own equipment in an employee's home to monitor certain channels because cable service was not yet available at the time at the agency's headquarters. *(CG Decision No. B-239774, July 22, 1991)*

The Air Force improperly placed 131 on-call employees in a non-pay status, where they stayed for about six months. The action was improper because management failed to notify the union of this change in working conditions, the Federal Labor Relations Authority ruled. *(41 FLRA No. 66, July 18, 1991)*

The Merit Systems Protection Board ordered the Navy to reinstate a policeman that it ordered fired on grounds of refusing to salute a Navy captain entering through a gate. MSPB said that although it was the police officer's third such offense within a year, he had a good work record and has the potential for "rehabilitation" since he promised to salute in the future. *(Carney v. Dept. of the Navy, MSPB Doc. No. PH07539010103, July 18, 1991)*

Federal agencies may reimburse employees for the purchase of safety shoes when they are required to work in "industrial environments where heavy objects are moved and lifted using various types of equipment . . . and the employees' supervisors verify that the shoes are needed and authorize the employees to buy them prior to the actual purchase . . . ," the U.S. Comptroller General ruled. *(CG Decision No. B-242082, June 17, 1991)*

Federal employees who sometimes must work in "extremely cold weather" can be required to supply their own protective clothing, the Federal Labor Relations Authority said, rejecting a union contention that the agency should be responsible. *(40 FLRA No. 80, May 24, 1991)*

An agency has the right to require employees to wear electronic pagers if it can prove such a policy is necessary to its mission, the Federal Labor Relations Authority said. *(40 FLRA No. 65, May 6, 1991)*

The Federal Labor Relations Authority, saying the office environment is "at the very heart" of a federal worker's conditions of employment, upheld bargaining on a variety of proposals regarding the safety and attractiveness of a workplace. *(39 FLRA No. 22, January 31, 1991)*

Federal agencies may use appropriated funds to purchase "access" for their employees to physical fitness centers, the U.S. Comptroller General ruled, as long as it's part of an official agency program to improve the health of their workers. *(CG Decision No. B-240371, January 18, 1991)*

The Federal Service Impasses Panel refused to order an agency to provide shuttle bus service for employees who fear being mugged as they travel between two work sites, suggesting instead that they employ "other less costly means such as traveling in groups." *(90 FSIP No. 161, December 27, 1990)*

An agency may require that employees who must be available on short call while off-duty to wear pagers, but that doesn't mean those employees will be eligible for premium pay for time spent on-call, said the Federal Service Impasses Panel. *(90 FSIP No. 153, December 21, 1990)*

After numerous administrative delays that ate up three years, a federal union finally succeeded in forcing the Labor Department's Boston office to return several water coolers it had removed over the union's objections. *(37 FLRA No. 2, September 7, 1990)*

Where a bargaining unit employee sits in his office can't be changed without negotiating with the union, ruled the Federal Labor Relations Authority in a case involving a Health and Human Services office that changed seating when it got new furniture. *(36 FLRA No. 71, August 16, 1990)*

A management order to turn off the radios in a Manhattan Health and Human Services office is out of tune with federal labor law and must be readjusted, ruled the Federal Labor Relations Authority. *(36 FLRA No. 55, July 26, 1990)*

A federal employee who charges official travel expenses on a personal charge card and who received a rebate for purchases made on that card during the calendar year, is entitled to keep the entire rebate, the U.S. Comptroller General ruled. *(CG Decision No. B-236219, May 4, 1990)*

On orders from an appeals court, the Federal Labor Relations Authority said an agency must negotiate with a union over the cancellation of the annual agency picnic if it has become such an ingrained part of the working there that it has become a "condition of employment." *(35 FLRA No. 70, April 24, 1990)*

The Federal Service Impasses Panel adopted a union request to block a proposal by the veterans hospital in Philadelphia to charge employees a parking fee. *(FSIP Nos. 90-32 and 90-57, March 30, 1990)*

The Federal Labor Relations Authority dismissed an unfair labor practice charge that a Department of Veterans Affairs hospital unilaterally discontinued a 17-year practice of allowing its dietary service employees to drink surplus coffee. *(35 FLRA No 23, March 22, 1990)*

An agency that required employees operating their motorcycles on its property to wear reflective vests didn't have to pay for them, the Federal Labor Relations Authority ruled, because the union agreement addressed protective gear used in performance of official duties—not for employee commuting. FLRA ruled against the union. *(FLRA 3-CA-80352, January 29, 1990)*

The Federal Labor Relations Authority ruled that a government agency did not violate its union contract when it forbade an employee to bring her radio to work. *(34 FLRA No. 107, January 29, 1990)*

The U.S. Comptroller General said there's no law against a federal agency obtaining charge cards for its employees for government business with the bills going directly to Uncle Sam. The cards, according to he agency that requested them, would be embossed with the employee's name and the words "For Official Use Only," and Census would provide other safeguards against abuse, the CG noted. *(No. B-237883, January 5, 1990)*

The government cannot reimburse employees for the cost of heating and electricity used in their home "work stations." *(CG Decision No. B-225159, June 19, 1989)*

The purchase of business cards is "personal" and employees who want them must pay for them themselves. *(CG Decision No. B-231830, June 5, 1989)*

The government may pay for installing telephone service in the residence of an employee who was required to temporarily vacate his agency-furnished residence during a renovation. *(CG Decision No. B-227727, March 7, 1989)*

The U.S. Court of Appeals for the District of Columbia ruled that agencies may set dress codes, including required neckties, to make their employees more professional in appearance. *(AFGE Local 2441 v. FLRA, 87-1820, December 30, 1988)*

An agency may reimburse an employee for charges and fees relating to official government phone calls from an official's personal automobile. But the agency may not use appropriated funds to pay for the phone, in whole or in part. *(CG Decision No. B-229406, December 9, 1988)*

Federal "dual-status" civilian employees must "observe military customs and courtesies" whenever they are in uniform while at work, even when off-duty. *(32 FLRA No. 160, Sept. 16, 1988)*